Parimutuel Applications in Finance

Parimutuel Applications in Finance

New Markets for New Risks

KEN BARON
AND
JEFFREY LANGE

First published in 2007 by
PALGRAVE MACMILLAN
Houndmills, Basingstoke, Hampshire RG21 6XS and
175 Fifth Avenue, New York, N.Y. 10010
Companies and representatives throughout the world.

PALGRAVE MACMILLAN is the global academic imprint of the Palgrave Macmillan division of St. Martin's Press, LLC and of Palgrave Macmillan Ltd. Macmillan® is a registered trademark in the United States, United Kingdom and other countries. Palgrave is a registered trademark in the European Union and other countries.

ISBN-13: 978–1–4039–3950–0 hardback
ISBN-10: 1–4039–3950–0 hardback

This book is printed on paper suitable for recycling and made from fully managed and sustained forest sources.

A catalogue record for this book is available from the British Library.

Library of Congress Cataloging-in-Publication Data

Baron, Ken, 1966–
    Parimutuel applications in finance / by Ken Baron and Jeffrey Lange.
        p. cm.
    Includes bibliographical references and index.
    ISBN 1–4039–3950–0 (cloth)
    1. Derivative securities – Mathematical models. 2. Risk
  management – Mathematical models. I. Lange, Jeffrey. II. Title.
HG6024.A3B373 2007
332.64′57015195—dc22   2006049422

10 9 8 7 6 5 4 3 2
16 15 14 13 12 11 10 09 08 07

Printed and bound in Great Britain by
Antony Rowe Ltd, Chippenham and Eastbourne

Ken Baron: *To Debbie*
Jeff Lange: *To my wife Liz*

Contents

List of Figures

List of Tables

List of Symbols

This section defines the symbols that are in the main text of the book. We have excluded notation that is used only in appendices and footnotes.

$\mathbf{A}$ a J by S matrix whose element in the jth row and sth column is $a_{j,s}$ for $j = 1, 2, \ldots, J$ and $s = 1, 2, \ldots, S$;

$a_{j,s}$ a scalar representing the replication weight for customer order j on the sth state claim for $j = 1, 2, \ldots, J$ and $s = 1, 2, \ldots, S$;

a_s a scalar representing the replication weight on a particular derivative strategy for the sth state claim for $s = 1, 2, \ldots, S$;

b_j a scalar representing whether customer order j is a buy or a sell order for $j = 1, 2, \ldots, J$;

$\mathbf{c}$ a column vector of length J with element c_j in the jth row for $j = 1, 2, \ldots, J$;

$\mathbf{C}$ a non-empty subset of $\{1, 2, \ldots, J\}$;

c_j a scalar representing the number of contracts based on the derivative strategy specified in the jth customer order for $j = 1, 2, \ldots, J$;

d a function of U representing the payout on a derivative strategy;

$\underline{d}$ a scalar representing the minimum payout on a derivative strategy;

$\overline{d}$ a scalar representing the maximum payout on a derivative strategy;

$\mathbf{D}$ a $J + S$ by $J + S$ matrix representing the first derivatives of state prices with respect to customer fills;

d_j a function of U representing the payout on the derivative strategy requested in customer order j for $j = 1, 2, \ldots, J$;

$\overline{d}_j$ a scalar representing the maximum payout on the derivative strategy requested in customer order j for $j = 1, 2, \ldots, J$;

$\tilde{d}_s$ a function of U representing the payout on the sth state claim for $s = 1, 2, \ldots, S$;

e a scalar that indexes the E strikes in a parimutuel derivatives auction;

$\tilde{e}$ a scalar that indexes the E strikes in a parimutuel derivatives auction;

E a scalar representing the number of strikes in a parimutuel derivatives auction;

f a function of U representing the P&L on a particular customer order;

F a function of the fills vector $\mathbf{x}$ for the BVIP representation of the GPEP whose jth element is F_j for $j = 1, 2, \ldots, J + S$;

f_j a function of U representing the P&L on the jth customer for $j = 1, 2, \ldots, J$;

F_j a function of the fills vector $\mathbf{x}$ for the BVIP representation of the GPEP for $j = 1, 2, \ldots, J + S$;

$\mathbf{H}$ an S by S matrix relating the PEP to an eigensystem;

j a scalar that indexes the J customer orders in a parimutuel derivatives auction;

J a scalar representing the number of customer orders in a parimutuel derivatives auction;

k a scalar representing an option strike;

k_e a scalar representing the eth strike in a parimutuel derivatives auction for $e = 1, 2, \ldots, E$;

$k_{\tilde{e}}$ a scalar representing the $\tilde{e}$th strike in a parimutuel derivatives auction for $\tilde{e} = 1, 2, \ldots, E$;

M a scalar representing the premium paid in a parimutuel auction;

$\tilde{M}$ a scalar representing the total amount of market exposure in a parimutuel derivatives auction;

m_s a scalar representing the premium invested in the sth state claim for $s = 1, 2, \ldots, S$;

$m_{\tilde{s}}$ a scalar representing the premium invested in the $\tilde{s}$th state claim for $\tilde{s} = 1, 2, \ldots, S$;

n a scalar that indexes vectors of customer fills;

o_s a scalar representing the odds on the sth horse to win a race for $s = 1, 2, \ldots, S$;

$\mathbf{p}$ a column vector of length S representing the prices of the state claims;

p_s a scalar representing the price of the sth state claim for $s = 1, 2, \ldots, S$;

$p_{\tilde{s}}$ a scalar representing the price of the $\tilde{s}$th state claim for $\tilde{s} = 1, 2, \ldots, S$;

r a scalar representing the requested number of contracts for a customer order;

r_j a scalar representing the requested number of contracts for customer order j for $j = 1, 2, \ldots, J$;

s a scalar that indexes the S states or state claims in a parimutuel auction;

$\tilde{s}$ a scalar that indexes the S states or state claims in a parimutuel auction;

S a scalar representing the number of states or state claims in a parimutuel auction;

SD the standard deviation operator;

s_e a scalar representing the state in which $U = k_e$;

$s_{\tilde{e}}$ a scalar representing the state in which $U = k_{\tilde{e}}$;

t a scalar indexing the observations in a time series;

T   the transpose operator;

u a scalar representing a possible value of U;

U a random variable representing the value of an underlying of interest;

$\tilde{U}$ a random variable that is a function of U;

u_s a scalar representing a possible value of U if the sth state occurs for $s = 1, 2, \ldots, S$;

u_t a scalar representing the value of U at time t;

V a scalar representing the total limit-order violations of the customer orders;

v_j a scalar representing the amount of the limit-order violation for customer order j for $j = 1, 2, \ldots, J$;

w a scalar representing the limit price for a customer order;

$\mathbf{w}$ a column vector of length J whose element in row j is w_j for $j = 1, 2, \ldots, J$;

w_j a scalar representing the limit price for customer order j for $j = 1, 2, \ldots, J$;

x a scalar representing the number of filled contracts for a customer order;

$\mathbf{x}$ a column vector of customer fills;

X a $(J + S)$-dimensional box representing possible fills for the GPEP;

x_j a scalar representing the number of filled contracts for customer order j for $j = 1, 2, \ldots, J$;

$\mathbf{x}_n$ a column vector of length J of possible customer fills;

$\mathbf{x}_{n,j}$ a scalar representing the customer fill from the nth vector of customer fills for the jth customer order for $j = 1, 2, \ldots, J$;

$y_{n,s}$ a scalar representing the net customer payout from the nth vector of customer fills for the sth state for $s = 1, 2, \ldots, S$;

y_s a scalar representing the amount of customer payouts required if the sth state occurs for $s = 1, 2, \ldots, S$;

$\mathbf{z}$ a column vector of length $J + S$;

α a scalar representing a constant strictly between zero and one;

β a scalar representing a constant;

δ_j a scalar representing the amount used to adjust the fill on the jth customer order on a particular iteration in part one of the PEP solution algorithm for $j = 1, 2, \ldots, J$;

Δx_j a scalar representing the change in the fill on the jth customer order between part one and part two of the PEP solution algorithm for $j = 1, 2, \ldots, J$;

ε_t a scalar representing the error in a time-series model at time t;

κ a constant that is independent of the state s;

λ_j a scalar representing the amount of premium paid by customer order j for $j = 1, 2, \ldots, J$;

$\tilde{\lambda}_j$ a scalar representing the amount of market exposure for customer order j for $j = 1, 2, \ldots, J$;

Ω a set representing the sample space of the random variable U;

π a scalar representing the price of a derivative strategy;

π^{f} a scalar representing the price of a forward;

π_j a scalar representing the price of the derivative strategy requested in customer order j for $j = 1, 2, \ldots, J$;

π^{rf} a scalar representing the price of a range forward;

ρ a scalar representing the tick size of U;

θ_s a scalar representing the amount of opening order premium invested in the sth state claim for $s = 1, 2, \ldots, S$;

ψ_t a scalar representing the surprise of the underlying at time t;

φ_t a scalar representing the market's consensus forecast for the value of the underlying at time t;

$\mathbf{0}$ a column vector of length J of all zeros;

$\leftarrow$ an operator that denotes adjusting the variable immediately to the left of the arrow iteratively based on the formula immediately to the right of the arrow.

List of Acronyms

BIS	Bank for International Settlements
BLS	Bureau of Labor Statistics
BVIP	Box Constrained Variational Inequality Problem
CBOT	Chicago Board of Trade
CEA	Commodities Exchange Act
CFMA	Commodity Futures Modernization Act
CFTC	Commodity Futures Trading Commission
CME	Chicago Mercantile Exchange
CPCAM	Convex Parimutuel Call Auction Mechanism
CPI	Consumer Price Index
DARPA	Defense Advanced Research Projects Agency
DPM	Dynamic Parimutuel Market
EIA	Energy Information Administration
FCM	Futures Commission Merchant
GPEP	Generalized Parimutuel Equilibrium Problem
GWS	Gu, Whinston, and Stallaert
LIFFE	London International Financial Futures and Options Exchange
LP	Linear Program
NA	Not Applicable
NFP	Monthly Change in US Nonfarm Payrolls
NYMEX	New York Mercantile Exchange
NYSE	New York Stock Exchange
OTC	Over the Counter
PEP	Parimutuel Equilibrium Problem
P&L	Profit and Loss
SPEP	Simplified Parimutuel Equilibrium Problem
TIPS	United States Treasury Inflation-Protected Securities
UK	United Kingdom
US	United States
USPTO	United States Patent and Technology Office
VIP	Variational Inequality Problem

Foreword

This book is about the technology for managing risks, and about a particular advance in risk management: parimutuel financial markets, the first example of which came into being in 2002 with the Economic Derivatives Market. The market continues today, sponsored by Goldman Sachs, at the service of traders around the world. The authors of this book were responsible for much of the technological innovation that made this historic market possible, and this book explains their methods and reasoning in impressive detail.

The parimutuel technology is fundamentally new in that it stretches the horizons of what can be traded on our risk markets. As such technology is further disseminated, it will mean better management of the widest variety of possible risks, and greater human welfare.

Risk management is important – anyone who has ever collected on an insurance policy will tell you that. But it could be a lot more important. The problem with risk management has been that, while we manage some risks very well, we still do not effectively manage most of our economic risks.

If all risks were really perfectly managed around the world, then, in theory, all idiosyncratic risks would be eliminated, and only shocks that hit the whole world would affect individuals' consumption. Changes in individual consumption in this ideal world of perfect risk management would be perfectly correlated across the nations of the world, since they would only be driven by the irreducible undiversifiable risk that affects everyone. But, in fact the correlation of consumption changes across countries is closer to zero than to one. This means that, for all our sophistication in risk management, we have only just begun the game.

It should be no surprise that most risks are not managed. There simply have been no markets for most of the risks we face. Our principal financial markets represent claims on the revenues after costs of corporations and governments, and we have futures markets on a few commodities, and derivatives piled on these. That sounds like a lot, but it is hardly everything.

Economic theorists Kenneth Arrow and Gerard Debreu had much more imagination about what could be traded: there could in principle be a market for every state of nature that affects human welfare. That is the theorist's dream.

The ruminations of economic theorists about what *might* be traded in markets may strike practical people as farfetched. People say: if these risks are not represented in markets, there must be a good reason why not. Perhaps. But quite likely the reason why not often has to do with the current state of development of the technology of markets.

The first economic risk that was traded on the world's first parimutuel financial market when it was opened in 2002 represents one of the most important risks that up to that date had never been traded. The nonfarm payroll market that opened in 2002 is a market for the risks to our jobs, to our livelihoods. Creating such a market is a radical departure from our normal ways of managing risks.

There is a fundamental puzzle. Why is it that we have markets for a million little risks (we have a market for pork bellies, for example) but not for some of the biggest risks (until 2002, the market for our jobs). We can live without bacon pretty easily, just substitute hamburger for example, but we can't so easily live without our jobs.

Starting markets for important risks faces some important ironies. It is not possible to get people to trade in a market unless it has liquidity. But, equally, it is not possible to get liquidity in a market unless it gets a lot of people to trade in it. So, it sounds impossible to get any new market started. Markets *do* get started, but they need all the help they can get.

The parimutuel structure for financial markets is an important invention in part because it deals with some of the barriers to achieving liquidity that have stymied would-be founders of markets. It achieves this by a fundamental structure that does not require a continuous two-sided market for every risk that is traded, but that conveniently allows people to express their demands for what amounts to complicated bundles of the primitive risks being traded and to add these demands up and offset them against demands for other incommensurable bundles of risks. So, liquidity does not need to be achieved separately in every single nook and cranny of the market; instead there is a system liquidity that can be managed and maintained with modern information technology.

The parimutuel concept is an exciting one that the world is only just beginning to appreciate. This book is the definitive treatise on this technology, as it is emerging today, and as it will be developed in the future. It is a book to be studied over future years as markets proliferate and become more and more important in our lives.

Robert J. Shiller, Stanley B. Resor Professor of Economics, Yale University.

Acknowledgments

First, we would like to thank the team at Palgrave Macmillan. Thanks to Andrea Hartill who suggested and encouraged us to write a book for Palgrave on parimutuel matching. Additionally, we are grateful to Anna Van Boxel and Alexandra Dawe for helping us to see the book through to publication.

Much of the work associated with this book was done while we were working at Longitude. We thank our colleagues at Longitude for making Longitude a truly unique and fun place to work. In particular our gratitude goes to Andrew Lawrence and Charlie Walden for leading Longitude and assembling such a great team. Thanks to Ben Holzman for many productive technical discussions and for a careful proof reading of several chapters of this book. Marcus Harte provided much technical expertise over the years and also assisted with some of the examples in this book. Further, we acknowledge the support of Longitude's shareholders, the Board of Directors, and the Academic Advisors.

Professor Robert Shiller has been a strong advocate of our work, and we would like to thank him for his long-standing support and for writing the thoughtful foreword for this book. The material in this book benefited from multiple technical discussions and encouragement from Dimtri Bertesekas, Bing Chin, Darrell Duffie, Nicholas Economides, and Michael Overton. Ken Garbade made extensive comments on almost every chapter in the book, often reviewing chapters more than once. His suggestions and advice have led to immense improvements in our exposition. Marvin Nakayama read several chapters with impressive thoroughness and made many useful comments. Peter Cotton and Randy Cieslak provided helpful remarks on the material in this book. Miki Yaran and Jasmatee Chandrakuar did a diligent job creating the figures in this book. Further, our thanks to Jennifer Yeske McCabe for her research assistance.

Longitude's efforts to bring parimutuel matching to the financial markets have been aided by the vision and support of Longitude's clients. We would like to specifically acknowledge the following people of various firms:

- Chicago Mercantile Exchange (CME): Mark Fields, Ed Gogol, John Pietrowicz, Rick Redding, Jerry Roberts, Scott Robinson, and Kim Taylor.

- Deutsche Bank: David Neumann, Neehal Shah, Mark Stafford, Francesco Tonin, and Torquil Wheatley.

- Goldman Sachs: Carlos Arena, Bill Cassano, Laurie Ferber, Oliver Frankel, Peter Gerhardt, Kevin Keating, and Irene Tse.

- ICAP: James Adam, Lisa Causarano, Chris Edmonds, Patrick Morgan, Rich Rosenberg, Andrew Samawi, and Carole Server.

- International Securities Exchange (ISE): Tom Ascher and Mike Knesevitch.

- New York Mercantile Exchange (NYMEX): Bo Collins, John D'Agostino, Bob Levin, Dan McElduff, Mike Milano, Matt Morano, Paul Sacristan, and Joe Raia.

We would like to thank the following financial market professionals who made practical suggestions or asked useful questions that led to improvements in our work: Bill Cassano, David Heatley, Kevin Heerdt, Steve Nixon, John O'Brien, Pavel Pinkava, and Will Romaro.

We welcome comments from readers. Please email us at ken.baron@yahoo.com and Jeffrey.lange@guggenheimpartners.com.

Personal Acknowledgements from Ken Baron: I thank Debbie, Eleanor, and Walter for their patience while I spent time away from them writing this book: my work on this would not have been possible without their unflagging encouragement. Thanks to Mom and Dad for supporting and cultivating my interest in mathematics from the beginning. Also, I thank Arthur, Caryl, Dad, Joan, and Mom for helping out with the grandchildren, time and again. I thank Ken Garbade for being a strong supporter of this book from the very beginning. Thanks to Andrew Lawrence and Jeff Lange for recruiting me into Longitude and for creating a terrific company. Thanks to Charlie Walden for his friendship and indefatigable spirit throughout our many Longitude adventures. In addition, I'd like to thank Andrew, Charlie, Jeff, and the following Longitude colleagues for many productive and enjoyable discussions over the last several years: Jennifer Berrent, Annette Donofrio, Marcus Harte, Ben Holzman, Seph Huber, Mark Selby, and Carolyn Taylor. Finally, thanks to Alan Kanter, Corey Mertes, Matt Morris, Bill O'Connell, Doug Robinson, Susanne

Robinson, and Roy Schuster for many fun field trips to study the more applied aspects of parimutuel wagering.

Personal Acknowledgements from Jeffrey Lange: I thank Liz, Gus, and Alice for their support and for letting me use the last piece of printer paper throughout the writing of this book. I also thank Andrew Lawrence for years of productive collaboration. Darrell Duffie provided a critical dose of encouragement when the material in this book could still fit on a lunch napkin. Robert Shiller was extremely generous with his time and invaluable advice and insights – thank you Bob! Finally, thanks to Ronald A. Howard of Stanford University, who taught me how to think (in general) and think rigorously about the topics herein (in particular).

Introduction

This book studies parimutuel matching, a new and useful approach for trading financial derivatives. Parimutuel matching has several unique properties that distinguish it from the traditional method of matching buyers with sellers. In particular,

- Parimutuel matching does not require a buyer to be matched with a seller for trades to occur. In fact, parimutuel matching can generate trades with only buyers (or with only sellers for that matter) of derivatives. This flexibility for matching trades can help increase traded volume in derivatives markets.

- Parimutuel matching enforces no-arbitrage restrictions, which can lead to lower costs for derivatives end-users.

- Parimutuel matching aggregates orders across different types of derivatives. Consequently, in the parimutuel framework, an order for one derivative can directly increase the liquidity for other derivatives.

Because of its ability to aggregate liquidity, parimutuel matching is in use today in new and otherwise illiquid derivatives markets.

- The Chicago Mercantile Exchange ("CME") uses parimutuel matching for trading options on economic statistics. Releases of economic statistics are widely followed by financial market participants and can have a dramatic impact on the prices of financial assets. Currently, CME's customers can trade options on ten economic releases per month. In particular, the CME offers parimutuel trading of options on US nonfarm payrolls, the most widely followed economic indicator in the US.

- Crude oil and natural gas prices can move sharply in response to the weekly releases of energy inventory statistics. Parimutuel matching is currently in use for the over-the-counter trading of options on these energy inventory figures. These energy-related markets are cleared and settled through the New York Mercentile Exchange (NYMEX) and the NYMEX clearinghouse.

These markets are organized and run in conjunction with Goldman Sachs. Additionally, ICAP PLC's brokers solicit and receive orders in these markets.

Markets on economic statistics and energy inventory statistics are examples of the new and growing area of "event markets." Event-market underlyings are either outcomes of events (such as who wins a presidential election) or values of computed statistics (such as nonfarm payrolls), instead of traditional markets where underlyings are prices of financial instruments. Event markets are of significant academic interest, as academic researchers are interested in these markets' ability to accurately predict future outcomes. Further, event markets have received growing attention from the financial community. Witness, for example, the growth in recent years of the market for weather derivatives. It is difficult for market makers and financial intermediaries to offer derivatives on event-market underlyings, as traditional methods of hedging are ineffective (this is due to the fact that event markets typically do not have a continuously traded underlying that can be used for "delta hedging"). Because of its ability to aggregate liquidity, parimutuel matching lessens the need for derivatives market makers and is well suited for use in trading event-market derivatives.

Parimutuel matching is relatively new to the derivatives markets, being first introduced in 2002 for trading derivatives on economic statistics. However, parimutuel matching has had a long and colorful history, having been used for wagering on horse races for over one hundred years. In fact, over $100 *billion* in premium is wagered annually on horse races and other types of races using parimutuel matching.

Overview of the Material: The material in this book is divided into two parts. Part I – Chapters 1 through 4 – introduces the parimutuel matching framework in a simple and straightforward setting. This part illustrates the unique liquidity aggregation properties of parimutuel matching with a minimum of mathematics and notation. As noted above, parimutuel matching has helped create new derivatives markets such as derivatives on economic statistics and energy inventory statistics. Part I describes those markets and their operation in some detail. Part II – Chapters 5 through 9 – presents an in-depth mathematical treatment of the parimutuel matching of derivatives. We show how the simple parimutuel framework used for wagering can be enhanced to handle a variety of important financial market features, including limit orders and orders for standard options. In addition, we derive several of the mathematical properties of a parimutuel equilibrium. As the book's co-authors, we believe that we bring a unique perspective to the material in this book: through our involvement with the company Longitude (more on that in Chapter 3), we have both helped create the parimutuel derivatives markets on the CME and NYMEX, and we have developed many of the mathematical techniques required for the parimutuel trading of derivatives.

Our Intended Audience: Who might be interested in this book? Professors and students who focus on the derivatives markets may find the material in Part I to be informative, since parimutuel matching is a new and useful way of trading derivatives. Also, there may be general interest from the academic community in the new markets that have been created based on parimutuel matching. Portfolio managers, economists, and policy makers that forecast and follow US economic statistics might use this book to better understand trading in economic derivatives. Similarly, energy traders and energy analysts might use this material to learn the uses of energy inventory derivatives. Professors and quantitative derivatives professionals ("quants" as they are often called on Wall Street) may wish to learn the mathematics of parimutuel pricing and trading.

Requirements for Readers: Although we provide some basic material on derivatives markets in Chapter 1, readers should have at least some knowledge of the financial markets in general, and derivatives markets in particular. We expect readers to have taken at least one university level financial markets class or to have had some professional derivatives experience. Part I requires fairly limited technical expertise, and it does not rely on calculus or other higher mathematics. Thus, readers with a variety of mathematical backgrounds can follow the main features of parimutuel matching and can learn about current parimutuel applications. Part II provides a more rigorous mathematical treatment of parimutuel matching and additional mathematical skills are required. For this material, readers are expected to have an MBA with a quantitative focus, or a masters or PhD in a quantitative field. Although Part II is mathematically more challenging, we rely heavily on examples to illustrate the main properties of parimutuel matching. Further, to keep the exposition as smooth as possible and to keep notation to the minimum amount possible, we relegate all proofs to the appendices.

PART I

Introduction to Parimutuel Markets

CHAPTER 1

Introduction to Derivatives

This chapter introduces the various aspects of derivatives trading, focusing on topics that we will draw on later in the book. Section 1.1 reviews the basics of derivatives contracts, and Section 1.2 discusses derivatives trading. Section 1.3 describes the recent growth in derivatives markets, and Section 1.4 discusses some of the causes of that recent growth. In these sections and throughout the remainder of the book, we assume that the reader has some familiarity with derivatives as is found, for example, in Chapters 1, 2, and 8 of Hull (2006). Where relevant, we provide additional references for readers interested in exploring specific topics in more detail.

1.1   REVIEW OF DERIVATIVES CONTRACTS

A derivative contact, or simply a "derivative" is a financial instrument whose value depends on the value of an "underlying variable." An underlying variable might be, for example, the price of a commodity such as corn or the price of a financial instrument such as a bond. We refer to a participant who has written the contract as being "short" the contract. We say that the holder or owner of the contract is "long" the contract.

Derivatives contracts can be settled either via "physical delivery" or via "cash settlement." In the case of physical delivery, a party who is short a derivative contract delivers the underlying to a party with a long position.[1] If the underlying is a commodity such as corn, then the person with the short position must deliver corn, while if the underlying is a financial instrument such as a bond, then the short delivers that bond. In the case of cash settlement, the underlying is not delivered. Instead, cash is exchanged based on the value of the underlying at expiration. Since this book focuses primarily on cash-settled derivatives, we now describe different types of cash-settled derivatives based on the amount they pay out on their expiration date.

The most widely traded type of derivatives are "futures," which are traded on an exchange, and "forwards," which are traded over the counter (OTC). These are similar derivatives in that they have payouts that are linear functions of the value of the underlying on expiration.[2] Typically, no cash is exchanged up front between the buyer and seller of these contracts because at the time the trade is executed, the net present value of the contract is generally zero.[3]

"Options" are another widely traded type of derivative. An option, or contingent claim as it is often called in the academic literature, gives the holder the right, but not the obligation, to buy or sell the underlying. The holder of a cash-settled option typically pays cash or premium up front in return for a possible payout from exercising the option at some date in the future. A party with a short position in a cash-settled option typically receives premium up front and may have to pay out cash to a holder exercising the option at some date in the future. This book focuses on cash-settled options that are "European-style," which means that the option holder can act to exercise the option only at the option's expiration.[4] For terminology, we say that a cash-settled European-style option is "out-of-the-money" if the holder of the option receives no payout upon expiration of the option. Alternatively, we say that a cash-settled European-style option is "in-the-money" if the option holder receives a payout upon expiration of the option.[5] The value of the underlying at which the option goes from being out-of-the-money to being in-the-money is typically called the option's "strike."

This book focuses on options that can be classified as either "digital options" or "vanilla options" based on their payout functions. A cash-settled European-style digital option pays the option holder the same amount in all cases as long as the option expires in-the-money.[6] A digital option expires in-the-money if the value of the underlying is at or above the strike for a "digital call," below the strike for a "digital put," or between two strikes for a "digital range." In contrast, a cash-settled European-style vanilla option that expires in-the-money pays the option holder different amounts based on the value of the underlying on expiration. For example, a "vanilla call" with a strike of k on an underlying U pays out max $[0, U - k]$, while a "vanilla put" with a strike of k pays out max $[0, k - U]$.[7] The adjective "vanilla" is a contraction of the phrase "plain vanilla." Financial-market participants consider vanilla options plain or standard, in contrast to digital options, which are considered exotic.[8] Like all options, payouts on vanilla calls and puts are nonlinear functions. Table 1.1 summarizes some features of these derivatives.

Table 1.1 Characteristics of cash-settled derivatives contracts

Derivative type	Payout function	Up front premium?
Futures and forwards	Linear	No
Vanilla options and digital options	Nonlinear	Yes

Table 1.2 Characteristics of derivatives-market participants

Category	Subcategory	Description
Market maker	None	Quotes bids and offers to customers and typically delta hedges the resulting trade
Customer	Hedger	Trades derivatives to reduce overall risk
	Speculator	Trades derivatives to generate a profit, while increasing overall risk
	Arbitrageur	Trades derivatives to try to profit based on small mispricings between different instruments

1.2   REVIEW OF DERIVATIVES TRADING

We divide parties that trade derivatives into two broad categories – "customers" and "market makers." A market maker provides a customer with a "bid price," the price at which the market maker stands ready to buy, and an "offer price," the price at which the market maker stands ready to sell. If the customer buys a derivative from the market maker, then the market maker sells the customer the derivative at the offer price, while if the customer sells a derivative, then the market maker buys the derivative from the customer at the bid price. Note that when a derivative trade occurs in this setting, there is both a buyer and a seller of that derivative, and we refer to this method of transacting as "bilateral matching." Customers may include "hedgers," who trade derivatives to reduce their overall risk, "speculators," who trade derivatives to generate a profit, and "arbitrageurs," who try to profit on small mispricings between different instruments. A derivatives customer might work as a portfolio manager, a corporate treasurer, or a hedge-fund trader. A market maker might work at a financial intermediary such as a bank, a broker-dealer, or for himself/herself.[9] Table 1.2 summarizes some of the properties of derivatives-market participants.

Based on his/her trades with customers, a derivatives market maker can have significant exposure to changes in the value of the underlying. To limit this risk, the market maker usually hedges in one of two ways. If the derivative is an option, the market maker will typically employ a dynamic hedge by trading in the underlying using the technique called "delta hedging." Delta hedging is based on the Greek variable delta, which measures changes in an option's price relative to changes in the price of the underlying based on a valuation model such as Black and Scholes (1973).[10] Alternatively, the market maker may employ a static hedge, whereby the market maker locates an offsetting transaction with another customer or another derivatives dealer.

Derivatives may be traded on an exchange such as the Chicago Mercantile Exchange (CME) or the New York Mercantile Exchange (NYMEX). Alternatively, derivatives may be traded OTC between a customer and a market maker at a financial intermediary such as a broker-dealer like Goldman Sachs. Customers who trade derivatives on an exchange have the advantage that their trades receive the credit of the exchange's clearinghouse, an entity that provides a performance guarantee to customers to insure that the derivatives contracts are honored. Because the exchange's clearinghouse is typically a well-capitalized entity, the risk of a default on an exchange-traded derivatives contract is negligible. Customers who trade derivatives OTC have the advantage that intermediaries can often offer them derivatives with a greater variety of terms than exchange-traded derivatives.

Historically, derivatives trades have been executed via verbal communication between a buyer and a seller. For example, exchange trading of derivatives has been done primarily via the open-outcry system used in trading on an exchange floor, and OTC trading of derivatives has been done primarily via the phone. In the last six or seven years, however, *electronic* trading of derivatives has grown significantly and is in many cases replacing the more traditional verbal means of trading.[11] In a well-known illustration of this, Eurex, which uses electronic trading, in 1998 became the primary market for trading German bund futures. Eurex displaced the former leader London International Financial Futures and Options Exchange (LIFFE) where German bund futures were traded via open outcry on the exchange floor. As a more recent illustration of the growth of electronic trading, Sutphen and Burns (2005) report that electronic trading of Eurodollar futures on the CME has grown from 10% of total contract volume to over 60% of contract volume over the calendar year 2004.

Most derivatives are traded *continuously* throughout the trading day, which means that participants arrange derivatives trades whenever the

Table 1.3 Characteristics of derivatives trading

Characteristic	Description
Trading venue	Exchange or OTC
Trading medium	Verbal or electronic
Trading session	Continuous or call auction
Order	Market order or limit order

market is open. Continuous trading allows customers to transact almost instantaneously during the trading day. An alternative mechanism for trading derivatives is a "call auction," where trading is done at specific times, that is, when the market is "called." Participants in a call auction sacrifice transaction immediacy in exchange for lower transaction costs.[12] In the financial markets, call auctions are used most notably to auction new US Treasury securities[13] and to open equities traded on the New York Stock Exchange (NYSE).[14] Section 3.5 will describe some of these applications in more detail.

In trading derivatives, customers can submit different types of orders. With a "market order," the customer requests that the trade be executed immediately at the best price available. Alternatively, a customer may submit a "limit order," in which case the customer requests that the order be filled at or better than the specific limit price.[15] A market order offers the customer the benefit of knowing that the transaction will be executed immediately if possible, whereas a limit order gives the customer control over the ultimate price paid for the derivative. Table 1.3 summarizes some of these features of derivatives trading.

1.3 RECENT GROWTH IN DERIVATIVES MARKETS

This section provides a brief history of the growth in derivatives trading, and Section 1.4 discusses the innovations that led to that growth. These topics provide important background information for us because many of the innovations that spurred the recent growth in derivatives trading also relate to the recent introduction of parimutuel matching to the financial markets. We will return to this material in that context in Section 3.6.

Derivatives have been traded for several hundred years.[16] The Dutch traded futures and options on tulip bulbs during the tulip bubble of the 1630s.[17] In the late 1600s, the Japanese traded rice forwards on the Dojima Exchange.[18] In the US, Americans first traded options in the late 1700s, and they first traded futures and forwards on an organized exchange in 1848 on the Chicago Board of Trade (CBOT).[19] Up until the 1970s, the underlyings used for derivatives trading were primarily agricultural commodities and the vast majority of these derivatives were settled upon expiration via physical delivery.

The introduction of new underlyings beginning in the 1970s set the stage for the dramatic growth in derivatives trading over the last 30 years.[20] In 1972, the CME introduced the world's first futures contracts on financial instruments with futures on seven foreign currencies versus the US dollar. The CBOT introduced their first financial future, the Government National Mortgage Association ("Ginnie Mae") futures contract, in 1975. In 1981, the CME introduced trading on Eurodollar futures, the first modern US futures contract to be cash-settled rather than settled via physical delivery.[21]

In the last 30 years, derivatives markets have grown dramatically in terms of the number of exchanges in existence and the volume traded. Today, there are over 60 futures and options exchanges. Burghardt (2005) reports that 8.9 billion derivatives contracts were traded in 2004 on futures and option exchanges with 60% of those contracts being option contracts. The Bank for International Settlements (BIS) surveys OTC derivatives trading across 52 countries or regions. The BIS estimates that in 2004, $305 trillion notional of OTC foreign exchange and OTC interest-rate derivatives were traded, and of that, $71 trillion notional of options were traded.[22]

While derivatives trading in the early 1970s was primarily done on agricultural products, today, derivatives trading takes place mainly on financial underlyings, such as stock indexes, bonds, foreign exchange, and short-term interest rates. Trading of derivatives and options worldwide has grown dramatically not only in terms of volume, but also in terms of the number and breadth of underlying risks. As an illustration, we note that the list of Commodity Futures Trading Commission (CFTC) approved underlyings for exchange trading in the US takes up 29 pages.[23] Recently introduced products include catastrophe derivatives, credit-default derivatives, economic derivatives (more on these in later chapters), and weather derivatives. Rapid innovation continues today. For example, in the US, exchanges filed with the CFTC to trade 207 new futures and option contracts in 2004.[24]

1.4 INNOVATIONS ASSOCIATED WITH THE RECENT GROWTH IN DERIVATIVES MARKETS

What has lead to the recent increase in derivatives trading and the new derivatives products? The overview papers by Tufano (2003) and

Frame and White (2004) detail much of the work that has been done on this question.[25] Researchers have shown that such financial innovation is often a result of several factors including changes in tax laws, increases in economic activity, increases in asset-price volatility and inflation, changes in regulation, advances in intellectual knowledge, and improvements in information technology. Though all of these are probably contributing factors to the growth in derivatives trading, we now discuss the last three reasons, which we believe are the primary factors.

Changes in US regulations have helped to spur the growth in derivatives trading. In 1974, Congress passed the Commodities Exchange Act (CEA) and created the CFTC. The CEA gave the CFTC jurisdiction over futures markets with the right to approve or restrict trading of different underlyings.[26] Whereas cash-settled futures markets would have been illegal under state and bucket shop laws up until that time, any such contracts from the CEA of 1974 onwards only require CFTC approval for trading.[27] After receiving CFTC approval in 1981, the CME began trading Eurodollars, the first futures contract to be cash-settled in the US. Since that time, cash settlement has become widely used. For example, in 2004, six of the top ten exchange-traded contracts (ranked by number of contracts traded) were cash-settled.[28] In an overhaul of the CEA of 1974, the Commodity Futures Modernization Act (CFMA) became law in the US in December 2000. Among its many implications, the CFMA allows for the trading of futures contracts on single stocks. Further, the CFMA affirms the legality of the OTC trading of derivatives on numerous types of underlyings, including measures of inflation and economic statistics.[29]

Recent intellectual advances in pricing and valuing derivatives have helped create demand and additional uses for derivatives. Beginning with the seminal paper of Black and Scholes (1973), academics have made numerous important contributions to this field. For example, over 95% of the references in Hull (2006), which is widely used by practitioners for pricing derivatives, are to writings published after Black and Scholes (1973).

Another likely spur to derivatives trading has come from advances in information technology, that is, the use of computers for derivatives trading. The growth in electronic trading discussed above has lead to decreased execution costs and quicker execution times for derivatives traders, which has in turn led to increased trading of derivatives. Chapters 17, 19, and 24 of Hull (2006) discuss computer models used by practitioners to value derivatives. The growth of fast and cheap computing allows derivatives practitioners to implement these models relatively easily or purchase inexpensive software packages that implement these models for them.

Today, most liquid option markets are on instruments that have a tradable underlying, allowing market makers to delta hedge their trades with customers. Correspondingly, there has been relatively limited growth in option markets on underlyings that are not traded. For example, option markets on credit defaults, economic statistics, and weather events, have been slow to develop, even though there may be customer demand for options on such underlyings. We believe that part of the reason for this slow development is that it is very expensive if not impossible for a market maker to hedge in markets where there is no tradable underlying. The work of Jameson and Wilhelm (1992) and Cho and Engle (1999) support this hypothesis by showing that a market maker quotes a wide bid-offer spread to customers when it is costly to delta hedge the resulting risk. Such option markets with wide bid-offer spreads are of limited utility to derivatives customers and thus resulting volume is likely to be low. Beginning in the next chapter, we discuss parimutuel matching, a useful method to generate volume and provide lower transaction costs to customers when there is no tradable underlying.

CHAPTER 2

Introduction to Parimutuel Matching

This chapter introduces the main features of parimutuel matching. Parimutuel matching has been used successfully for over 100 years for wagering on horse races, and it has been in use in the derivatives markets since October 2002. This chapter describes parimutuel matching in its simplest form, because doing so allows us to introduce most of the main features of parimutuel matching without too much detailed mathematics and notation. We defer the more detailed mathematics of parimutuel matching to the later chapters in this book.

This chapter proceeds as follows. Section 2.1 develops the basic mathematics behind parimutuel matching, and it illustrates these mathematical concepts with an example based on the US Consumer Price Index (CPI). Section 2.2 compares parimutuel matching and bilateral matching. Section 2.3 concludes the chapter with a review of the academic research on parimutuel matching.

2.1 THE BASIC MATHEMATICS OF PARIMUTUEL MATCHING

This section describes the basic mathematics of parimutuel matching. Section 2.1.1 introduces the setup and the "states" for this analysis. Section 2.1.2 presents the customer orders. Section 2.1.3 describes the assumptions for the analysis. Section 2.1.4 discusses the two main mathematical principles of parimutuel pricing in this framework, and Section 2.1.5 concludes by showing what these mathematical principles imply about parimutuel prices. Throughout this section, we illustrate our general discussion using an example where the underlying is the monthly percentage change in the US CPI.

Table 2.1 State claims for a CPI example

State and state-claim number	State	State-claim strategy type
1	$U < 0.2$	Digital put
2	$U = 0.2$	Digital range
3	$U = 0.3$	Digital range
4	$U \geq 0.4$	Digital call

2.1.1 The setup and the states

Assume that we want to match orders on cash-settled European-style derivatives that pay out based on a particular underlying. Let U be a random variable that denotes the value of that underlying upon expiration, and let Ω denote the sample space of possible values of U. Divide Ω into a set of mutually exclusive and collectively exhaustive subsets or "states." Each state corresponds to a single value or multiple values of U. With multiple values in certain states, we can partition the sample space so that the total number of states is finite, making the mathematics tractable. Let S denote the number of those states, and let s and $\tilde{s}$ denote state index numbers. If $s < \tilde{s}$, we require that all values of U in state s are less than all values of U in state $\tilde{s}$. Thus, a higher state number implies a higher value of the underlying U.

The CPI example: Assume that the underlying U is the monthly change in US CPI measured in percentage terms over a specified month. Consequently, a value of $U = 0.3$ means that US CPI over the month of interest increased by 0.3%. The Bureau of Labor Statistics (BLS) measures CPI to the nearest one tenth of 1%. Our example has the following $S = 4$ states: U is less than 0.2; U equals 0.2; U equals 0.3; and U is greater than or equal to 0.4.[1] These states represent a mutually exclusive and collectively exhaustive set of finite outcomes for CPI. The first two columns of Table 2.1 summarize information on these states.

2.1.2 The customer orders

Customers can trade S "state claims," which are associated with the S states in the following way.[2] The sth state claim expires in-the-money if and only if the sth state occurs for $s = 1, 2, \ldots, S$. A customer who buys one contract of the sth state claim pays premium up front. Upon expiration, the customer receives one dollar if the sth state occurs. If the

sth state does not occur, then the sth state claim expires out-of-the-money and the customer who purchased it receives no payout, losing the premium that he/she paid. A state claim is an example of a digital option (introduced in Section 1.1) since each state claim pays out a fixed amount if the state claim expires in-the-money. State claims are at the foundation of financial theory and are discussed in, among many, Duffie (1988) and LeRoy and Werner (2001).

The CPI example: The third column of Table 2.1 displays the strategy types of the four state claims for our CPI example. The first state claim is a digital put, which pays out if CPI is below 0.2 upon expiration. The second and third state claims pay out a fixed amount if CPI equals a specific value upon expiration. These state claims are digital ranges, since they pay out if CPI is within a range, albeit a narrow one. The fourth state claim is a digital call, which pays out if CPI is 0.4 or higher upon expiration.

2.1.3   Assumptions for the analysis

We now describe assumptions that help us introduce the main features of parimutuel matching without too much mathematical complexity. Assume that the interest rate between the dates that premiums are collected and payouts are made is zero, or equivalently assume that premium and payouts are exchanged on the same date.[3] Next, assume that all participants meet their financial obligations, so there is no credit risk. Further, assume that there are no fees associated with any derivatives transactions. These assumptions let us avoid incorporating an interest rate or a transaction fee into our formulas, and we will use these three assumptions throughout this book.

We next introduce three somewhat restrictive assumptions that we will relax in the later chapters. First, we only allow customers to make purchases and all purchases must be of state claims. Thus, customers cannot sell state claims,[4] and customers cannot buy or sell any derivatives that pay out across multiple states. This implies that customers cannot trade vanilla options (which were introduced in Section 1.1), for instance. Returning to our CPI example, we only allow customers to buy from among the four state claims described above and listed in Table 2.1. Second, we only allow customers to submit market orders, and so customers cannot submit limit orders. Third, we require that all customers specify the premium to invest at the time the order is placed. In practice, most derivatives customers request a specific number of contracts when they submit their order, which is equivalent to requesting a specific payout based on different values of the underlying. Table 2.2 summarizes

Table 2.2 Setup for parimutuel matching in this chapter

Customers can	Customers cannot
Buy state claims	Sell state claims, buy vanilla options, or sell vanilla options
Submit market orders	Submit limit orders
Request a specific amount of premium to invest	Request a specific number of contracts

these three simplifying assumptions. It is worth noting that parimutuel matching under these simplifying assumptions closely resembles how parimutuel matching is used today for wagering on horse races.

2.1.4   The mathematical principles of parimutuel pricing

Parimutuel matching is done in a call-auction format (which was discussed in Section 1.2). Assume that such a parimutuel auction is run by a financial intermediary, who handles all monies and settles all contracts. Assume that customers submit market orders to buy state claims that pay out based on U, the value of the underlying at expiration. During the auction, a customer submits a market order by requesting a particular state claim and by specifying the premium to invest. Customers know their premium at risk at the time the order is submitted since all orders are market orders and will be fully filled. The number of contracts that the customer receives, or equivalently the payout if the state claim expires in-the-money, is the customer's premium amount divided by the price of that state claim. With parimutuel matching, the prices of the state claims are not known until the auction closes so, at the time the customer submits an order, the premium at risk is known, while the number of contracts that the customer receives is not known. With parimutuel matching, all customer orders for the same state claim pay the same price per contract, regardless of the time during the auction that each customer order is submitted (because the auction is a call auction).

For notation, let m_s denote the total amount of customer premium invested in the sth state claim in the auction for $s = 1, 2, \ldots, S$. We assume that m_s is positive for $s = 1, 2, \ldots, S$, so [5]

$$m_s > 0 \quad s = 1, 2, \ldots, S. \tag{2.1}$$

Let M denote the total amount of premium invested across all the state claims in the auction. Thus,

$$M = \sum_{s=1}^{S} m_s. \tag{2.2}$$

Let p_s denote the price of one contract of the sth state claim (which pays out one dollar if the sth state occurs) for $s = 1, 2, \ldots, S$. Based on the amount of premium invested in the sth state claim and the price of that state claim, we have that

$$y_s = \frac{m_s}{p_s} \quad s = 1, 2, \ldots, S, \tag{2.3}$$

where y_s denotes the total amount paid out to those customers who own the sth state claim if the sth state claim expires in-the-money for $s = 1, 2, \ldots, S$. The payout to buyers of the sth state claim if the sth state claim expires in-the-money is simply the premium invested in the sth state claim divided by the price of the sth state claim.

We now describe the mathematical principles used to determine the parimutuel prices. First, we require the following restriction:

$$p_s > 0 \quad s = 1, 2, \ldots, S. \tag{2.4}$$

Equation (2.4) says that all state claims have positive prices, and so customers cannot buy a state claim with a price that is less than or equal to zero.[6] Next, consider a portfolio that contains one contract of every state claim. Regardless of what state occurs, this portfolio will pay out one dollar, and so it is a risk-free portfolio, since we assumed above that all participants will meet their financial obligations. The cost of this portfolio is simply the sum of the prices of the state claims. Our second restriction is that

$$\sum_{s=1}^{S} p_s = 1. \tag{2.5}$$

Thus, Equation (2.5) is that this risk-free portfolio that pays out one dollar also costs one dollar. Equations (2.4) and (2.5) imply that parimutuel prices are "arbitrage-free" in the sense that customers cannot buy a derivative that both makes money in at least one state and never loses money.[7] The fact that parimutuel prices are arbitrage-free is the first mathematical principle of parimutuel matching.

The second mathematical principle of parimutuel matching is based on the following requirement:

$$y_s = M \quad s = 1, 2, \ldots, S. \tag{2.6}$$

The principle is that the amount that is paid out if the sth state claim expires in-the-money is simply the total amount of premium in the auction, and this is true regardless of the state s. Equation (2.6) requires that irrespective of which state occurs, total payouts to in-the-money state-claim holders equal M, the total premium in the auction. With parimutuel matching, the profits to the in-the-money option holders come from the premium paid by out-of-the-money option holders. Thus, the aggregate of all investments form what we call a closed "self-hedging" system. We refer to Equation (2.6) as the self-hedging equation, which is the second mathematical principle of parimutuel matching. The self-hedging feature of parimutuel matching is an attractive and important feature for the financial intermediary running the call auction, because the intermediary does not take on any risk associated with those investments. If no fees are charged in this call auction as assumed above, then a parimutuel market is a zero-sum game, like most derivatives markets net of fees. However, we can say something stronger about a parimutuel market – it creates a set of trades that in combination have *zero risk*. Table 2.3 presents the two mathematical principles of parimutuel matching (in this framework) and the main equations associated with those principles.

The CPI example: Table 2.4 displays relevant auction statistics for the CPI example. Column two of Table 2.4 lists the states and column three

Table 2.3 The mathematical principles of parimutuel matching in this simplified framework

Principle 1	Statement of principle	Prices satisfy no-arbitrage restrictions
	The no-arbitrage equations	$p_s > 0 \qquad s = 1, 2, \ldots, S$
		$\sum_{s=1}^{S} p_s = 1$
	Related restriction	$m_s > 0 \qquad s = 1, 2, \ldots, S$
Principle 2	Statement of principle	Prices and fills satisfy self-hedging restrictions
	The self-hedging equation	$y_s = M \qquad s = 1, 2, \ldots, S$
	Related equations	$M = \sum_{s=1}^{S} m_s$
		$y_s = \frac{m_s}{p_s} \qquad s = 1, 2, \ldots, S$

Table 2.4 Statistics for the CPI auction

State claim s	State	Amount invested in the sth state claim m_s in $	Price of the sth state claim p_s	Number of contracts per $1 in premium invested in the sth state claim	Payout if the sth state claim expires in-the-money y_s in $
1	$U < 0.2$	80,000	0.20	5	400,000
2	$U = 0.2$	200,000	0.50	2	400,000
3	$U = 0.3$	100,000	0.25	4	400,000
4	$U \geq 0.4$	20,000	0.05	20	400,000

shows the amount of premium invested in each state claim. The total amount invested across all four state claims, which is the sum of the values in this third column, is $M = \$400,000$. Column four shows the state-claim prices. One can easily check the no-arbitrage conditions of Equations (2.4) and (2.5), that is, that the state prices are all positive and sum to one. The fifth column of Table 2.4 displays the number of contracts a customer receives for one dollar of premium invested in a state claim, which is simply the inverse of the state claim's price. The sixth column shows the total dollar payouts if each state occurs based on Equation (2.3). Note that $400,000 must be paid out to in-the-money state-claim holders regardless of the state that occurs. Since the total premium collected is $400,000, regardless of the state that occurs, the payouts to in-the-money option holders are exactly funded by the premium collected, and so the self-hedging condition of Equation (2.6) holds.

2.1.5   Implications of the parimutuel principles

What do the no-arbitrage and the self-hedging conditions imply about the prices of the state claims in parimutuel matching? Equations (2.1), (2.2), (2.3), and (2.6) imply that

$$p_s = \frac{m_s}{M} \quad s = 1, 2, \ldots, S. \tag{2.7}$$

Examine Equation (2.7) and note that the more premium that is invested in the sth state claim relative to the total premium invested across all state claims in the auction, or the larger m_s is relative to M, the higher the price of the sth state claim p_s. The payout or number of contracts for a one dollar investment in the sth state claim is simply the inverse of the price of the sth state claim, or M divided by m_s. Note that the financial intermediary running the auction does not require any expertise with regard to setting the prices: the prices are determined mathematically by Equation (2.7). The state price p_s is often interpreted as the "implied probability" that the sth state occurs, where the implied probability is based on the premium invested by auction participants. Equations (2.1), (2.4), and (2.7) together imply that

$$\frac{m_s}{m_{\tilde{s}}} = \frac{p_s}{p_{\tilde{s}}} \quad s, \tilde{s} = 1, 2, \ldots, S. \tag{2.8}$$

Thus, in parimutuel matching, the relative amount of premium invested in two state claims determines the relative prices of these claims: the more that is invested in one state claim relative to a second state claim, the higher the price of the first state claim relative to the price of the second state claim.[8] For example, if the first state claim has twice as much premium invested in it as the second state claim, then the price of the first state claim will be twice the price of the second state claim. Since the amount of premium invested in a state claim can be considered a measure of demand for that state claim, we refer to this property as the "relative-demand pricing" feature of parimutuel matching. Although relative-demand pricing will be new to many derivative-market participants, it helps customers understand how parimutuel matching determines prices based on the orders.[9]

The CPI example: It is straightforward to check the state-pricing formula of Equation (2.7) for each value of s. Let us do so for state $s = 2$.

$$p_2 = 0.5$$
$$= \frac{200,000}{400,000}$$
$$= \frac{m_2}{M}. \tag{2.9}$$

Next, we verify the relative-demand pricing of Equation (2.8) for states $s = 2$ and $\tilde{s} = 3$. Here, we need to check that

$$\frac{m_2}{m_3} = \frac{p_2}{p_3}. \tag{2.10}$$

In this case,

$$
\begin{aligned}
\frac{m_2}{m_3} &= \frac{200,000}{100,000} \\
&= \frac{0.50}{0.25} \\
&= \frac{p_2}{p_3}.
\end{aligned}
\tag{2.11}
$$

Thus, relative-demand pricing holds for states $s = 2$ and $\tilde{s} = 3$. The second state claim is twice as valuable as the third state claim because it has twice the premium invested in it. One could verify relative-demand pricing for other values of s and $\tilde{s}$.

2.2 COMPARING PARIMUTUEL MATCHING AND BILATERAL MATCHING

The CPI example from Section 2.1 can be used to illustrate many of the main properties of parimutuel matching. Using this example as a springboard, we now compare parimutuel matching and bilateral matching.

2.2.1 Matching buyers and sellers

As discussed in Section 1.2, bilateral matching requires a buyer for every seller. Consider a call auction where customers trade the four state claims in the CPI example. Since the customer orders in Section 2.1 are all buy orders, bilateral matching cannot transfer risk or generate trades between these buy orders.[10] With bilateral matching, for every buyer, there is a seller whose payout function is the opposite of the buyer's payout function, and this seller has the exact opposite risk as the buyer. Parimutuel matching, in contrast, does not require a buyer for every seller. As the example in Section 2.1 illustrates, parimutuel matching can transfer risk with only buyers of options. Consider the buyer of the first state claim in the parimutuel auction on CPI. This customer receives a payout if the first state occurs and receives no payout if the second, third, or fourth states occur. This order gets filled because the buyers of the other state claims are all effectively short the first claim. The in-the-money payout for the buyer of the first state claim is based on the total premium in the auction, which is his/her premium invested plus the premium of the other buyers of state claims in the auction. In parimutuel matching, all trades in an auction are executed at the same instant in time (when the auction is called), and this allows orders to be filled across multiple parties and multiple derivatives. Thus, with parimutuel matching, there does not necessarily exist a party with the exact opposite risk to each buyer.

2.2.2   Pricing and liquidity

With bilateral matching, prices and liquidity are based on bids and offers for each derivative separately. Consequently, an order on one derivative does not directly impact pricing or liquidity on other derivatives. To see the impact an order can have on all derivative prices in a parimutuel auction, consider the scenario that all amounts invested in the different state claims remain the same as those in Table 2.4 except that an additional $100,000 investment is made in the second state claim right before the call auction closes. Table 2.5 displays the statistics from this auction example, and Table 2.6 shows the changes in auction statistics based on this new order.[11] Column three of Table 2.6 shows the change in state-claim prices with the new investment. Note that the price of the second state claim rises while the prices of the other state claims fall. Because of the relative-demand pricing of parimutuel matching (Equation (2.8)), an order on one derivative can impact the prices of all other derivatives.

With the additional $100,000 investment in the second state claim, buyers of the second state claim receive fewer contracts per one dollar of premium invested, and buyers of the other state claims receive more contracts per one dollar of premium invested. For example, the number of filled contracts for a customer who invests one dollar in the fourth

Table 2.5 Statistics for the CPI auction with an additional $100,000 investment in the second state claim

State claim s	State	Amount invested in the sth state claim m_s in $	Price of the sth state claim p_s	Number of contracts per $1 in premium invested in the sth state claim	Payout if the sth state claim expires in-the-money y_s in $
1	$U < 0.2$	80,000	0.16	6.67	500,000
2	$U = 0.2$	300,000	0.60	1.67	500,000
3	$U = 0.3$	100,000	0.20	5.00	500,000
4	$U \geq 0.4$	20,000	0.04	25.00	500,000

Table 2.6 Change in auction quantities with the additional $100,000 investment in the second state claim for the CPI auction

State claim s	Change in amount invested in the sth state claim m_s in $	Change in price of the sth state claim p_s	Change in number of contracts per $1 in premium invested in the sth state claim
1	0	−0.04	1.67
2	100,000	0.10	−0.33
3	0	−0.05	1.00
4	0	−0.01	5.00

state claim increases from 20 to 25. As this example illustrates, the additional order on second state claim increases fills for orders on the other state claims. In this way, parimutuel matching aggregates liquidity across different derivatives.

2.2.3   No-arbitrage restrictions

With bilateral matching, prices are based on bids and offers for each derivative separately, and so no-arbitrage restrictions such as those of Equations (2.4) and (2.5) are not enforced across different derivatives. Because prices are based on bids and offers for each derivative separately, bilateral matching can lead to risk-free profits or arbitrage opportunities across different derivatives.

For example, consider customer orders submitted to buy each of the four state claims. Since bilateral matching treats orders on different derivatives separately, these four orders cannot help generate trades with each other using bilateral matching. Now, consider a theoretical arbitrageur who executes trades instantaneously, pays no transaction fees, and has zero cost of capital. If this arbitrageur sells one contract of each of the four state claims and collects more than one dollar in premium, then this arbitrageur will generate a risk-free profit or lock in an arbitrage opportunity. In practice, arbitrageurs cannot guarantee execution of all four trades simultaneously, and arbitrageurs pay transaction costs.[12] Thus, the total premium that the arbitrageur expects to collect for selling the four contracts must be bigger than one to compensate an arbitrageur for the risk that he/she will not be able to execute all four trades, and to compensate the arbitrageur for his/her efforts. Without enforcing the no-arbitrage restrictions, these four orders would likely be filled at prices that sum to greater than one in a bilateral system. Consequently, with bilateral matching, such frictions hinder the ability of these orders to be executed and at the best possible prices.[13]

In contrast, parimutuel matching enforces no-arbitrage restrictions on derivatives on the same underlying with the same expiration date. In particular, parimutuel matching forces prices to sum to one, as expressed in Equation (2.5). Thus, the orders on the four state claims are all filled using parimutuel matching and the state prices sum to one. Eliminating such arbitrage opportunities is likely to lead to improved prices for hedgers and speculators, although it may limit profit opportunities for market markers and arbitrageurs.[14]

2.2.4   Liquidity for low-delta options

Although option prices are based in part on valuation models such as Black and Scholes (1973), Figlewski (1989a) shows that due to market imperfections, prices can differ significantly from such model values. Figlewski (1989b) and Canina and Figlewski (1993) argue that supply and demand play an important role in determining option prices. Hodges, Tompkins, and Ziemba (2003) and Bollen and Whaley (2004) empirically verify the importance of supply and demand for determining option prices. Because of the importance of supply and demand, option liquidity with bilateral matching may be hindered if at the current price there are many interested buyers and few sellers, and so few trades are executed.

For instance, consider an option that has a very low probability of expiring in-the-money but has a large payout if it does expire in-the-money. Such an option is often called a low-delta option, because of the option's low exposure to changes in the underlying as measured by delta from the Black and Scholes model (1973). Figlewski (1989b) argues that such an option should sell above its theoretical value as computed by an option-pricing model, because buyers find the large potential payout favorable and sellers find the substantial risks unfavorable. Hodges, Tompkins, and Ziemba (2003) find empirical support for Figlewski's hypothesis. When a customer wants to buy a low-delta option with a lottery-ticket-like payout, he/she may only be able to buy it at a price significantly above fair value from a market maker because of the option's risky profile. This may discourage buyers of these derivative strategies and so bilateral matches for such options may only occur rarely.

Let us return to the example from Section 2.1, and consider a buyer of the fourth state claim. For each dollar of premium invested, a buyer will receive a payout of $20 if the option expires in-the-money, giving a buyer a high degree of leverage, as is typically the case with low-delta options. In bilateral matching, a market maker would be required to take on the exact opposite payout profile to a buyer of the fourth state claim, which is an unattractive risk-return proposition for most market makers. As discussed above in Section 2.2.1, there is no customer in the CPI auction who has to pay out $20 if the fourth state occurs and who also receives one dollar if the first, second, or third state occurs (although the buyers of the first three state claims have this position collectively). Put another way, there is no customer who has a worst loss that is 20 times larger than their potential gain. Thus, there is no one who has the exact opposite risk to the buyer of the fourth state claim, and so there is no one that is short an option with a lottery-ticket-like payout. The price of this claim (like the price of all state claims in parimutuel matching) is not based solely on bids and offers for this derivative and is instead based on relative demand using the orders across all the state claims. Since no one has to be short the fourth state claim, customers may be able to pay a lower price on such a low-delta option, which may increase traded volume in the auction. Section 2.3.5 reviews the academic literature on this topic, which confirms our hypothesis and finds that parimutuel matching often leads to fairer prices on such low-delta options. This aspect of parimutuel matching is likely to contribute to increased trading volume and risk transfer.

2.2.5 Liquidity without a tradable underlying

As discussed above, market makers generally play a very important role in providing liquidity to option markets by quoting bids and offers for prospective customers. After executing a trade with a customer, market makers often hedge the resulting option exposure by delta hedging through trading in the underlying. Jameson and Wilhelm (1992) and Cho and Engle (1999) show that a market maker quotes a wide bid-offer spread when it is costly to hedge the resulting risk. For instance, when there is no continuously-tradable underlying for delta hedging, hedging costs increase for market makers, and these costs get passed along to customers in the form of wider bid-offer spreads on their option quotes. With bilateral matching, it is difficult to create a liquid options market without a tradable underlying, since delta hedging is not a viable hedging approach for market makers in such a scenario.

Parimutuel matching does not require a buyer for every seller to execute trades, and its flexibility may help create a liquid options market when there is no tradable underlying for delta hedging. This can lead to lower all in costs for customers trading options when there is no tradable underlying. With parimutuel matching, the customer trades form a zero-risk book, and so there is less of a reliance on an intermediary to quote bids and offers and then hedge by trading in the underlying. This can lead to more efficient risk transfer for customers trading options when there is

Table 2.7 The main properties of parimutuel matching

Property #	Property
1	No need to match a buyer with a seller
2	Risk can be transferred and trades executed with just buyers of options
3	One new order can change the prices of *all* other derivatives in the auction
4	Orders on one derivative can improve the liquidity on other derivatives

no tradable underlying. For instance, over $100 billion in volume trades each year in parimutuel wagering on horse and other types of races, a case where there is no tradable underlying. Further, the economic derivatives market has used parimutuel matching successfully for more than four years without a tradable underlying. We discuss these topics in greater detail in Chapter 3.

2.2.6   Summary

Based on our discussion above, Table 2.7 highlights some of the key aspects of parimutuel matching, all of which may be new to derivatives-market participants. Table 2.8 summarizes the differences between bilateral matching and parimutuel matching.

2.3   ACADEMIC RESEARCH ON PARIMUTUEL WAGERING

Researchers have studied parimutuel wagering on horse races for over 50 years. One reason that researchers have been attracted to this topic is that wagering on horse races provides a simple framework for studying how individuals make decisions under uncertainty. Researchers can readily obtain data on both the amount wagered on different horses and the outcome of each race. Thus, empirical analysis is straightforward. Another advantage of parimutuel wagering is that it is easy to explain and to implement, and so economists have studied the properties of parimutuel matching in the laboratory – research that is part of a growing body of work in the field of experimental economics. The results of academic research on parimutuel matching are important, because they tell us if trading derivatives using parimutuel matching is likely to be efficient. As shown below,

Table 2.8 Comparing bilateral matching and parimutuel matching

Topic	Bilateral matching	Parimutuel matching
Conditions for a trade	A trade occurs when a buyer of a derivative is matched with a seller of that derivative	A trade occurs when orders are matched across (possibly) different derivatives
Pricing	Based on the bids and offers for each derivative separately	Based on the bids and offers across different derivatives
Liquidity across derivatives	Orders on one derivative do not improve liquidity for other similar derivatives	Orders on one derivative may improve liquidity for other similar derivatives
Arbitrage	Arbitrage exists, which increases costs for hedgers and speculators and hurts price discovery	Arbitrage can be eliminated, which decreases costs for hedgers and speculators and improves price discovery
Low-delta options	Customers may pay higher prices on low-delta options to compensate sellers for being short these risky options	Customers may pay lower prices on low-delta options because there is no seller required for trades to take place
Tradable underlying	Option bid-offer spreads may be wider when there is no tradable underlying for market makers to use for delta hedging	Option bid-offer spreads may be narrower when there is no tradable underlying for market makers to use for delta hedging

many properties of parimutuel matching are favorable, suggesting that parimutuel matching may be useful for trading derivatives.

We now describe some of main conclusions of academic research on parimutuel wagering. Since most parimutuel research has been done on wagering on horse races, Section 2.3.1 provides background on parimutuel horse-race wagering. Section 2.3.2 reviews the accuracy of parimutuel win odds in predicting the winner of a horse race. Section 2.3.3 discusses if it is possible to systematically make money wagering on horse races. Section 2.3.4 describes the mathematical properties of parimutuel matching. Section 2.3.5 comments briefly on some additional topics, and Section 2.3.6 provides a summary. Throughout this discussion, we refer to some of the relevant research articles, many of which can be found in Hausch, Lo, and Ziemba (1994a).[15]

2.3.1   Parimutuel wagering on horse races

We now illustrate how parimutuel matching works for wagering on horses to win a particular race, which is essentially the framework discussed in Section 2.1.[16] The wagering period or call auction takes place in the several minutes leading up to the start of the race and ends exactly when the race begins. A customer submits a wager during that period by specifying which horse will win and a premium amount to risk. Let S denote the number of horses that are in the race of interest and assume that the horses are indexed $s = 1, 2, \ldots, S$. Let U denote the random variable that represents the number of the horse that wins the race. The sth state claim pays out if and only if the sth horse wins the race for $s = 1, 2, \ldots, S$. After the race is completed and the results are official, the payout amounts to those who selected the winning horse are announced. An important and widely discussed quantity at the racetrack is the "odds" for each horse to win, which are inversely related to the state prices in the following way. Let o_s denote the odds on the sth horse to win for $s = 1, 2, \ldots, S$. Then, the odds are

$$o_s = \frac{1}{p_s} - 1 \quad s = 1, 2, \ldots, S. \tag{2.12}$$

The odds represent the profit to the bettor per one dollar wagered if the specified horse wins the race. By the principle of relative demand, wagers on a specific horse to win decrease the odds on that horse to win (increase the price) and increase the odds (lower the prices) on other horses to win.

In addition to wagering on a horse to win, bettors can make a number of other types of wagers on a horse race. For example, bettors can also wager on a horse to "place" or to "show." A place wager pays out if the selected horse finishes either first or second, and a show wager pays out if the selected horse finishes first, second, or third. In current parimutuel wagering, win, place, and show wagers each have their own separate pools, and the payouts on these wagers depend on the amounts in these respective pools. Handling the pools separately makes calculating payouts to customers very easy mathematically, but has two shortcomings. First, separate pools lead to arbitrage opportunities across different types of wagers.[17] For instance, Willis (1964) describes how to construct such an arbitrage by wagering on horses to win and on horses to place.[18] Second, separate pools are not an efficient way to aggregate liquidity, and so large wagers in one pool are likely to receive a lower winning payout than if wagers of all types were combined into one pool.

2.3.2   Accuracy of parimutuel pricing

How accurate are the odds or equivalently the prices at the racetrack in terms of predicting the actual winner in a horse race? Researchers have found evidence in the past that "favorites" (horses that are favored to win a race) tend to be underbet and "long shots" (horses that are not expected to win a race) tend to be overbet at the racetrack, and this pricing anomaly is often called the "favorite-longshot" bias. The favorite-longshot bias was discovered by Griffith (1949) and has been found in numerous subsequent papers analyzing parimutuel wagering on horse races run in the US and elsewhere. Hausch, Lo, and Ziemba (1994b) and Sauer (1998) provide a summary and analysis of much of this work.[19]

The most recent empirical evidence, however, suggests that the favorite-longshot bias may not be as robust in parimutuel wagering as was originally believed. Busche and Walls (2000) and Bjorkman and Bukszar (2003) show that the favorite-longshot bias has not been statistically significant in the US in recent years. Researchers have also found limited evidence of the favorite-longshot bias in parimutuel wagering in other countries. Bruce and Johnson (2000) find only very weak recent evidence for the favorite-longshot bias in wagering on UK horse races. Busche and Hall (1988), Busche (1994), and Gandar, Zuber, and Johnson (2001) find no statistical evidence of the favorite-longshot bias in wagering on horse races in Hong Kong, Japan, or New Zealand, respectively.

As described in Wolfers and Zitzewitz (2004), there is widespread academic interest in how well markets do at forecasting future events versus experts. Figlewski (1979) shows that parimutuel prices at the racetrack are more accurate on average than those put forth by professional handicappers. Sections 4.4 and 6.3 will discuss related work that shows that parimutuel matching does a better job in forecasting upcoming economic statistics than professional economists. Economic theory provides a basis as to why parimutuel auctions may be better than experts at forecasting. Eisenberg and Gale (1959) and Owen (1997) show that the parimutuel state prices can be viewed as weighted averages of the bettors' individual subjective probabilities of different outcomes. Thus, the state prices from a parimutuel auction can be viewed as consensus measures of the participants' forecasts, as will be discussed further in Section 2.3.4. To the extent that those participants have better information than the experts (and often times bettors have access to expert opinions before they make a wager), then the parimutuel prices are likely to provide better forecasts than the experts.

2.3.3   Beating the racetrack

Researchers have extensively studied if there is a systematic way to make money wagering on horse races. Most horse racing associations take approximately 20 cents of every dollar in premium wagered before entering the remaining 80 cents into the parimutuel pool to fund payouts. With customers paying such high transaction costs, finding a wagering strategy that can consistently overcome this disadvantage seems quite daunting. In addressing this issue, academic economists have tested the profitability of several strategies based on information in the wagering pools and the odds. In looking at such "pool strategies," Ziemba and Hausch (1987, pp. 45–47), among many others, conclude that it is difficult to make money consistently by making wagers to win. This result may not be too surprising, given that bettors are on average good forecasters of which horse wins a race.

Much of the evidence of profitable pool strategies comes from strategies that make place and show bets. Researchers have developed at least two such approaches, both of which use information from the win pool. The most widely known such system is the "Dr. Z System," named after William Ziemba. As described by Hausch, Ziemba, and Rubinstein (1981), Hausch and Ziemba (1985), and Ziemba and Hausch (1987), this strategy capitalizes on the empirical finding that horses likely to win a race are often underbet in the place and show pools. Ziemba and Hausch (1987) confirm with historical data and with several trips to the racetrack that selectively wagering on the favorite or the near favorite to place or show can yield profitable results. Asch, Malkiel, and Quandt (1984 and 1986) and Asch and Quandt (1986) develop a related system. Their strategy is based on their finding that bettors making wagers just before the start of the race tend to be more informed than the general wagering public. Thus, these researchers postulate that a drop in a horse's win odds just before the start of the race reflects informed wagering. Based on this strategy, they document historical profits from wagering on a favorite or near favorite horse to place or show after a relative large amount of money is wagered on that horse late in the wagering period.

Ritter (1994), however, shows that profitably implementing such pool strategies in real time can be difficult. These systems often rely on knowing or approximately knowing the final amounts in the pools, and consequently they require wagering at the last possible moment in the wagering period. Changes in the amounts in the pools after a wager has been made can adversely affect the profitability of a strategy. In addition,

Lo, Bacon-Shone, and Busche (1995) note in recent years that the number of people employing such wagering strategies for place and show betting has risen significantly. Because of this, they argue that the profitability of these strategies is likely to be significantly less than earlier studies indicate. In financial parlance, one might say that bettors that currently employ these strategies have arbitraged out much of the profits.

The two place and show strategies described above utilize the fact that the win pool is separate from the place and show pools. However, using separate parimutuel pools for different types of wagers is not necessarily inherent to parimutuel matching. In the parimutuel matching approach introduced in the later chapters, all orders are entered into one pool of liquidity, and it is possible to use a similar technique to combine all win, place, and show wagers into one parimutuel pool. Our intuition is that combining into one all the pools for wagering on a horse race would likely reduce the profitability of these place and show strategies: the combined pool approach enforces no-arbitrage restrictions, which will likely help to limit the profitability of such strategies. Thus, pricing anomalies between the win, place, and show pools are not necessarily inherent to parimutuel matching, but are at least in part created by using separate pools for related types of wagers.[20]

2.3.4   Mathematical properties of parimutuel pricing

Eisenberg and Gale (1959) were the first to study the mathematical properties of parimutuel pricing. In their seminal paper, they examine the properties of wagers and state prices (or equivalently implied state probabilities) under the conditions where:

1.   Each bettor is endowed with a budget;

2.   Each bettor has his/her own subjective probability estimate of each outcome in the state space; and

3.   Each bettor seeks to maximize his/her expected payout (i.e., each bettor is risk neutral).

Eisenberg and Gale (1959) find that, under these three conditions, the parimutuel equilibrium prices are unique and are guaranteed to exist.[21] Furthermore, the equilibrium wagers and prices have an interesting interpretation: the equilibrium is equivalent to a social planner maximizing an objective function that is the weighted sum of each bettor's logarithmic expected value – which can be interpreted as a total return – where the weights are proportional to each bettor's budget. So if a social planner maximizes the bettors' budget weighted expected return, then this exactly corresponds to the competitive equilibrium whereby each bettor acts individually through the parimutuel mechanism.[22]

Owen (1997) generalizes Eisenberg and Gale's (1959) results for bettors that have general concave utility functions, instead of just being risk neutral. Owen's results are particularly interesting for some commonly used utility functions. If each bettor has logarithmic utility, then Owen (1997) shows that the parimutuel equilibrium state prices are a weighted *arithmetic* average of each bettor's individual subjective state probabilities, where the weights are based in part on each bettor's wealth. If each bettor has exponential utility, then Owen (1997) shows that the parimutuel equilibrium state prices are a weighted *geometric* average of each individual bettor's subjective probability, where the weights are based on each bettor's risk tolerance.[23]

These results bear on another important area of research. Economists have studied combining individual – oftentimes "expert" – probability assessments into an aggregate probability distribution. Economists refer to the method in which forecasts are combined as a "scoring rule," and Chen, Chu, Mullen, and Pennock (2005), for instance, describe and compare how various scoring rules do relative to market-based forecasts.[24] A standard scoring rule is "LinOP," which is a weighted average of individual probability forecasts. When participants in a parimutuel auction have logarithmic utility functions, Owen's (1997) results show that the equilibrium state prices can be thought of as LinOP forecasts. Weighted geometric averages of experts – which are known as "LogOP" scoring rules – are then closely related to the parimutuel equilibrium prices when participants have exponential utility. Thus, we can interpret parimutuel equilibrium state prices as scoring rules based on individual participants' probabilities and utility functions. To the extent that parimutuel auction participants have as good as or have better information than experts, then we can expect forecasts that are based on parimutuel auctions to be more accurate than scoring rules.

2.3.5   Additional topics on parimutuel pricing

This section describes research on three additional features of parimutuel matching.

Parimutuel odds versus bookmaker odds: Horse racing in Ireland and the UK provide a unique environment to compare parimutuel matching with bilateral matching. In these countries, bettors can legally wager on a horse race either parimutuelly or bilaterally with a bookmaker. Gabriel and Marsden (1990, 1991) and Bruce and Johnson (2000) study wagering in the UK, and they find that bettors in general get higher odds on long shots with the parimutuel mechanism than with bookmakers. A model of Shin (1993) suggests that bookmakers offer worse odds on long shots to protect themselves against informed bettors. Fingleton and Waldron (2001) generalize Shin's model. Using wagering data from horse races in Ireland, they find that risk aversion and anti-competitive behavior by Irish bookmakers are also contributing factors to bookmakers offering lower odds on long shots. Long-shot wagers are effectively equivalent to low-delta options discussed in Section 2.2.4. Thus, consistent with our comments in that section, parimutuel matching tends to provide higher odds (lower prices) on such low-delta option strategies.

Difficulty in manipulating parimutuel prices: Camerer (1998) makes several trips to racetracks to attempt to manipulate the win odds. Camerer (1998) makes wagers in horse races where there are two horses with similar probabilities of winning the race. Camerer (1998) randomly chooses one of the two horses and makes a $500 or $1000 wager on that horse about twenty minutes before the start of the race and then cancels that wager about seven minutes before the start of the race. Camerer (1998) compares the odds on the horses with the temporary wagers against the odds on the horses in the control group, and he shows the temporary wagers have no statistical impact on the final odds. Camerer (1998) concludes that the parimutuel mechanism is difficult to manipulate.[25]

Information aggregation: Plott, Wit, and Yang (2003) examined the parimutuel mechanism's ability to aggregate information with a study from the experimental economics field. In their experiments, they give each participant a small piece of private information regarding the actual outcome of a lottery (e.g., "the winning lottery number is not number 4"). Plott, Wit, and Yang (2003) distribute private information in such a way that if every piece of private information became public, then the lottery outcome would be known. So, in aggregate, the participants have enough information to know exactly which outcome will occur in the lottery. Consequently, if the parimutuel mechanism is an efficient means of aggregating information, all money should be wagered on that outcome and no money should be wagered on the other outcomes. Plott, Wit, and Yang's (2003) experimental results show that the parimutuel mechanism does not quite achieve this goal of perfect information aggregation, yet the parimutuel mechanism does aggregate enough information to make it difficult for each investor to make consistent profits based upon his/her own information. Plott, Wit, and Yang (2003) conclude that the parimutuel mechanism is generally an efficient means of information aggregation and price discovery.

2.3.6 Summary of academic research

Based on the evidence, we find that the parimutuel odds to win provide a fairly accurate measure, on average, of a horse's probability of winning a race, since evidence of pricing anomalies such as the favorite-longshot bias is fairly weak in recent years. Research shows that some bettors can earn consistent profits betting parimutuelly on horses to place and show, but these profits are likely due in part to the fact that these pools are treated separately from the win pool. Separate pools are not a required feature of parimutuel wagering, but instead are a result of how parimutuel horse-race wagering has been historically implemented. Research has shown that the parimutuel pricing equilibrium has some favorable mathematical properties. Further, evidence suggests that the parimutuel mechanism can provide higher odds on long shots than bilateral matching with bookmakers, is difficult to manipulate, and is a fairly efficient means of aggregating information for price discovery. Thus, we conclude that the parimutuel mechanism has a number of favorable properties which may make it a useful mechanism for trading derivatives.

CHAPTER 3

Parimutuel Applications

Parimutuel matching has been used successfully for over 100 years for wagering on horse races, and it has been in use for trading derivatives in the financial markets since October 2002. This chapter describes these applications in more detail. Section 3.1 discusses how parimutuel matching has been used in the wagering arena to date. Section 3.2 reviews recent mathematical innovations that make parimutuel matching more suitable for trading derivatives. Section 3.3 provides an overview of how parimutuel matching is applied today in the derivatives markets. Section 3.4 discusses some closely related derivatives markets to those that use parimutuel matching, and Section 3.5 describes other trading mechanisms that are similar to parimutuel matching. Section 3.6 concludes with possible reasons for the relatively tardy introduction of parimutuel matching to the derivatives markets.

3.1 PARIMUTUEL WAGERING APPLICATIONS

Pierre Oller first put parimutuel matching into practice in Paris, France in 1872 for wagering on horse races.[1] Since that time, parimutuel wagering has grown significantly. Today, legal parimutuel wagering is conducted in at least 37 countries worldwide with over $100 billion wagered each year.[2] Japan has the highest amount of parimutuel wagering with $53 billion wagered in 2003.[3] The majority of parimutuel wagering in Japan is on horse races, but Japan also has parimutuel wagering on bicycle races, motorcycle races, and motorboat races. The US has the second highest amount of parimutuel wagering worldwide with $17.9 billion wagered in 2003, as reported by the Association of Racing Commissioners International (2005). In the US, parimutuel wagering is done on horse races, greyhound dog races, and jai alai contests.[4] In Hong Kong, $8.3 billion was wagered parimutuelly in 2003 on horse races.[5] Hong Kong has a population of 6.8 million people,[6] so $1,200 is wagered on average per person, which is by far the highest amount wagered per capita of any major country.

The parimutuel framework in use today for wagering on horse races was described in Sections 2.1 and 2.3.1. This framework is virtually unchanged from the system first formulated by Oller in nineteenth-century France, and it has somewhat limited application for trading derivatives as:

1. Customers cannot trade vanilla options;

2. Customers can only buy (and cannot sell) derivatives;

3. Customers cannot submit limit orders;[7]

4. Customers must submit orders in premium terms; and

5. Liquidity is not aggregated across all types of derivative strategies.[8]

Though the parimutuel framework used at the racetrack is quite successful for wagering, these limitations hinder the usefulness of the parimutuel framework for trading derivatives. Fortunately, these shortcomings are not inherent to parimutuel matching and can be addressed using more advanced mathematics and sufficient computing power.

3.2　LONGITUDE'S PARIMUTUEL INNOVATIONS

Jeffrey Lange, a coauthor of this book, and Andrew Lawrence founded the company Longitude in 1999 with the goal of introducing parimutuel matching and related techniques to the derivatives markets. They established the company with the view that applying parimutuel techniques to derivatives trading seems natural, since it allows financial institutions to offer derivatives to their customers without taking on market risk. Longitude has developed techniques to make parimutuel matching more compatible with derivatives trading, and these extensions have been described in part in Baron and Lange (2003) and Lange and Economides (2005). The first column of Table 3.1 shows the current parimutuel wagering framework, and the second column of Table 3.1 summarizes Longitude's extensions to parimutuel matching, which include allowing customers to submit limit orders and orders for vanilla options. Chapters 5 and 6 will describe these refinements in further detail. We refer to an auction that has the functionality described in column two of Table 3.1 as a "parimutuel derivatives auction."

Table 3.1 The parimutuel wagering framework and parimutuel innovations by Longitude

In parimutuel wagering, customers can	With Longitude's parimutuel innovations, customers can
Buy digital options	Buy and sell digital and vanilla options
Submit market orders	Submit market and limit orders
Request a specific amount of premium to invest	Request a specific number of contracts to buy and sell
Submit orders into separate parimutuel pools	Submit orders into one common pool of liquidity

To protect its intellectual property, Longitude has applied for patent protection on its parimutuel advances. Inventors on these patent filing include Jeffrey Lange, Ken Baron (a coauthor of this book), Marcus Harte, and Charles Walden. In November 2001, the US Patent and Technology Office (USPTO) granted Longitude's first patent, Lange (1999). It is worth noting that patent protection for financial methods is relatively new in the US and elsewhere. The 1998 landmark case of *State Street Bank and Trust* v. *Signature Financial Group*, 149 F.3d 1368 (Fed. Cir. 1998), established that inventors could patent financial methods in the US.[9]

Longitude has developed a software implementation of its parimutuel matching engine that prices derivatives using its mathematical innovations. Longitude currently licenses that software to the Chicago Mercantile Exchange (CME), Goldman Sachs, the New York Mercantile Exchange (NYMEX), and ICAP for running parimutuel derivatives auctions for each of their respective customers. (The assets of Longitude were purchased by the International Securities Exchange and Goldman Sachs in the spring of 2006.) Regarding this business strategy, it is worth recalling that financial intermediaries typically offer derivative products to their customers only when they can hedge the underlying risks associated with those trades. Parimutuel matching does not require hedging by the financial intermediary, and this has led Longitude to work with its partners to offer derivatives in two broad areas where hedging is difficult.[10]

One area in which Longitude's parimutuel technology has been used is for trading derivatives on non-tradable underlyings, such as derivatives on economic statistics (more on those in the next section). Offering derivatives on such new underlyings has three comparative advantages. First, it allows Longitude and its partners to work on derivative products where there are no pre-existing competitors and no pre-existing products. Second, for risks where there are no tradable underlyings such as economic statistics, transaction immediacy is likely to be less important to investors since information is less likely to be revealed continuously throughout the day. Thus, the call-auction aspect of parimutuel derivatives auctions is likely to be not inappropriate for trading such underlying risks. Third, with new underlyings, derivatives traders and customers may be more open to accepting the call-auction feature, a mechanism that they are likely to be unaccustomed to using.

Longitude and its partners are also currently running parimutuel derivatives auctions for trading short-dated options on liquid underlyings. Short-dated options, particularly short-dated digital options, are difficult for market makers to delta hedge since the deltas of these options can change dramatically based on small movements in the underlying.[11] Consequently, short-dated options are a natural product for parimutuel derivatives auctions. As discussed in more detail in the next section, Longitude's matching engine is currently used for trading options that expire on the same day that they are traded, and these options are cash-settled based on the NYMEX settlement prices of crude oil and natural gas. These underlyings are widely followed by market participants. Such short-dated options can be of interest to both speculators and hedgers because their potential payout is greater than their price. The next section discusses these applications in more detail.

3.3 PARIMUTUEL DERIVATIVES APPLICATIONS

This section describes the three derivative markets that currently employ parimutuel matching – economic derivatives, energy inventory derivatives, and daily settlement derivatives. All three of these markets are traded using Longitude's parimutuel matching engine.

Economic derivatives: Many economic releases are widely followed by financial-market participants and can significantly impact prices in the financial markets. Because of this, Goldman Sachs and CME in conjunction with ICAP run parimutuel derivatives auctions using Longitude's matching engine on several economic statistics. They refer to derivatives on economic statistics as the "economic derivatives" market. Some

Table 3.2 Details on economic derivatives

Product	Economic derivatives
Date of first auction	1 October 2002
Current underlyings with measurement agencies in parenthesis	US nonfarm payrolls (US Department of Labor) US consumer price index (US Department of Labor) US initial jobless claims (US Department of Labor) US retail sales excluding autos (US Department of Commerce) US purchasing managers index (Institute for Supply Management) US international trade balance (US Department of Commerce) US gross domestic product (US Department of Commerce) European harmonized inflation (Eurostat)
Auction organizer	Goldman Sachs
Matching engine	Provided by Longitude
Brokering	Provided by ICAP
Clearing	CME Clearinghouse

of the most widely followed auctions are on the monthly change in US nonfarm payrolls (NFP), as measured by the Bureau of Labor Statistics (BLS), which is a division of the US Department of Labor. Goldman Sachs "organizes" auctions on economic derivatives, which means that Goldman Sachs determines the option strikes, the auction times, and the underlyings for the auctions. Customers of Goldman Sachs and CME participate in these parimutuel derivatives auctions, and ICAP solic-its or "brokers" orders from other dealers. Trades are cleared through CME's clearinghouse.[12] The first parimutuel economic derivatives auc-tion, which was held in conjunction with Deutsche Bank, was on NFP for September 2002 and it took place on 1 October 2002.[13] This was the first time that derivatives were traded parimutuelly. Table 3.2 summa-rizes the main aspects of parimutuel auctions on economic derivatives. Chapter 4 will present a case study of parimutuel derivatives auctions on NFP.

Energy inventory derivatives: On 2 June 2004, Goldman Sachs, ICAP Energy, and NYMEX in partnership began using Longitude's parimutuel matching engine for over-the-counter (OTC) trading of derivatives on energy inventory statistics released by the Energy Information Adminis-tration (EIA), a division of the Department of Energy. Currently, these parties hold parimutuel auctions on derivatives that are based on weekly changes in crude oil and natural gas inventories. These weekly inventory releases are closely followed by participants in the crude oil and natural gas markets. These statistics are important measures of market supply and demand conditions, and surprises in these numbers can cause significant

Table 3.3 Details on energy inventory derivatives

Product	Energy inventory derivatives
Date of first auction	2 June 2004
Current underlyings	Crude oil and natural gas inventory statistics
Measurement agency	The Energy Information Administration
Auction organizer	Goldman Sachs
Matching engine	Provided by Longitude
Brokering	Provided by ICAP Energy
Clearing	NYMEX Clearinghouse

moves in the energy markets. Goldman Sachs organizes these parimutuel derivatives auctions. All auction customers have a NYMEX Futures Commission Merchant (FCM), and these FCMs provide performance guarantees on all trades through use of the NYMEX Clearinghouse. ICAP Energy, a subsidiary of ICAP, provides brokering services for these derivatives. The newspaper article by Jakab ("New ICAP–NYMEX Derivatives Have U.S. Gas Market's Number," *Wall Street Journal*, 4 August 2004) and the articles by Baron (2004) and Sodergreen (2005) describe energy inventory derivatives in more detail. Table 3.3 summarizes the main aspects of these parimutuel auctions on energy inventory derivatives.

Daily settlement derivatives: Goldman Sachs, ICAP Energy, and NYMEX began using Longitude's parimutuel matching engine on 18 July 2005 for the OTC trading of crude oil and natural gas derivatives. Each business day before trading on the NYMEX floor begins, an auction is run for crude oil derivatives and an auction is run for natural gas derivatives. Derivatives in these auctions are cash-settled at day's end based on the NYMEX closing price for the nearby crude oil and natural gas contracts. Thus, these derivatives expire the same day that they are first traded, and they are referred to as "daily settlement derivatives." Using these derivatives, customers can express a short-term view on crude oil or natural gas or hedge exposure to fluctuations in crude oil or natural gas. Goldman Sachs organizes these auctions, and ICAP Energy brokers these derivatives. All trades are cleared through the NYMEX clearinghouse. Table 3.4 summarizes the main features of these parimutuel derivatives auctions.

Table 3.4 Details on daily settlement derivatives

Product	Daily settlement derivatives
Date of first auction	18 July 2005
Current underlyings	NYMEX crude oil and NYMEX natural gas settlement prices
Auction organizer	Goldman Sachs
Matching engine	Provided by Longitude
Brokering	Provided by ICAP Energy
Clearing	NYMEX Clearinghouse

3.4 RELATED FINANCIAL MARKETS

Economic derivatives and energy inventory derivatives differ from traditional derivatives markets in that each underlying is a *measured* quantity, as opposed to being the *price* of a traded instrument. Although these types of markets are not commonplace, other derivatives markets exist today where underlyings are measured quantities. Each of these markets use, by necessity, cash settlement since there is no deliverable underlying, and each of these markets rely on an unbiased measurement agency to determine the value of the underlying. Although none of these other markets are traded via parimutuel derivatives auctions, it is worth describing some of these markets to better understand the context in which economic derivatives and energy inventory derivatives are traded.

In early 2004, the CME launched futures trading on the US Consumer Price Index (CPI).[14] Similar to the economic derivatives underlyings, the underlying for this contract is an economic statistic, and the CME settles their contract based on measurements from the BLS.[15] There are, however, three significant differences between economic derivatives and the CPI contract. First, the CPI futures market differs from the economic derivatives market in that the CME does not trade options on CPI futures. Second, trading of CPI futures is done bilaterally in continuous time, as opposed to parimutuelly in a call auction. Interestingly, Miller (1986) suggests a call-auction structure as a more efficient way to trade CPI futures, because he argues that customers do not require transaction immediacy for this underlying.[16] Third, while the economic derivatives market seeks to capture the event-driven flavor of the release of economic statistics, the CPI futures contract is structured to complement the inflation-protected bond market in the US, formally known as US Treasury Inflation-Protected Securities (TIPS).[17] Thus, while economic derivatives typically have only several hours to expiration when they are traded, CPI futures have typically several months to expiration, corresponding to coupon payments on TIPS.

As reported in Brockett, Wang, and Yang (2005), weather exposure of US companies is often measured in trillions of dollars. Such exposure to weather has helped to drive growth in the OTC and exchange-traded weather derivatives market in the last few years. In most cases, weather derivatives contracts are settled based on daily temperatures measured at specified weather stations. The weather market is exchange-traded on the CME, where contracts are cash settled based on measurements taken by the Earth Satellite Company.

Hedgestreet (web site http://www.hedgestreet.com), which began operating in 2004, offers *retail investors* the ability to trade a variety of derivatives in small size via the Internet. In the realm of underlyings that are prices of financial instruments, Hedgestreet allows retail investors to trade short-dated options on the prices of various commodities and currencies. In the sphere of measured underlyings, Hedgestreet offers options on NFP (like Longitude and its partners), and options on price indexes of single-family homes in major US metropolitan areas.

Markets that settle based on future events, which are often called "event markets" as described in Gorham (2004), have also grown in recent years with trading by retail and other non-institutional players.[18] The oldest event market in operation is the Iowa Electronic Markets, which is run by the University of Iowa Tippie College of Business on their web site http://www.biz.uiowa.edu/iem. This academic initiative allows people to trade in small size in underlyings based on political events such as the winner of the US Presidential elections. As detailed by Wolfers and Zitzewitz (2004), markets have a long history of making better forecasts than individual experts or polls, and so such markets are of significant interest to academics. In 2003, the Defense Advanced Research Projects Agency (DARPA) planned to create markets on political events as a research tool. This project was stopped in 2003 after significant negative publicity.[19] As described in Foroohar (2005), for-profit Internet businesses called "bet exchanges" have begun trading event markets including Betfair (web site http://www.betfair.com) and Intrade (web site http://www.intrade.com). So far, most trading of event markets has avoided US financial regulations by either being an academic initiative (and restricting trading to be in small size) or by operating outside of the US.[20]

3.5 RELATED MATCHING ENGINES

This section reviews other matching mechanisms that (1) are similar to parimutuel derivatives auctions; and (2) have been used or proposed for use in the financial markets. Section 3.5.1 describes call auctions, a feature embedded in parimutuel derivatives auctions. Section 3.5.2 introduces "combinatorial auctions," and Section 3.5.3 compares combinatorial auctions to parimutuel derivatives auctions. Section 3.5.4 describes combinatorial applications in the financial markets, and Section 3.5.5 presents three other trading methods proposed for use in the financial markets.

3.5.1   Call auctions

Introduced in Section 1.2, call auctions are a useful means of aggregating liquidity and reducing transaction costs for participants. For trading equities, the New York Stock Exchange (NYSE) opens trading each day with call auctions on individual stocks, as described in Domowitz and Madhavan (2001). In another important use of call auctions for trading equities, Economides and Schwartz (1995) describe POSIT, which is run by the financial company ITG. POSIT crosses orders on individual equities using NYSE equity prices at fixed times throughout the trading day.[21] In the fixed-income markets, call auctions are used most notably to auction new US Treasury securities.[22]

Derivatives exchanges, such as the CME and London International Financial Futures and Options Exchange (LIFFE), use call auctions to open electronic markets on many of the underlyings that are traded on their exchanges. Domowitz and Madhavan (2001) describe an early implementation of the call auction on Globex, the CME's electronic trading system. In another example of a derivatives call auction, Brenner, Eldor, and Hauser (2001) study auctions held by the Central Bank of Israel for options on the exchange rate between the Israeli shekel and the US dollar. In all of these aforementioned call auctions, there is a single *item* (i.e., a US Treasury note with a particular coupon rate and maturity date) to be bought and/or sold with multiple *units* (i.e., billions of dollars in principal) of the item to be bought and/or sold. Although parimutuel matching is done in a call-auction framework, it differs from these call auctions as it has multiple items (derivatives) being bought and/or sold at one instant in time.

3.5.2   Combinatorial auctions

Much research has been done on auctions where multiple *items* are sold. In some auctions with multiple items on offer, a bidder may be allowed to submit bids on combinations or "bundles" of these items, and such auctions are called combinatorial auctions. In a combinatorial auction, a bidder requests a specific bundle of items and specifies a single limit price to be paid for all items requested. If a bid is accepted, then the bidder pays no higher than their limit price and the bidder receives *all* the items in the bundle. From the bids received, the auctioneer picks those that maximize the total revenue from selling the items on auction. As an illustration of a combinatorial auction, de Vries and Vohra (2003) use the example of selling a dining room set of a table and four chairs, where bidders can bid on all five items or any subset of these five items. For example, a bidder can bid for just the table, just one of the chairs, for the table and two chairs, and so on. The bidder's limit price represents the maximum price that the bidder is willing to pay for the specified bundle of the table and the chairs.

As described in the excellent overview by de Vries and Vohra (2003), there is a substantial and growing literature on combinatorial auctions.[23] Combinatorial auctions are particularly useful when bidders in the auctions have preferences not just for particular items but for sets of such items, due to items on auction being complementary or substitutable for one another. Combinatorial auctions are not just a theoretical construct of academic interest, but they are useful practical tools as well. Typically held in a call-auction format, combinatorial auctions have been used for FCC spectrum rights, logistics services such as delivery or bus routes, airport time slots, and railroad segments.[24]

3.5.3 Combinatorial auctions versus parimutuel derivatives auctions

As will be shown in Section 4.4.2, every traded derivative in a parimutuel derivatives auction can be represented as a bundle of state claims (state claims were first described in Section 2.1.2). Thus, one can think of the items up for auction in a parimutuel derivatives auction as the state claims with participants bidding and offering derivatives – such as digital options or vanilla options – comprising bundles of these state claims. Customers can submit limit prices for their requested bundle of state claims in parimutuel derivatives auctions. In this sense, a parimutuel derivatives auction is an example of a multiple-item, multiple-unit combinatorial auction.[25,26]

There are, however, some significant design differences between a standard combinatorial auction and a parimutuel derivatives auction, and it is worth highlighting two such differences:

1. In a standard combinatorial auction, the equilibrium price of each individual item on offer is unrestricted as long as the resulting equilibrium maximizes revenue. In contrast, in a parimutuel derivatives auction, each equilibrium state price is positive (Equation (2.4))

and the state prices sum to one (Equation (2.5)). These no-arbitrage restrictions are often called "side constraints" in the combinatorial-auction literature, as discussed for example in Sandholm and Suri (2006).

2. In a standard combinatorial auction, each customer's requested amount is restricted to be a whole number and all customer fills must be "all-or-nothing." In the dining room set example, this means that no customer can bid for or buy half a chair. In contrast, a customer *cannot* submit all-or-nothing orders in a parimutuel derivatives auction, as customers must be willing to accept partial fills for fractional amounts.[27]

The fact that parimutuel derivatives auctions have no-arbitrage restrictions and require partial fills has two important practical implications:

1. In general, computing equilibrium prices and fills quickly can help a customer follow auction activity in real time and see the impact of any order that the customer submits. Computation times in a standard combinatorial auction may be quite long, and Pekeč and Rothkopf (2003) argue that this can create significant difficulties for using combinatorial auctions in practice. In contrast, computation times for typical parimutuel derivatives auctions can be fast.[28]

2. Having *unique* equilibrium prices is a favorable feature of a pricing methodology as this gives each customer comfort that prices will be fair (as opposed to picked arbitrarily or based on an exogenous rule). Prices in a standard combinatorial auction may not be unique, while Chapter 8 will prove that the prices in a parimutuel derivatives auction are unique.

Thus, although a parimutuel derivatives auction is similar to a standard combinatorial auction, it has two advantages – faster computation of equilibrium quantities and unique prices.

3.5.4   Combinatorial auctions in the financial markets

Though they have not been used in the financial markets to date, combinatorial auctions have been *proposed* in several different formats for trading bundles of securities. Srinivasan, Stallaert, and Whinston (1998), and Fan, Stallaert, and Whinston (1999, 2000) suggest and describe a combinatorial-auction design for trading bundles or portfolios of equity securities based on a linear program. Polk and Schulman (2000) argue that bundle trading can enhance liquidity for bond trading. Bossaerts, Fine, and Ledyard (2002), using a method they call "combined value trading," show experimentally that bundle trading can improve liquidity in a thin or illiquid market. Abrache, Crainic, and Gendreau (2005) extend previous financial combinatorial models and address the case where bidders can submit multiple conditional bids, that is, they allow participants to submit bids such that if one bid gets filled then other bids from the same bidder are automatically cancelled.

Gu, Whinston, and Stallaert (2001) – hereafter GWS – describe a combinatorial model for trading equity derivatives in which vanilla options are traded on multiple equities and with multiple expiration dates. Using option-replication theory as described in Merton (1992a), each option can be thought of as being composed of a bundle of several risky assets and the risk-free asset. Consequently, bidding on an option in a combinatorial auction can be thought of as bidding for a weighted bundle of those assets. In GWS's proposal, all option trades are exactly hedged at the time the trades are executed, which is at the end of the auction. However, the weights of the assets for each option change over time, and there must be dynamic trading or "rebalancing" over time to keep the hedge perfect. Thus, running such a combinatorial auction requires that the costs associated with rebalancing be explicitly or implicitly charged to the auction participants.

It is worth comparing a parimutuel derivatives auction with GWS's combinatorial proposal. GWS's proposal is more ambitious in that it handles trading of options on multiple underlyings with multiple expiration dates, while a parimutuel derivatives auction only handles options on a single underlying with a single expiration date. However, a parimutuel derivatives auction has the advantage that it does not require dynamic trading, as the set of trades from the parimutuel match have zero risk for the entire life of the options (see Equation (2.6), the self-hedging expression for parimutuel matching).

3.5.5   Other proposed approaches for trading

This section describes three additional trading proposals. Each proposal can be used in the financial markets and has a combinatorial auction-like flavor.

Hanson (2003) proposes a combinatorial trading mechanism when the state space of possible outcomes is quite large. At the start of trading, a participant sets an initial probability distribution for the underlying, and then trading proceeds as follows. At any time, a trader who believes that the current probability distribution is incorrect can change any part of the distribution by buying an option that pays out according to a specific scoring rule (see Section 2.3.4 for a brief discussion of scoring rules), as long as that trader also agrees to pay the most recent trader to change the probability distribution. Hanson (2003) refers to this market mechanism as a "market-scoring rule." In addition to being a method for trading, as the number of trades increase, the market-scoring rule produces a combined estimate of the probability of various outcomes and so, it functions in a way similar to a scoring rule (hence its name). Hanson (2003) argues that a market where trading is done via a market-scoring rule is a useful means of aggregating information in event markets. This approach was planned for use with the DARPA Policy Analysis Market, described in Section 3.4, before that project was halted due to bad publicity.

Fortnow, Kilian, Pennock, and Wellman (2005) propose trading what they call "compound securities," which pay out based on logical formulas. To illustrate, consider two measurable events A and B. Compound securities might make fixed payouts if A and B both occur, if either A or B occurs, if A occurs but not B, and so on. Therefore, compound securities are digital options that pay out based on Boolean combinations of events. Fortnow, Kilian, Pennock, and Wellman (2005) argue that a market in which participants trade compound securities allows participants a high degree of customization in constructing their bids, and they motivate this framework as a means to reduce the number of financial instruments required to support Pareto optimal allocations of risk.

Pennock (2004) proposes a combinatorial mechanism for options trading which he calls a Dynamic Parimutuel Market (DPM). This is a hybrid mechanism that is one part parimutuel matching and one part continuous market. DPM is parimutuel in that the total payouts equal the total cash collected, and it has continuous-market features in that traders can enter and exit trades. In a DPM, a trader's payout depends not only on the price at the time the trade is made but also on orders submitted in the future. Since the payout of a trade depends on future trading activity, this makes evaluating the profitability of potential trades somewhat difficult. Yahoo! and O'Reilly Media use a DPM for their Tech Buzz game (no real money changes hands) for predicting trends in high-tech.[29]

All three of these approaches have fundamental differences from how current options markets operate today: (1) instead of requesting a particular option and a limit price, Hanson (2003) proposes that a trader submits his/her probability distribution using a market-scoring rule; (2) while standard financial options are numerical functions of an underlying, Fortnow, Kilian, Pennock, and Wellman (2005) propose trading securities that are based on logical formulas; (3) while most traders know their payout function at the time a trade is made, in Pennock's (2004) DPM, the payout function is stochastic. Thus, to implement any of these three proposals requires educating financial-market participants regarding these novel features, which is likely to hinder or slow successful adoption of these mechanisms.

3.6 REASONS FOR THE RECENT INTRODUCTION OF PARIMUTUEL MATCHING TO THE DERIVATIVES MARKETS

As argued in Section 2.2, parimutuel matching can, in certain cases, be an efficient means of risk transfer relative to bilateral matching. Academic research, summarized in Section 2.3, shows that parimutuel matching is a fairly efficient means of aggregating information for price discovery, is difficult to manipulate, and tends to provide lower prices than bilateral matching to buyers of low-delta options. Given the favorable properties of parimutuel matching and its use in wagering for over 100 years, it may seem surprising that parimutuel matching only started being used in the derivatives markets in 2002. Why wasn't parimutuel matching introduced in the derivatives markets in 1992, or 1902 for that matter? Of course, first someone had to think that the matching of derivatives parimutuelly was a good idea, which to our knowledge, occurred with the founding of Longitude in 1999. In addition, however, certain specific changes have helped pave the way for the recent introduction of parimutuel derivatives auctions. Following up on the material in Section 1.4, which described various derivatives innovations, this section now highlights how changes in regulation, advances in intellectual technology, and advances in information technology helped contribute to the recent introduction of parimutuel matching to the derivatives markets.

Changes in regulation have helped spur numerous derivatives innovations, and consequently it is not surprising that regulatory changes – three changes in particular – have helped lead to the introduction of parimutuel matching. First, as discussed in Section 1.4, the growth of the trading of cash-settled derivatives in the last 20 years could not have taken place without the Commodities Exchange Act (CEA) of 1974 and the subsequent creation of the Commodity Futures Trading Commission (CFTC) in 1975. Although derivatives markets have been around for centuries, the growth of the trading of cash-settled derivatives in the last 20 years is a helpful trend for parimutuel matching, since parimutuel matching is well suited for pricing and trading cash-settled derivatives. Second, the 1998 case of *State Street Bank and Trust* v. *Signature Financial Group*, which established the patentability of financial methods in the US, provides protection and incentive for small companies such as Longitude to pursue innovations in financial markets. A third regulatory change, the Commodity Futures Modernization Act (CFMA) of 2000, confirms the legality of OTC derivatives trading based on a wide range of underlyings (including macroeconomic and other economic indexes). As argued in Section 3.2, customers are unlikely to require a high degree of transaction immediacy in trading these underlyings, and so they are natural underlyings for the call auction embedded in a parimutuel derivatives auction.

In terms of intellectual advances, beginning with Black and Scholes (1973), academics and practitioners have developed many tools for valuing and trading derivatives. Longitude's recent mathematical advances (see Section 3.2 and the remainder of this book) are in that vein, making parimutuel matching a more powerful and flexible tool for trading derivatives.

Advances in information technology have helped facilitate the introduction of parimutuel matching in two important respects. Customers expect to know their trade prices and fills in a timely manner, whether trading electronically or otherwise. Longitude's parimutuel matching engine solves for prices and fills when customers submit limit orders using an iterative algorithm.[30] Thus, to provide customers with timely pricing updates requires sufficient computing power. With computers that only cost tens of thousands of dollars, Longitude computes prices and fills in typically half a second or less. Even ten years ago, the cost of

Table 3.5 Related events and trends leading up to the introduction of parimutuel matching to the derivatives markets in October 2002

Date	Description of innovation
1973–Present	Black and Scholes publish their landmark paper on option pricing, starting the growth of tools for pricing and trading derivatives
1974–75	CEA of 1974 and the founding of the CFTC. Subsequent growth of derivatives trading
1977–Present	Introduction of the first personal computers and the growth of fast, inexpensive computing
1981	Eurodollars become the first legal cash-settled contract in the US. Subsequent growth of trading of cash-settled derivatives
1997–Present	Growth of electronic trading of derivatives
1998	*State Street Bank and Trust* v. *Signature Financial Group* establishes the patentability of financial methods in the US
1999–Present	Parimutuel advances by Longitude
2000	CFMA of 2000 allows for the OTC trading of derivatives based on macroeconomic and other economic indexes

obtaining this type of computing speed would have likely been 50 to 100 times more expensive. The current availability of inexpensive computing power makes running parimutuel derivatives auctions a more cost effective business.[31]

Next, note that until recently, a high percentage of derivatives were traded using the open-outcry system, in which buyers and sellers arrange trades bilaterally and verbally on the exchange floor. However, since parimutuel matching does not necessarily match buyers with sellers, parimutuel matching cannot use the open-outcry system of floor trading. Parimutuel derivatives auctions are done most naturally when orders are entered into an electronic system, which then computes prices and fills. Today, customers trading in parimutuel derivatives auctions submit a significant percentage of orders electronically, and the recent growth in electronic trading is a further help to parimutuel derivatives auctions.[32] Table 3.5 summarizes these changes and trends.

CHAPTER 4

A Case Study Using Nonfarm Payrolls

This chapter analyzes parimutuel derivatives auctions in more detail, presenting a case study on the monthly change in nonfarm payrolls (NFP), a particularly influential US economic statistic. We proceed as follows. Section 4.1 provides background on NFP. Section 4.2 discusses why hedgers and speculators trade short-dated derivatives on NFP. Section 4.3 argues that parimutuel derivatives auctions have a comparative advantage over bilateral matching for trading NFP derivatives. Section 4.4 describes the design, mathematics, and dynamics of parimutuel derivatives auctions on NFP.

4.1 BACKGROUND AND DATA ON NFP

Each month, the Bureau of Labor Statistics (BLS), which is a division of the US Department of Labor, compiles the "employment report." Although this report contains a large amount of employment-related data, NFP is the most important statistic.[1] The BLS calculates the monthly change in the total number of full-time or part-time jobs in US non-farm establishments to the nearest one thousand jobs, and we refer to this quantity as NFP.[2] The BLS typically releases the employment report at 8:30 AM New York time on the first Friday of the month, providing employment-related figures for the previous month. For example, on Friday 2 September 2005 at 8:30 AM New York time, the BLS reported that the number of jobs in the nonfarm sector increased by 169 thousand in the month of August 2005. In each employment report, the BLS may revise the prior two months of NFP values, though these revised values are of lesser importance.[3] Throughout the remainder of this chapter, the abbreviation "NFP" will refer specifically to the first released value

Table 4.1 Information on the monthly change in US NFP

Statistic	Monthly change in the number of jobs in the US's nonfarm sector
Compiled by	The Bureau of Labor Statistics (BLS)
Periodicity	Monthly
Release date	Typically the first Friday of each month for the previous month's data
Release time	8:30 AM New York time
Precision	In thousands of jobs
Recent value	+169 thousand jobs for August 2005 released on 2 September 2005
Revised?	Yes, up to two times after the initial release, but the initial value is the most widely followed

(as opposed to either of the revisions), which is also called NFP's "first print," unless otherwise stated. Table 4.1 summarizes this basic information on NFP.

Table 4.2 displays data on NFP for the last three years. This time series begins with NFP for September 2002, which was the first underlying ever used in a parimutuel derivatives auction. Column one displays the index of the 36 NFP releases in the time series. Columns two and three show the measurement month and the release date, respectively, for each NFP release. Column four presents the actual values (unrevised) of NFP. Since the BLS measures NFP in thousands of jobs, the data in column four is written in thousands of jobs to avoid displaying three zeros at the end of each number. Upcoming sections of this chapter will refer back to this table. Figure 4.1 graphs the last three years of values of NFP.

4.2　DEMAND FOR DERIVATIVES ON NFP

Academics have done much research, beginning with Working (1953), on what factors lead to a successful futures market. In an extensive overview of this literature, Black (1986) notes that demand for derivatives by hedgers and speculators is crucial to the success of a futures market.[4] This section presents four indicators that suggest that hedgers and speculators have demand for short-dated NFP derivatives. Indicator 1 relates to how widely market participants forecast and follow the release of NFP. Indicators 2 and 3 hinge on the ability of NFP derivatives to complement

Table 4.2 Information on the value of NFP from September 2002
to August 2005

Index t	Measurement month	Date of release	NFP value in thousands of jobs u_t	Range forward price in thousands of jobs φ_t	Surprise in thousands of jobs ψ_t	Release day return on 10-year US Treasury note futures (%)
1	September 2002	4 October 2002	−43	−18	−25	0.04
2	October 2002	1 November 2002	−5	−14	9	−0.41
3	November 2002	6 December 2002	−40	67	−107	0.35
4	December 2002	10 January 2003	−101	36	−137	−0.03
5	January 2003	7 February 2003	143	62	81	0.20
6	February 2003	7 March 2003	−308	−13	−295	0.23
7	March 2003	4 April 2003	−108	−61	−47	−0.14
8	April 2003	2 May 2003	−48	−118	70	−0.39
9	May 2003	6 June 2003	−17	−45	28	−0.13
10	June 2003	3 July 2003	−30	3	−33	−0.61
11	July 2003	1 August 2003	−44	17	−61	−0.07
12	August 2003	5 September 2003	−93	8	−101	1.32
13	September 2003	3 October 2003	57	−5	62	−1.34
14	October 2003	7 November 2003	126	88	38	−0.24
15	November 2003	5 December 2003	57	160	−103	1.10
16	December 2003	9 January 2004	1	160	−159	1.24
17	January 2004	6 February 2004	112	171	−59	0.69
18	February 2004	5 March 2004	21	129	−108	1.33
19	March 2004	2 April 2004	308	138	170	−1.69
20	April 2004	7 May 2004	288	186	102	−1.22
21	May 2004	4 June 2004	248	255	−7	−0.46
22	June 2004	2 July 2004	112	225	−113	0.76
23	July 2004	6 August 2004	32	239	−207	1.33
24	August 2004	3 September 2004	144	152	−8	−0.62
25	September 2004	8 October 2004	96	114	−18	0.71
26	October 2004	5 November 2004	337	168	169	−0.74
27	November 2004	3 December 2004	112	220	−108	0.81
28	December 2004	7 January 2005	157	165	−8	−0.10
29	January 2005	4 February 2005	146	193	−47	0.56
30	February 2005	4 March 2005	262	243	19	0.37
31	March 2005	1 April 2005	110	209	−99	0.24
32	April 2005	6 May 2005	274	187	87	−0.73
33	May 2005	3 June 2005	78	174	−96	−0.52
34	June 2005	8 July 2005	146	191	−45	−0.49
35	July 2005	5 August 2005	207	179	29	−0.51
36	August 2005	2 September 2005	169	194	−25	−0.01

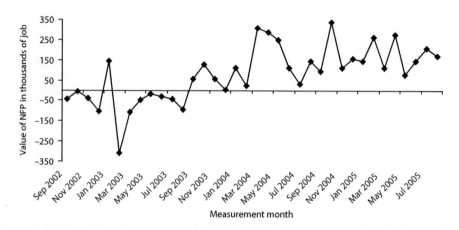

Figure 4.1 Historical values of NFP from September 2002 to August 2005

trading in financial underlyings. Indicator 4 is that NFP derivatives can be cash-settled in a fair way.

4.2.1 Indicator 1: The value of NFP is widely followed and forecasted

Several articles in widely read financial publications discuss NFP in the days before the number is released. For example, the *Wall Street Journal* ran no less than six stories in their Money and Investing Section on Friday 4 June 2004 that discussed the upcoming release of NFP that morning.[5] In addition, several economists from banks, broker-dealers, and economic research firms devote significant resources to forecasting NFP. Over the last three years, an average of 70 economists per month contributed forecasts to a Bloomberg survey on the upcoming release of NFP.[6] Such interest by the financial media and financial institutions suggests that financial-market participants may closely follow the NFP release and have interest in trading NFP derivatives.

Why is NFP widely followed by the financial media, and why do so many economists forecast NFP? The US economy is the world's largest economy, and the US employment situation is an important barometer of both the health of the US economy and of US inflationary pressures. Consequently, NFP's release can have a dramatic effect on many financial markets, as discussed in more detail in the Sections 4.2.2 and 4.2.3 below on indicators 2 and 3. Part of the reason for NFP's significance relates to the timing of its release. NFP is released in the early part of the month, and it is one of the first statistics to measure the prior month's economic activity. Jones (1982) argues that financial-market participants look most closely at the statistics that provide the first indicators of the direction of the US economy, and Andersen, Bollerslev, Diebold, and Vega (2003) show empirically that the statistics that are the first to measure economic activity in a month have the greatest impact on the prices of financial assets.

4.2.2   Indicator 2: The release of NFP increases volatility in financial markets

Academic researchers have done much work on the impact of economic releases on financial markets. For example, Andersen, Bollerslev, Diebold, and Vega (2005) refer to over 20 papers that use intraday data to analyze the impact of economic statistics on financial markets. What does this literature say about the impact of the employment report? Using tick data from 1982 to 2000, Fair (2003) examines the largest moves in six liquid financial markets. He categorizes an event as a one-minute or a five-minute price change greater than or equal to 0.75% in absolute value in any of these markets. Of the 221 events identified, 58 or 26% are due to the employment report, illustrating the influence this report can have on financial markets. The employment report has a particularly dramatic impact on US fixed-income markets, as described in Ederington and Lee (1993), Fleming and Remolona (1997, 1999), and Balduzzi, Elton, and Green (2001). For example, Balduzzi, Elton, and Green (2001) show that the volatility of cash 10-year Treasury notes between 8:30 AM and 8:35 AM New York time on a day when the employment report is released is *ten times higher* than normal volatility, and they argue that "a jump component is a needed ingredient in a realistic model of interest rate dynamics." Andersen and Bollerslev (1998, p. 240) note that the employment report is referred to as the "king of kings" among economic announcements because of its propensity to cause financial markets to move quickly and dramatically after it is released. Although academic studies do not always break out the impact of NFP versus other statistics from the employment report, NFP is typically considered the most important statistic, and it is referred to as the "headline" number. Because NFP has a significant effect on financial markets, speculators in those markets are likely to have an opinion on an upcoming release of NFP, and they may be interested in trading NFP derivatives.[7]

As evidence of speculative interest in NFP, note that financial-market participants with a short-term trading horizon often "trade the number," which means that they take a position in a financial market based on their view on the upcoming value of a US economic number and the market's likely response to that number. In trading the number, a trader can have an accurate call on the economic number but lose money because the market reacts in an unpredictable way. Using NFP derivatives instead of financial instruments to trade the number avoids this shortcoming, allowing traders to take positions that have payouts that are *directly* tied to the economic number.

Today, "macroeconomic hedge funds" are significant players in the financial markets. As reported by Peltz (2005), macroeconomic hedge funds have an estimated $100 billion in assets under management. One of the primary investment approaches of these funds is to forecast economic variables and then take a position in the financial markets based on their economic forecasts. Trading NFP derivatives allow portfolio managers at these hedge funds to profit directly based on their forecasts for US employment.

4.2.3 Indicator 3: The release of NFP impacts financial markets in a predictable way

The volatility of many financial markets is high in the minutes and hours after the release of NFP, and so financial-market participants may wish to hedge out this resulting volatility.[8] Consider, for example, a US fixed-income portfolio manager who is overweight US Treasury securities right before NFP is released. This manager might consider selling Treasury futures, which are traded on the Chicago Board of Trade (CBOT), before NFP is released to limit short-term swings in the value of his/her portfolio. Although this trading strategy reduces the portfolio's potential downside losses, it also equally limits the portfolio's upside gains. As an alternative strategy that maintains more potential upside, the portfolio manager might consider buying very short-dated put options on US Treasuries or US Treasury futures. Unfortunately, opportunities to purchase such options are limited. Exchanges and dealers generally do not offer options with maturities of five minutes, one hour, or one day, and so the portfolio manager may not be able to trade Treasury options with a short enough time horizon to match his/her exposure to NFP's release. Even if such options are available, it is risky for market makers to delta hedge such options, since the release of NFP can cause gap moves or sharp price changes in the fixed-income markets. Consequently, to offset hedging risks, market makers may need to offer such options at very high and unfavorable prices to customers. Thus, even if appropriate options are available for a portfolio manager to buy for hedging purposes, those options may be so expensive that the portfolio manager may not find economic value in purchasing them.

Are NFP options a useful tool for hedgers? As Black (1986, p. 23) points out, most hedgers prefer a poor hedge that is cheap to a more exact hedge that is expensive. Thus, NFP options must be fairly priced to attract interest from hedgers. On this topic, Section 2.2.3 pointed out that parimutuel prices are arbitrage-free, which provides a degree of fairness in pricing (see also Section 4.4.2). In addition, Section 2.3.4 argued that parimutuel matching can lead to lower prices for buyers of low-delta options. Of course to be useful for hedging, NFP options must also provide some protection to potential hedgers against moves in the financial markets to which they have exposure.[9] We now look at how well NFP options hedge moves in different financial markets.

For notation, let t index the NFP releases in the time series, so t goes from 1 to 36 since there are three years of monthly data. Let u_t denote the tth release of NFP in thousands of jobs. Further, let φ_t denote the market consensus forecast for the tth NFP release right before NFP is released, also in units of thousands of jobs. To estimate φ_t, we proceed as follows. The "range forward" is a tradable derivative in a parimutuel derivatives auction, and its payout function is very similar to a futures or forward contract. The range forward's price is a market-driven forecast (based on all filled orders in the auction) of the upcoming value of NFP.[10] As our estimate of φ_t, we use the price of the range forward from the parimutuel derivatives auction on NFP that closes 30 min before NFP is released. Such a forecast is useful because it is derived just before NFP is released, and it is based on committed capital from market participants, which can often lead to the most accurate forecast possible.[11] Column five of Table 4.2 displays these range forward prices in thousands of jobs. Consequently, $\varphi_{36} = 194$ means that the parimutuel derivatives auction predicted an increase in nonfarm payrolls of 194 thousand jobs for August 2005. Define the "surprise" ψ_t for month t as follows:

$$\psi_t \equiv u_t - \varphi_t. \tag{4.1}$$

The surprise is the actual value of NFP minus the price of the range forward from the parimutuel derivatives auction on NFP. Column six shows the value of ψ_t in units of thousands of jobs. For the August 2005 value of NFP, note that

$$\psi_{36} = u_{36} - \varphi_{36} = 169 - 194 = -25. \tag{4.2}$$

Therefore, ψ_{36} equals -25, which means that the August 2005 release was 25 thousand jobs below the price of the range forward. The surprise is a widely used measure in various studies of economic data releases, and it is discussed in, for example, Balduzzi, Elton, and Green (2001). The standard deviation of surprises for NFP is a measure of the market's uncertainty regarding the value of NFP right before NFP is released. Using the data from column six of Table 4.2, we calculate that the standard deviation of surprises equals 98 thousand jobs.[12]

Now, consider using NFP options to hedge changes in 10-year Treasury note futures. Column seven of Table 4.2 displays the percentage change in 10-year Treasury note futures between their close the day before NFP is released and their close on the day that NFP is released. The sample correlation between the NFP surprises and the percentage changes is −70%. Thus, the price of 10-year Treasury note futures tends to decrease (resp., increase) when NFP is higher (resp., lower) than expected. The price of Treasury note futures react somewhat predictably to NFP surprises, and so NFP options may offer some protection for fixed-income market participants against adverse movements in fixed-income markets. Although they are not perfect hedges, NFP options may be less expensive and thus preferable to very short-term options on fixed-income instruments.

Next, consider using NFP options to hedge changes in US equity indexes. Historically, the correlation between NFP surprises and changes in most equity markets has been close to zero. Quite recently, however, Andersen, Bollerslev, Diebold, and Vega (2005) and Boyd, Hu, and Jagannathan (2005) have observed that equity market returns are positively correlated with surprises in NFP during economic expansions and negatively correlated with surprises in NFP during recessions. Although this relationship makes any full period correlation low, using NFP options to hedge changes in equity indexes may be useful, as hedgers can establish the appropriate hedge position based on the state of the economy.[13]

4.2.4   Indicator 4: Derivatives based on NFP can be cash-settled in a fair way

NFP derivatives must be cash-settled (instead of settled via physical delivery) since there is no underlying to deliver. For a cash-settled derivatives contract to exhibit sufficient demand from hedgers and speculators, the underlying must meet a number of specific requirements. Paul (1985) argues that to successfully create a marketplace for cash-settled derivatives based on a calculated underlying requires confidence in the organization that determines the underlying's value. In particular, market participants must believe that the organization is immune to influence from outside parties and will not leak the value of the underlying in advance.[14]

As discussed above, NFP is measured and released by the BLS. The BLS is generally considered by market participants to be immune to manipulation and data leaks are rare.[15] Fleming and Remolona (1999, p. 1905) describe the BLS's detailed procedures for keeping the value of NFP secure in the minutes leading up to its release at 8:30 AM New York time. Further, Green (2004, p. 1212) presents empirical evidence that the number is not leaked in the half hour before its release. This

Table 4.3 Indicators that suggest demand from hedgers and speculators for short-dated derivatives on NFP

Indicator number	Indicator description
1	The value of NFP is widely followed and forecasted
2	The release of NFP increases volatility in financial markets
3	The release of NFP impacts financial markets in a predictable way
4	Derivatives based on NFP can be cash-settled in a fair way

evidence implies that NFP derivatives can be cash-settled in a fair way. Table 4.3 presents the four indicators that suggest that there is demand from hedgers and speculators for short-dated derivatives on NFP.

4.3   COMPARATIVE ADVANTAGES OF PARIMUTUEL TRADING OF NFP DERIVATIVES

This section continues with our case study, describing four properties of NFP that give parimutuel derivatives auctions a comparative advantage over bilateral matching in continuous time for trading NFP derivatives. Properties 1 and 2 imply that NFP derivatives are well suited to the call-auction aspect of parimutuel matching. Property 3 relates to the fact that it is difficult (or impossible) for market makers to delta hedge NFP options. Property 4 of NFP is based on market participants having a diverse set of views on NFP, which implies that it is useful that parimutuel derivatives auctions can aggregate liquidity across NFP options with different strikes.

4.3.1   Property 1: Information on NFP is released periodically

Parimutuel matching is done in a call-auction framework. A call auction is most effective at aggregating liquidity when no or very limited information regarding the value of the underlying comes out during the auction period, or when market participants do not need to transact immediately when trading the underlying. How well does NFP satisfy these conditions?

Information Flow: To measure the rate of information flow on NFP, we examine the uncertainty around NFP just before it is released relative to the uncertainty around NFP one month before it is released. As a measure of uncertainty just before NFP is released, we use the standard deviation of NFP surprises, which is 98 thousand jobs (as described above). To measure the uncertainty around NFP one month before it is released, we now employ techniques from "time-series analysis."[16] Let $SD_{t-1}[u_t]$ denote the standard deviation of u_t "conditioned" on all previous values of NFP. To estimate $SD_{t-1}[u_t]$ while accurately modeling the autocorrelation in NFP (see Figure 4.1), we fit the following "autoregressive model of lag one" to u_t:

$$u_t = 49.23 + 0.45 \times u_{t-1} + \varepsilon_t. \tag{4.3}$$

In this case, $SD_{t-1}[u_t]$ is the standard error of the residuals ε_t, which is estimated to be 125 thousand jobs. Thus, the standard error of a forecast for NFP based on previous values of NFP is 125 thousand jobs. Forecasting NFP right before its release (using the economic derivatives auction) has a standard error of 98 thousand jobs while forecasting NFP one month before its release (using the time-series model in Equation (4.3)) has a standard error of 125 thousand jobs. Consequently, the forecast accuracy right before NFP is released is not much lower than the forecast accuracy one month before NFP is released.[17] Thus, in the month before NFP is released, a fairly limited amount of information comes out that bears on the value of NFP. Krueger and Fortson (2003) show that much of the information used to forecast NFP is based on prior values of NFP and US jobless claims surveys. This evidence suggests that information on the value of NFP, however limited it is, comes out primarily when related economic statistics are released, which occurs at scheduled times.[18] Therefore, as long it does not take place during the release of another related economic statistic, a call auction on NFP is likely to be good at aggregating liquidity.

Transaction immediacy: A call auction can be effective for aggregating liquidity when traders do not require a high degree of transaction immediacy regarding the item on auction. Miller (1986, pp. 469–470) argues that there is a limited need for transaction immediacy for trading Consumer Price Index (CPI) futures. He suggests that floor trading is inefficient for trading CPI futures and instead proposes an auction framework. Similarly, one can argue that market participants trading NFP derivatives are not likely to require a high degree of transaction immediacy.

Given that significant information about the value of the underlying is unlikely to come out during an auction on NFP (as long as that auction does not take place during the release of related economic statistics), and given that there may be a limited need for transaction immediacy, NFP derivatives are suitable for trading in a call-auction framework.

4.3.2   Property 2: Interest in NFP peaks close to its release

If market participants generally have interest in trading an underlying at a specific point in time, then holding a derivatives auction at that time is a natural way to aggregate liquidity. Further, if interest in that underlying peaks shortly before the release of that underlying, then an auction can be held shortly before the value of the underlying is released. Such timing is likely to be attractive to potential auction participants because it ensures that all derivatives positions will be promptly liquidated through cash settlement (once the value of the underlying is known), and financial-market professionals will not have to worry that derivatives positions may be difficult to exit in a timely manner and at a fair price.[19] Thus, financial-market participants are more likely to participate in such an auction if it is held close in time to the release of the value of the underlying. In the day or two leading up to the release of NFP, financial periodicals and news services publish several articles on NFP, and the interest of financial-market participants is high (see the discussion in Section 4.2.1). Since trading interest in NFP peaks close to the release of the value of NFP, this provides a comparative advantage for parimutuel derivatives auctions on short-dated NFP derivatives over bilateral matching in continuous time.

4.3.3   Property 3: There is no tradable underlying based on NFP

As described in Section 2.2.5, a market maker typically trades derivatives with a customer when the market maker can hedge the risk associated with such a trade. Jameson and Wilhelm (1992) and Cho and Engle (1999) show that a market maker quotes a wide bid-offer spread when it is costly for the market maker to hedge such a derivatives transaction. Hedging is difficult when there is neither sufficient order flow for the market maker to perform a static hedge, nor a tradable underlying for the market maker to perform a dynamic hedge. A parimutuel derivatives auction on an underlying that is illiquid or is not traded seems natural since (1) a parimutuel derivatives auction does not require buyers to match with sellers; and (2) a parimutuel derivatives auction does not require any hedging by a financial intermediary. Since there is no tradable underlying based on NFP, parimutuel derivatives auctions have a comparative advantage over bilateral matching for trading NFP options.

As discussed in Section 4.2.3, the standard deviation of NFP surprises is 98 thousand jobs. Consequently, market expectations just before NFP is released can differ significantly from the actual value of NFP. Because of this, if there were a futures contract settled to a particular month's value of NFP, then one would expect it to gap by typically tens of thousands of jobs right after NFP is released. This gap risk renders the delta hedging of NFP options using NFP futures ineffective. Thus, even if there existed a futures contract on NFP, it would be hard for market makers to use it to delta hedge options on NFP.

4.3.4   Property 4: Demand exists for options with different strikes on NFP

In bilateral matching of derivatives, bids and offers for one option typically do not directly impact the liquidity on options with other strikes. As discussed in Section 2.2.2, parimutuel derivatives auctions can aggregate liquidity across multiple derivatives at a time. For example, consider a parimutuel derivatives auction on a single underlying for a specific expiration date: such an auction can aggregate liquidity across cash-settled European-style digital and vanilla options with different strikes. Thus, the more interest and trading there is across a variety of option strategies and option strikes on a single underlying, the greater the comparative advantage of parimutuel derivatives auctions over bilateral matching.

NFP forecasts by economists provide some evidence on the demand for NFP options with different strikes. Economists typically produce a diverse set of forecasts for each NFP release. For example, Figure 4.2 shows a histogram of the 72 economist forecasts from the Bloomberg survey for August 2005 NFP. The first bar in Figure 4.2 shows that the percentage of economist forecasts strictly below 150 thousand jobs is 1.4% (1 out of 72). The second bar shows that the percentage of economist forecasts greater than or equal to 150 thousand jobs and strictly less than 175 thousand jobs is 18.1% (13 out of 72). Other histogram bars are calculated in a similar way. Note that the economist forecasts cover a somewhat wide range of values for NFP. This diversity of opinion among economists is likely to correlate with a diversity of opinion among auction participants, suggesting that there may be interest in trading NFP options with a variety of strikes.[20] For further evidence in support of this hypothesis, we note that in most NFP auctions to date, participants have traded options with a broad range of strikes. This implies that there is demand for derivatives with different strikes on this underlying, and so parimutuel derivatives auctions are an appropriate method of trading NFP derivatives. Table 4.4 shows the four properties that suggest that NFP is well suited to trading using a parimutuel derivatives auction.

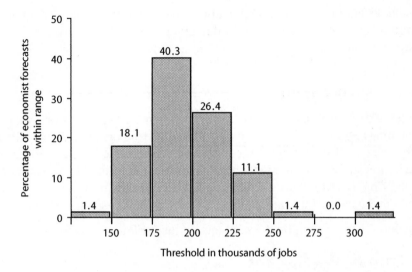

Figure 4.2 Economist forecasts for August 2005 NFP based on a Bloomberg survey of 72 economists

Source: Bloomberg LP

Table 4.4 Properties that suggest that NFP is well suited to trading via a parimutuel derivatives auction

Property number	Property description
1	Information on NFP is released periodically
2	Interest in NFP peaks close to its release
3	There is no tradable underlying based on NFP
4	Demand exists for options with different strikes on NFP

4.4 DESIGN, MATHEMATICS, AND DYNAMICS OF PARIMUTUEL DERIVATIVES AUCTIONS ON NFP

This section completes our case study by illustrating how parimutuel derivatives auctions work for trading NFP derivatives, focusing in particular on derivatives auctions on August 2005 NFP. Section 4.4.1 describes the auction setup. Section 4.4.2 introduces the mathematical principles used to determine the auction prices and the customer fills. Section 4.4.3

discusses auction timing and dynamics. Section 4.4.4 concludes by presenting the implied distribution and the range forward, important pricing tools in a parimutuel derivatives auction.

4.4.1   Auction setup

Roles of different institutions: As discussed in Section 3.3, Longitude's matching engine determines the prices and fills for parimutuel derivatives auctions on NFP. Goldman Sachs is the auction organizer, determining the option strikes, the auction dates, and the auction times. The customers of the Chicago Mercantile Exchange (CME), Goldman Sachs, and ICAP trade in these auctions, and the CME's clearinghouse clears all trades.

Option strikes: Goldman Sachs sets up the NFP auctions so that

1.   The strikes are spaced 25 thousand jobs apart;

2.   The strikes are centered near the median economist forecast from the Bloomberg survey for NFP; and

3.   The range of strikes is wide enough so that it is unlikely that NFP will be below the lowest strike or above the highest strike.

For the auctions on August 2005 NFP, there were 16 option strikes: 0, 25, 50, ... , 350, and 375 thousand jobs.[21] These option strikes were centered close to the median from the Bloomberg economist survey, which predicted a 190 thousand jobs increase in August 2005 NFP.

Tradable derivatives: In a parimutuel derivatives auction, customers can trade a variety of derivative strategies. Because the premium collected needs to fund the payouts in parimutuel matching (see Equation (2.6), the self-hedging equation), all tradable derivatives in a parimutuel derivatives auction must have capped payouts. Consequently, derivatives that have uncapped payouts, which include vanilla calls, vanilla puts, and the forward, cannot be traded in a parimutuel derivatives auction. As substitutes, customers can trade vanilla capped calls, vanilla floored puts, and the range forward, which are identical to vanilla calls, vanilla puts, and the forward, respectively, except that their payouts are capped below the auction's lowest strike and above the auction's highest strike.[22] For the auctions on August 2005 NFP, this means that payouts on vanilla options and the range forward were capped below 0 jobs and above 375 thousand jobs. The fact that payouts are capped outside of a fairly wide range implies that these caps are not likely to play a big role in how auction participants price such vanilla options and the range forward.

4.4.2 The mathematical principles of a parimutuel derivatives auction

Chapter 2 introduced the mathematics for parimutuel wagering, which is a simple framework where only state claims are traded. Calculating prices in the parimutuel wagering framework is based on two mathematical principles – the principle of no-arbitrage and the principle of self-hedging. A parimutuel derivatives auction is a much more flexible framework for trading than parimutuel wagering, as highlighted in Table 3.1. We now describe the five mathematical principles used by Longitude's matching engine to determine the prices and customer fills in a parimutuel derivatives auction. Chapters 5 and 6 will provide further details on these five mathematical principles.

Principle 1- Limit-order logic: Just as with parimutuel wagering, a customer can submit a market order in a parimutuel derivatives auction. A market order is fully filled at the close of the auction regardless of the derivative's market price. In addition to submitting a market order, a customer can submit a limit order. For a limit order, the customer's fill is determined when the auction closes and the market prices are computed. In a parimutuel derivatives auction, all customers with fills on the same derivative get filled at the same price (before fees) for that derivative, regardless of their limit prices. Because of this feature, a parimutuel derivatives auction is an example of a "uniform-price auction" (which is also sometimes called a "Dutch auction"). Thus, in a parimutuel derivatives auction, a customer order may get filled at a price better than his/her limit price. The fact that all customers get filled at the same price for the same derivative encourages customers to submit more aggressive limit prices than they would in a discriminatory auction. We now describe the logic for a limit order to buy a derivative. If the customer's limit price is below the market price of the derivative requested, then the customer's order receives no fill. If the customer's limit price is exactly equal to the market price of the derivative requested, then the customer may receive a partial fill. If the customer's limit price is above the market price of the derivative requested, then the customer is fully filled. For notation, let w denote the customer's limit price, let r denote the number of contracts the customer requests, and let x denote the number of filled contracts.[23] Mathematically, then, the limit-order logic for a buy order is as follows:

$$\begin{cases} w < \pi & \Rightarrow \quad x = 0, \\ w = \pi & \Rightarrow \quad 0 \le x \le r, \\ w > \pi & \Rightarrow \quad x = r. \end{cases} \tag{4.4}$$

Similar logic to that in Equation (4.4) holds for a limit order to sell a derivative. These conditions represent principle 1 of a parimutuel derivatives auction – all customer fills in a parimutuel derivatives auction satisfy standard limit-order logic.

The state claims: As discussed in Section 2.1.1, the states for an auction represent a mutually exclusive and collectively exhaustive set of outcomes for the underlying. Let S denote the number of states in an auction, which equals the number of possible values of the underlying between the lowest and highest strikes in the auction plus two. For auctions on August 2005 NFP, the lowest strike is 0 jobs, and the highest strike is 375 thousand jobs. Since NFP is measured to the nearest 1 thousand jobs, the number of states S equals 377. Columns one and two of Table 4.5 show the states for the August 2005 NFP auctions. Associated

Table 4.5 The state claims for the parimutuel derivatives auctions on August 2005 NFP

State and state-claim number s	State in thousands of jobs	State-claim strategy type	State-claim strike(s) in thousands of jobs	Replication weight a_s for a digital call struck at 350 thousand jobs	Replication weight a_s for a vanilla capped call struck at 350 thousand jobs
1	$U < 0$	Digital put	0	0	0
2	$U = 0$	Digital range	0 and 1	0	0
3	$U = 1$	Digital range	1 and 2	0	0
4	$U = 2$	Digital range	2 and 3	0	0
⋮	⋮	⋮	⋮	⋮	⋮
350	$U = 348$	Digital range	348 and 349	0	0
351	$U = 349$	Digital range	349 and 350	0	0
352	$U = 350$	Digital range	350 and 351	1	0
353	$U = 351$	Digital range	351 and 352	1	1
354	$U = 352$	Digital range	352 and 353	1	2
355	$U = 353$	Digital range	353 and 354	1	3
⋮	⋮	⋮	⋮	⋮	⋮
375	$U = 373$	Digital range	373 and 374	1	23
376	$U = 374$	Digital range	374 and 375	1	24
377	$U \geq 375$	Digital call	375	1	25

with each state is a state claim that pays out if and only if a particular state occurs. Columns three and four of Table 4.5 display the strategies and strikes, respectively, for these state claims. As we now see, the state claims are the fundamental building blocks for a parimutuel derivatives auction.

Principle 2- Replicating derivatives using the state claims: In a parimutuel derivatives auction, each derivative is represented or "replicated" using a portfolio of the state claims,[24] where the weights are selected so that the portfolio's payout matches exactly the derivative's payouts for all values of the underlying. For notation, let a_s denote the "replication weight," which represents the amount of the sth state claim used to replicate a specified derivative for $s = 1, 2, \ldots, S$. As will be shown in Theorem 5.1 in Section 5.3.3, the sth replication weight is simply the derivative's payout in the sth state. For example, column five of Table 4.5 shows the replication weights for a digital call struck at 350 thousand jobs. Regardless of the value of NFP upon expiration, the portfolio of state claims based on these replication weights pays out the same amount as the digital call struck at 350 thousand jobs. Note that these replication weights are zero or one, which is the case for the replication weights on all digital option orders, since digital options pay out zero or one upon expiration. Column six of Table 4.5 shows the replication weights, or the a_s's, for a vanilla capped call struck at 350 thousand jobs. Because vanilla options generally pay out more the further in-the-money they are upon expiration, the replication weights for the vanilla capped call struck at 350 thousand jobs are larger in higher states. Replicating every derivative in a parimutuel derivatives auction using a portfolio of state claims allows *all* customer orders to be aggregated into *one* common pool of liquidity. This is a powerful approach for liquidity aggregation, as two options can help to increase each other's fills, even if the options have different strikes. This was discussed in some detail in Sections 2.2.2 and 4.3.4.

Principle 3- No-arbitrage pricing: Prices in a parimutuel derivatives auction satisfy three no-arbitrage conditions. The first no-arbitrage condition is that the price of every state claim is positive, that is,

$$p_s > 0 \quad s = 1, 2, \ldots, S, \tag{4.5}$$

where p_s denotes the price of the sth state claim for $s = 1, 2, \ldots, S$. This condition helps remove the possibility that an auction participant could pay zero premium (or receive premium) for an option purchase.[25] For the second no-arbitrage condition, note that a portfolio of one contract of every state claim is risk-free, paying out exactly one dollar regardless of the value of the underlying upon expiration. The second no-arbitrage condition is that this portfolio must cost one dollar.[26] In other words, the sum of the prices of the state claims equals one, that is,

$$\sum_{s=1}^{S} p_s = 1. \tag{4.6}$$

The third no-arbitrage condition is that the price of each option is a *weighted* sum of the prices of the state claims, where the weights are the replication weights for the option strategy. For notation, let π denote the market price of an option with replication weights $a_1, a_2, \ldots, a_S$. Then, this third no-arbitrage condition is that

$$\pi \equiv \sum_{s=1}^{S} a_s p_s. \tag{4.7}$$

This equation says that the price of the whole equals the sum of the prices of the parts. These three no-arbitrage restrictions insure a degree of fairness and consistency in prices in a parimutuel derivatives auction.[27]

Principle 4- Self-hedging: In parimutuel wagering, customers can only *buy* state claims, implying that all customers pay premium up front. In this case, prices and fills satisfy the principle of self-hedging, which means that the *total* amount of premium collected from customers fund the *total* amount of payouts required, regardless of the value of the underlying upon expiration (see Equation (2.6)). In a parimutuel derivatives auction, customers can buy *or sell* options. When selling an option, a customer typically receives premium up front (subject to margin requirements) but may have to make a payout if the option sold expires in-the-money. In a parimutuel derivatives auction, the *net* amount of premium collected from customers funds the *net* amount of payouts, regardless of the value of the underlying upon expiration. This represents the fourth mathematical principle of a parimutuel derivatives auction – the prices and fills satisfy this more general form of self-hedging.

Principle 5- Maximizing volume: Different sets of customer fills can sometimes be selected that satisfy the first four mathematical principles described above. From those set of possibilities, the customer fills are selected to make the total volume in a parimutuel derivatives auction as large as possible.[28] This represents the fifth and final mathematical principle in a parimutuel derivatives auction. Consequently, a parimutuel derivatives auction maximizes filled customer volume subject to standard limit-order logic, state-claim replication, no-arbitrage restrictions, and the self-hedging conditions. Table 4.6 summarizes these five

Table 4.6 The five mathematical principles used to determine prices and customer fills in a parimutuel derivatives auction

Principle number	Principle description
1	Customer fills obey standard limit-order logic
2	Derivatives are replicated using the state claims
3	Derivative prices satisfy no-arbitrage conditions
4	Prices and fills satisfy the parimutuel principle of self-hedging
5	Customer fills are chosen to maximize volume

mathematical principles, which are used to determine the prices and fills in a parimutuel derivatives auction.

Comparison to parimutuel wagering: The parimutuel wagering framework is based on the no-arbitrage conditions and on the self-hedging principle. A parimutuel derivatives auction uses a more flexible framework than parimutuel wagering, and thus, this framework is based on those two mathematical principles plus three additional mathematical principles. Specifically, the parimutuel derivatives auction uses limit-order logic (to handle limit orders), state-claim replication (to handle, for instance, vanilla options), and volume maximization (to pick the optimal customer fills).

Pricing implications: In parimutuel wagering, the price of a state claim is proportional to the *total* amount of premium invested in that state claim divided by the *total* amount of premium invested in all state claims (Equation (2.7)). Further, in parimutuel wagering, relative-demand pricing holds, which means that the ratio of total premium invested in each of two state claims determines the ratio of prices of these claims (Equation (2.8)). How do these results translate to a parimutuel derivatives auction? For notation, let m_s denote the *net* amount of customer premium invested in the sth state claim in the auction for $s = 1, 2, \ldots, S$, where the net premium is based on *all* filled orders (premium from both filled digital orders and filled vanilla orders) in the auction. Let M denote the *net* amount of premium in the auction, that is,

$$M = \sum_{s=1}^{S} m_s. \tag{4.8}$$

If M is non-zero, then the price of a state claim is equal to the net amount of premium invested in that state claim relative to the net amount of premium invested in the auction, that is,

$$p_s = \frac{m_s}{M} \quad s = 1, 2, \ldots, S. \tag{4.9}$$

This result is identical to Equation (2.7) of Section 2.1.5, except that here the result is based on the net premium instead of total premium. In a parimutuel derivatives auction, relative-demand pricing also holds but, once again, demand for a state claim is measured as the *net* premium invested in each state claim. If M is non-zero, then

$$\frac{m_s}{m_{\tilde{s}}} = \frac{p_s}{p_{\tilde{s}}} \quad s, \tilde{s} = 1, 2, \ldots, S. \tag{4.10}$$

These pricing conditions in Equations (4.9) and (4.10) do not represent separate mathematical principles for a parimutuel derivatives auction, as they can be derived from the no-arbitrage restrictions and the self-hedging principles above.[29] However, these two pricing conditions are useful as they give customers intuition as to how prices in a parimutuel derivatives auction are determined. Section 4.4.4 will discuss these pricing implications in more detail.

4.4.3 Auction timing and dynamics

Auction dates: Goldman Sachs announces the dates and times of NFP auctions several months in advance, and the auction schedule is published on the CME web site http://www.cme.com/clearing/clr/auctions. Parimutuel derivatives auctions on NFP are held in the couple of days leading up to NFP's release. Currently, auctions are held on Wednesday morning, Thursday morning, Thursday afternoon, and Friday morning just before the number is released. These auctions take place during the time period in which interest in NFP is highest (see the discussion in Section 4.3). Due to time-zone differences, customers located in Europe can most easily participate in the morning auctions, while customers located on the West Coast can most easily participate in the Thursday afternoon auction. Each auction has its own *separate* pool of liquidity, which allows customers to build positions across different auctions, or trade in and out of positions before NFP is released.

Auction times: NFP auctions are open for either 45 minutes or for one hour. Auctions are held early in the New York morning (ending often at 8 AM New York time) or near the end of the New York workday (ending at 4 PM New York time). At these times, most traders active in the US financial markets are at work, but many US financial markets are not actively trading. For example, there is neither floor trading of Eurodollar futures nor floor trading of US Treasury futures during the NFP auctions. Fleming (1997, chart 5, p. 17) shows that these periods are times of fairly low volatility in the US Treasury market, allowing auction participants to better focus on the NFP auctions.

Auction dynamics: While an auction is open, the public web site http://auctions.cme.com displays "indicative" prices on *all* tradable derivatives.[30] The indicative prices represent what *would be* the actual market prices if the auction were to close at that moment (or without any additional orders or order modifications being received).[31] Customers can submit new orders or modify their existing orders at any time while the auction is open. Since pricing is order-driven in a parimutuel derivatives auction, indicative prices of the tradable derivatives may change as new orders are received or existing orders are modified. Consequently, indicative prices are updated on the website in real time while the auction is open. After the auction closes, no new orders can be submitted and no existing orders may be modified. At that time, the market prices are determined and displayed on the web site. For illustration, Table 4.7 shows the market prices (before fees) of digital calls, digital puts, vanilla capped calls, and vanilla floored puts in the parimutuel derivatives auction held on Friday morning, 2 September 2005 from 7:00 AM to 8:00 AM New York time for August 2005 NFP.[32] The price to buy a derivative is that derivative's market price plus a fee, while the price to sell a derivative is that derivative's market price minus a fee.[33]

Using NFP's first print to settle derivatives: As described in Section 4.1, the BLS revises NFP up to twice in the two months after its initial release. Even though NFP is revised, the initial value of NFP is used to settle NFP derivatives contracts for two reasons. First, the initially released value of NFP is the most widely followed number in the employment report. As supporting evidence of this, Andersen, Bollerslev, Diebold, and Vega (2005) show that several financial markets respond in a statistically significant way to the first print of NFP, while Krueger and Fortson (2003, pp. 947–948) show that fixed-income markets respond in a statistically insignificant way to revisions on NFP. Second, settling derivatives based on NFP's first print allows each customer with an NFP derivatives position to find out his/her payouts fairly soon after initiating a position. A customer learns his/her payouts between 30 min (if the customer trades in the Friday morning auction) and two days (if the customer trades in the Wednesday morning auction) after entering a

Table 4.7 Prices of digital calls, digital puts, vanilla capped calls, and vanilla floored puts in the parimutuel derivatives auction held on 2 September 2005 for August 2005 NFP

Strike in thousands of jobs	Digital call price in $	Digital put price in $	Vanilla capped call price in $	Vanilla floored put price in $
0	0.996	0.004	194.30	NA
25	0.991	0.009	169.50	0.16
50	0.980	0.020	144.80	0.52
75	0.960	0.040	120.54	1.22
100	0.930	0.070	96.88	2.56
125	0.868	0.132	74.35	5.03
150	0.764	0.236	53.94	9.62
175	0.590	0.410	37.01	17.69
200	0.466	0.534	23.86	29.54
225	0.343	0.657	13.79	44.47
250	0.193	0.807	7.23	62.91
275	0.101	0.899	3.69	84.37
300	0.051	0.950	1.90	107.58
325	0.029	0.971	0.96	131.60
350	0.021	0.979	0.35	156.00
375	0.013	0.987	NA	180.70

position, instead of having to wait one or two months for settlement. The fact that NFP derivatives settle in a timely fashion is appealing to auction participants.

4.4.4   The Implied distribution and the range forward price

This section describes the "implied distribution" and the range forward price, both of which are useful trading tools for trading in a parimutuel derivatives auction.

The implied distribution and digital option prices: The implied distribution is a bar graph that is displayed and updated in real time during each NFP auction on the public web site http://auctions.cme.com. The height of each histogram bar in the implied distribution represents the price of the digital option that pays out if and only if NFP is within the associated

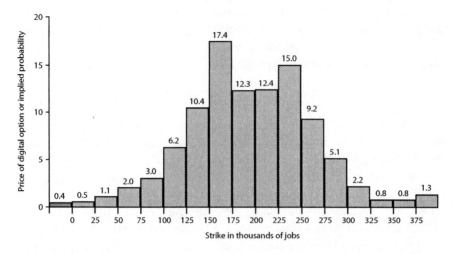

Figure 4.3 The implied distribution in the parimutuel derivatives auction held on 2 September 2005 for August 2005 NFP

histogram range, and the range associated with each histogram bar is based on the strikes in the auction. The digital prices are based on *all* filled orders in the auction. Figure 4.3 shows the implied distribution after the close for the auction that took place on Friday morning, 2 September 2005 for August 2005 NFP. In the NFP auction on 2 September 2005, the price of a digital put struck at 0 jobs equaled 0.004 (0.4% of a one dollar payout), and the price of the digital range with strikes of 0 and 25 thousand jobs equaled 0.005 (0.5% of a one dollar payout). Thus, the implied distribution provides a visual display of the prices of digital options that cover the range of possible NFP outcomes.[34] The implied distribution can be a useful trading tool as participants examine the shape of the implied distribution during the auction and may submit orders based on certain digital options looking cheap or rich relative to other nearby digital options.[35]

Implied probabilities: In addition to displaying pricing information, the height of each bar in the implied distribution can also be interpreted as the "implied probability" that NFP will fall within a particular range.[36] The implied probabilities are based on *all* filled orders in the auction. Based on the filled orders in the auction, the implied probability that August NFP was strictly less than 0 jobs equaled 0.4%. Similarly, the implied probability that August NFP was greater than or equal to 0 and strictly less than 25 thousand jobs equaled 0.5%. As discussed in Aït-Sahalia and Lo (1998), among many, the implied distribution (or the "state-price density" as it is often called in academia) is of significant academic interest, but it is not available in most financial markets. As shown in the study by Gürkaynak and Wolfers (2006), the implied probabilities from a parimutuel derivatives auction provide accurate measures of the probabilities of different outcomes for NFP.

No-arbitrage pricing: As discussed in Section 4.4.2, prices in a parimutuel derivatives auction are arbitrage-free, which implies that if a derivative has the same payouts as a portfolio of other derivatives, then the derivative and the portfolio will cost the same amount. For example, the digital call struck at 350 thousand jobs has the same payout for all values of NFP as a portfolio containing the digital range with strikes of 350 and 375 thousand jobs and the digital call with a strike of 375 thousand jobs. Consequently, arbitrage-free pricing implies that the price of the digital call struck at 350 thousand jobs (displayed in Table 4.7) equals the price of the digital range with strikes of 350 and 375 thousand jobs (displayed in Figure 4.3) plus the price of the digital call with a strike of 375 thousand jobs (displayed in Table 4.7 and Figure 4.3), that is, $0.021 = 0.008 + 0.013$. It is not hard to check that each tradable digital option in a parimutuel derivatives auction can be represented as a portfolio of digital options from the implied distribution.[37] Thus, the price of any digital option can be determined using the prices from the implied distribution. Therefore, the arbitrage-free nature of parimutuel derivatives prices means that the implied distribution provides information about *all* tradable digital options in the auction.

The range forward: The range forward is a tradable derivative in a parimutuel derivatives auction. The price of the range forward is based on *all* the filled orders in the auction, and the price of the range forward can be thought of as the approximate center of mass of the implied distribution.[38] In the auction on 2 September 2005 for August 2005 NFP, the range forward price equaled 194.3 thousand jobs, which is the approximate balancing point of the implied distribution. Gürkaynak and Wolfers (2006) show that the range forward price is generally more accurate than the median from a survey of economist forecasts (see box below) in predicting the value of NFP. Just as the implied distribution provides information on the probability of different outcomes for NFP, the price of the range forward can be thought of as the single best measure of the market's expectation for NFP. Consequently, it provides useful information to auction participants about the upcoming release of NFP.

The Auctions versus the Economists

Section 2.3.2 showed that the odds from parimutuel wagering are more accurate than professional handicappers in predicting the winner of a horse race. How do parimutuel derivatives auctions do versus economists at forecasting upcoming economic numbers? In a recent look at this question, Gürkaynak and Wolfers (2006) compare the range forward prices from economic derivatives auctions with the medians from economist surveys.[39] Using a data set of 153 economic releases (which includes NFP and several other economic statistics) in which there were both parimutuel derivatives auctions and economist forecasts, Gürkaynak and Wolfers (2006) employed a powerful regression-based methodology developed by Fair and Shiller (1990).[40] Gürkaynak and Wolfers (2006) find that the parimutuel derivatives auctions outperform the economists with statistical significance both in terms of predicting the value of the economic release more accurately and in terms of predicting the move in the US Treasury market and the S&P 500 in response to the data release.[41]

Pricing implications: As discussed in Section 4.4.2, the state-claim prices are proportional to the net amount of premium invested in each state (Equation (4.9)), and the state-claim prices satisfy the principle of relative demand (Equation (4.10)). In addition to the state-claim prices satisfying these two pricing results, each digital option in the implied distribution satisfies these results as well. To illustrate, note from the implied distribution in Figure 4.3 that the price of the digital range with strikes of 200 and 225 thousand jobs equals 0.124. Thus, 12.4% of the premium invested in the auction is invested in options that payout if NFP is greater than or equal to 200 thousand jobs or less than 225 thousand jobs. Further, note that the price of the digital range with strikes of 100 and 125 thousand jobs equals 0.062. The fact that the price of this first digital range is twice the price of the second implies (by relative-demand pricing) that there is twice the net premium invested in the first digital range as there is invested in the second digital range. Consequently, the implied distribution provides information about relative invested amounts in the auction, and thus, it measures auction activity.

PART II

The Mathematics of Parimutuel Derivatives Auctions

CHAPTER 5

Derivative Strategies and Customer Orders

Chapter 2 introduced parimutuel pricing in its most basic form, a framework in which customers can only trade single state claims (no trading of vanilla options) and customers can only submit market orders (no submitting of limit orders). In this framework, pricing was based on two mathematical principles – the principle of "no-arbitrage" and the principle of "self-hedging." Although this framework is widely used for wagering, it is not flexible enough to be useful for trading derivatives.

This chapter and the next expand the functionality of the parimutuel framework. In this new setting, customers can trade a variety of derivatives (including vanilla options), and customers can place both market orders and limit orders. We refer to this more advanced framework as the Parimutuel Equilibrium Problem (PEP). Prices and fills in the PEP are based on the two mathematical principles from Chapter 2 plus three additional mathematical principles.[1] This chapter and the next together present the five mathematical principles and the complete mathematical specification of the PEP, expressed as a type of mathematical programming problem.

This chapter starts by introducing payouts on various digital options,[2] vanilla options, and forwards in Section 5.1. Much of this material is also described in, for example, Hull (2006). Section 5.2 examines a set of hypothetical customer orders in a parimutuel derivatives auction on the US Consumer Price Index (CPI). We show that the parimutuel prices and fills for these customer orders satisfy standard limit-order logic, which represents the first mathematical principle of the PEP. Section 5.3 introduces the state claims, which are the fundamental building blocks for parimutuel derivatives auctions. Parimutuel derivatives auctions replicate tradable derivatives using the "state claims," and this represents the second mathematical principle of the PEP. This approach, which is often called a "state space" approach, allows liquidity to be aggregated across all order types and ensures that prices are arbitrage-free. These are important and unique features of parimutuel derivatives auctions.[3,4]

5.1 DIGITAL OPTIONS, VANILLA OPTIONS, AND FORWARDS

This section describes the derivatives that are tradable in a parimutuel derivatives auction. Section 5.1.1 discusses the setup for a parimutuel derivatives auction. Section 5.1.2 presents the general restrictions on tradable derivatives in a parimutuel derivatives auction, and Sections 5.1.3, 5.1.4, and 5.1.5 enumerate the payouts on digital options, vanilla options, and forwards, respectively.

5.1.1 Setup

As in earlier chapters, let U be the random variable that denotes the value of a one-dimensional underlying on a specific date and time in the future, and let Ω denote the sample space of the possible values of U. Let ρ be a positive quantity that denotes the "tick size" for U, which represents the minimum possible change in U, or equivalently the precision to which U is measured. Assume that all values of U are multiples of the tick size ρ. Because of the discrete nature of U, the sample space Ω contains either a finite number of elements or a countably infinite number of elements.

Assume there are E option strikes for the auction, where E is finite. Let $k_1, k_2, \ldots, k_E$ denote these strikes subscripted in increasing order, that is,

$$k_1 < k_2 < \cdots < k_E. \tag{5.1}$$

Assume that each option strike is a possible value of U, which implies that each strike is an element of the sample space Ω and a multiple of ρ.[5] Therefore, the strikes must all be at least one tick apart. Strikes may or may not be equally spaced. Table 5.1 summarizes the properties of the underlying and the strikes. It is worth noting that the assumptions in Table 5.1 are not restrictive in the sense that almost all financial underlyings and option markets satisfy these assumptions.

The CPI example: As a small-scale example that we will return to multiple times, consider the monthly percentage change in US CPI, the underlying introduced in Chapter 2. For this underlying, a value of $U = 0.3$ means that US CPI over the month of interest increased by 0.3%. The Bureau of Labor Statistics (BLS) measures CPI to the nearest one tenth

Table 5.1 Properties of the underlying and the strikes in a parimutuel derivatives auction

Attribute	Notation and restrictions
Value of the underlying upon expiration	U
Tick size of the underlying	ρ
Sample space of the underlying	Ω. All elements of Ω are multiples of ρ. Ω contains a finite number of elements or a countably infinite number of elements
Number of strikes	E
Possible strike values	Strikes must be elements of Ω
Subscripting	Strikes are subscripted in increasing order, that is, $k_1 < k_2 < \cdots < k_E$
Spacing between strikes	Strikes must be at least one tick apart

of 1% and so $\rho = 0.1$. For this underlying, the sample space Ω contains the elements 0, $\pm$ 0.1, $\pm$ 0.2, and so on. Suppose the strikes for this auction are $k_1 = 0.2$, $k_2 = 0.3$, and $k_3 = 0.4$, each of which are elements of the sample space Ω (as required). Consequently, adjacent strikes are one tick apart, and the auction has $E = 3$ strikes.[6]

5.1.2 Tradable derivatives in a parimutuel derivatives auction

As discussed in Chapter 2, each derivative in a parimutuel derivatives auction is cash-settled with European-style exercise. For notation, let the payout function of a derivative be denoted by d, which has Ω as its domain.[7] Let $\underline{d}$ and $\overline{d}$ denote the derivative's minimum and maximum payouts, respectively.[8] We assume that the derivative does not make the same payout in every state. Thus, the derivative's minimum payout is strictly less than the derivative's maximum payout. Recall from Sections 2.1 and 4.4.2 that parimutuel matching creates a self-hedged book, that is, the amount paid out is equal to the amount of premium collected. Since there is always a finite amount of premium collected, each derivative in a parimutuel derivatives auction must have bounded payouts.[9] Consequently, this setup requires that the minimum and maximum payout of *every* traded derivative must be finite, or symbolically that

$$-\infty < \underline{d} < \overline{d} < \infty. \tag{5.2}$$

Table 5.2 Assumptions regarding derivatives that are tradable in a parimutuel derivatives auction

Attribute	Assumption
Settlement	Cash settlement
Exercise style	European-style
Derivative type	Digital, vanilla, or other exotic
Min and max payouts	$-\infty < \underline{d} < \overline{d} < \infty$
Payouts when $U < k_1$	$d(k_1 - \rho) = d(k_1 - 2\rho) = d(k_1 - 3\rho) = \cdots$
Payouts when $U \geq k_E$	$d(k_E) = d(k_E + \rho) = d(k_E + 2\rho) = \cdots$

To help bound d, payouts are fixed when either U is strictly less than k_1 or U is equal to or above k_E. Mathematically, this requirement is that *every* tradable derivative must satisfy

$$d(k_1 - \rho) = d(k_1 - 2\rho) = d(k_1 - 3\rho) = \cdots , \tag{5.3}$$

$$d(k_E) = d(k_E + \rho) = d(k_E + 2\rho) = \cdots . \tag{5.4}$$

Because of these restrictions, k_1 is called the "floor" and k_E is called the "cap." There are no additional restrictions on d, and therefore customers can trade a variety of digital options and vanilla options based on the E strikes. Table 5.2 shows the assumptions regarding tradable derivatives in a parimutuel derivatives auction.

In the upcoming sections, we will describe several standard derivatives. Some of these derivatives satisfy the bounded payout assumptions in Table 5.2, but others do not. For those that do not satisfy the bounded payout assumptions, we create similar derivatives that have bounded payouts and satisfy all the assumptions in Table 5.2.

5.1.3   Digital options

This section presents the payout functions for three types of digital options. Though digital options are not as widely traded in traditional markets as vanilla options, they are commonly traded in parimutuel derivatives auctions. A "digital call" struck at k_e pays out one dollar if U is greater than or equal to k_e upon expiration. Therefore, the payout function for a digital call is

$$d(U) = \begin{cases} 0 & \text{if } U < k_e, \\ 1 & \text{if } k_e \leq U. \end{cases} \tag{5.5}$$

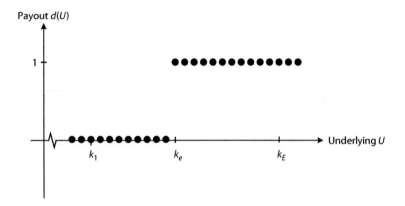

Figure 5.1 Payout of a digital call struck at k_e

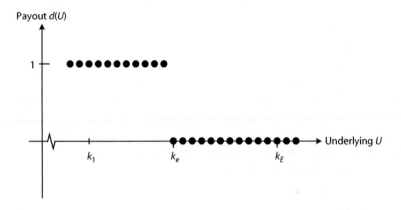

Figure 5.2 Payout of a digital put struck at k_e

A "digital put" struck at k_e pays out one dollar if U is strictly below k_e on expiration. The payout function for a digital put is

$$d(U) = \begin{cases} 1 & \text{if } U < k_e, \\ 0 & \text{if } k_e \leq U. \end{cases} \qquad (5.6)$$

Figures 5.1 and 5.2 are payout diagrams for a digital call and a digital put, respectively. Instead of using a continuous line to graph the payout functions in these figures (and all payout figures in this chapter), separated dots are used to highlight that U is a discrete random variable.

A "digital range" pays out one dollar if U is greater than or equal to the lower strike k_e and strictly less than the upper strike $k_{\tilde{e}}$, where k_e is

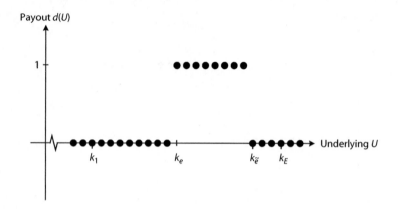

Figure 5.3 Payout of a digital range with strikes of k_e and $k_{\tilde{e}}$

strictly less than $k_{\tilde{e}}$. The payout function for a digital range is

$$d(U) = \begin{cases} 0 & \text{if } U < k_e, \\ 1 & \text{if } k_e \leq U < k_{\tilde{e}}, \\ 0 & \text{if } k_{\tilde{e}} \leq U. \end{cases} \tag{5.7}$$

Figure 5.3 is the payout diagram for a digital range. A long position in a digital range with strikes of k_e and $k_{\tilde{e}}$ is equivalent to being simultaneously long a digital call struck at k_e and short a digital call struck at $k_{\tilde{e}}$, which is also equivalent to being simultaneously short a digital put struck at k_e and long a digital put struck at $k_{\tilde{e}}$.

5.1.4 Vanilla options

Vanilla options are widely traded in financial markets. A "vanilla call" with a strike of k_e has a payout function of

$$d(U) = \begin{cases} 0 & \text{if } U < k_e, \\ U - k_e & \text{if } k_e \leq U. \end{cases} \tag{5.8}$$

In contrast to a digital call, a vanilla call pays out a greater amount when U is above the strike k_e upon expiration. A "vanilla put" with a strike of k_e has a payout function of

$$d(U) = \begin{cases} k_e - U & \text{if } U < k_e, \\ 0 & \text{if } k_e \leq U. \end{cases} \tag{5.9}$$

In contrast to a digital put, a vanilla put pays out a greater amount when U is below the strike k_e upon expiration. Figures 5.4 and 5.5 display the payouts on a vanilla call and a vanilla put, respectively. Although

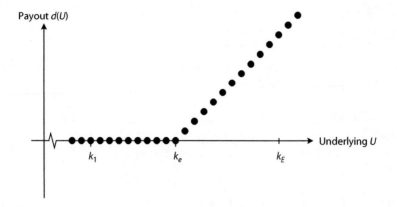

Figure 5.4 Payout of a vanilla call with a strike of k_e

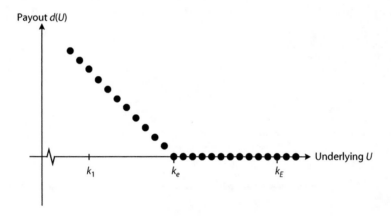

Figure 5.5 Payout of a vanilla put with a strike of k_e

financial-market participants will often refer to vanilla calls and vanilla puts simply as calls and puts, this book uses the modifier "vanilla" to differentiate these calls and puts from digital calls and digital puts.

The payouts on vanilla calls and vanilla puts are unbounded, and so Equations (5.2), (5.3), and (5.4) are violated for these options. Because derivatives that are traded in a parimutuel derivatives auction must have bounded payouts, this section now introduces options whose payouts closely resemble those of vanilla calls and vanilla puts, but the payouts on these derivatives are fixed when either U is strictly less than k_1 or U is equal to or above k_E. A "vanilla capped call" struck at k_e is an option strategy that is simultaneously long a vanilla call struck at k_e and short a vanilla call struck at the cap, k_E. The payout function for a vanilla capped call is[10]

$$d(U) = \begin{cases} 0 & \text{if } U < k_e, \\ U - k_e & \text{if } k_e \leq U < k_E, \\ k_E - k_e & \text{if } k_E \leq U. \end{cases} \tag{5.10}$$

A "vanilla floored put" struck at k_e is an option strategy that is simultaneously long a vanilla put struck at k_e and short a vanilla put struck at k_1. The payout function for a vanilla floored put is[11]

$$d(U) = \begin{cases} k_e - k_1 & \text{if } U < k_1, \\ k_e - U & \text{if } k_1 \leq U < k_e, \\ 0 & \text{if } k_e \leq U. \end{cases} \tag{5.11}$$

Figures 5.6 and 5.7 display the payouts on a vanilla capped call and a vanilla floored put, respectively. If the floor k_1 is low enough and

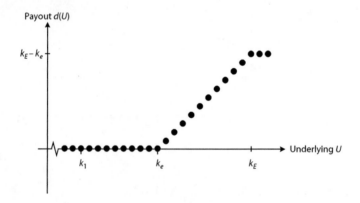

Figure 5.6 Payout of a vanilla capped call with a strike of k_e

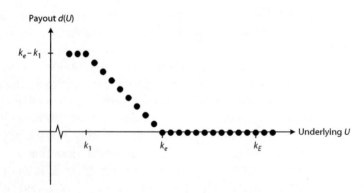

Figure 5.7 Payout of a vanilla floored put with a strike of k_e

the cap k_E is high enough, then the payouts of these two bounded options resemble the payouts of the corresponding unbounded options, and so these bounded options may serve as reasonable surrogates for their unbounded counterparts.

5.1.5 Forwards

A "forward" has a payout function as follows:

$$d(U) = U - \pi^f, \tag{5.12}$$

where π^f denotes the price of the forward.[12] The forward price is typically set so that a forward has a value of zero when it is created.[13] Figure 5.8 displays the payouts on a forward. The payouts on a forward are unbounded, so once again Equations (5.2), (5.3), and (5.4) are violated for the forward. To handle this, define a "range forward," which is a forward-like instrument with the following bounded payouts:

$$d(U) = \begin{cases} k_1 - \pi^{rf} & \text{if } U < k_1, \\ U - \pi^{rf} & \text{if } k_1 \leq U < k_E, \\ k_E - \pi^{rf} & \text{if } k_E \leq U. \end{cases} \tag{5.13}$$

where π^{rf} denotes the price of the range forward.[14] Just as with the forward, the price of the range forward is set so that it has a value of zero when it is created.[15] Figure 5.9 displays the payouts on a range forward.

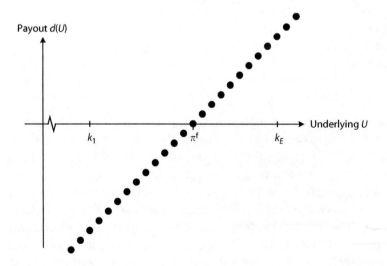

Figure 5.8 Payout of a forward

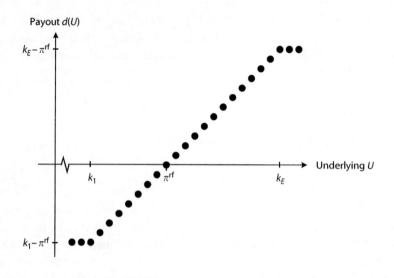

Figure 5.9 Payout of a range forward

Table 5.3 Properties of different derivatives that are tradable in a parimutuel derivatives auction

Derivative strategy	Strike(s)	Strike restrictions	Minimum payout $\underline{d}$	Maximum payout $\overline{d}$
Digital call	k_e	$k_1 \leq k_e \leq k_E$	0	1
Digital put	k_e	$k_1 \leq k_e \leq k_E$	0	1
Digital range	k_e and $k_{\tilde{e}}$	$k_1 \leq k_e < k_{\tilde{e}} \leq k_E$	0	1
Vanilla capped call	k_e	$k_1 \leq k_e < k_E$	0	$k_E - k_e$
Vanilla floored put	k_e	$k_1 < k_e \leq k_E$	0	$k_e - k_1$
Range forward	NA	NA	$k_1 - \pi^{rf}$	$k_E - \pi^{rf}$

If the floor k_1 is low enough and the cap k_E is high enough so that U is highly unlikely to be below k_1 or above k_E, then the payout of the range forward is likely to equal the payout of the forward, and so the range forward may serve as a reasonable proxy for the forward.

Table 5.3 summarizes the properties, including the minimum and maximum payouts, of the six derivatives described above that are tradable in a parimutuel derivatives auction. In addition to these six strategies, a number of other derivative strategies can be traded in a parimutuel derivatives auction including strategies that have bounded but similar payouts to "straddles," "strangles," and "butterflies."[16]

5.2   CUSTOMER ORDERS IN A PARIMUTUEL DERIVATIVES AUCTION

This section introduces the customer orders in a parimutuel derivatives auction. Section 5.2.1 describes the attributes that customers specify when submitting orders. Section 5.2.2 presents the limit-order constraints, which are important for determining the fills for the customer orders in a parimutuel derivatives auction. Throughout this section, we illustrate these concepts using the CPI example. Following Section 2.1, we assume the following regarding a parimutuel derivatives auction: any fees that the auction organizer charges are not included in the prices; there is no need to discount cash flows between the payout settlement date and the premium settlement date;[17] and all auction participants meet their financial obligations, so there is no credit risk associated with the orders in the auctions.

5.2.1   Customer orders

Assume that customers submit a total of J orders in a parimutuel derivatives auction, indexed by $j = 1, 2, \ldots, J$. Each customer order has five components, each of which we now describe. First, the customer specifies a derivative of interest, and second, the customer specifies the strike(s) if the order is for an option. Third, the customer specifies the *side*, that is, whether the order is a buy or a sell of the requested derivative. For notation, define b_j as follows:

$$b_j \equiv \begin{cases} 1 & \text{if customer order } j \text{ is a buy order,} \\ -1 & \text{if customer order } j \text{ is a sell order,} \end{cases} \quad j = 1, 2, \ldots, J.$$

$$(5.14)$$

Fourth, when submitting an order, the customer requests a specific "number of contracts," denoted by r_j for order j for $j = 1, 2, \ldots, J$. We adopt the following conventions: one digital option contract pays out $1 if the digital option expires in-the-money; one vanilla option contract pays out $1 per point up to the cap or floor that the option is in-the-money upon expiration;[18] and one range forward contract pays out $1 (resp., −$1) per point that the range forward is above (resp., below) the range forward price upon expiration up to the cap (resp., floor).[19] Fifth, each customer specifies if the order is a "market order" (which is to be filled regardless of the market price of that derivative), or if the order is a "limit order."[20] If the order is a limit order, then the customer specifies a "limit price," denoted as w_j, for customer order j. If customer order j is a limit order to buy a derivative ($b_j = 1$), then w_j represents the maximum price the

Table 5.4 The customer orders for the parimutuel derivatives auction on CPI

Customer order j	Derivative strategy	Strike(s)	Side b_j	Requested number of contracts r_j	Limit price w_j	Derivative price π_j	Customer fill x_j
1	Digital call	0.3	1	100,000	0.40	0.40	100,000
2	Digital put	0.2	1	150,000	0.20	0.20	99,833
3	Digital range	0.2 and 0.3	1	200,000	0.40	0.40	99,833
4	Vanilla capped call	0.2	1	2,000,000	0.05	0.05	1,496,667
5	Vanilla floored put	0.4	1	1,500,000	0.16	0.15	1,500,000
6	Range forward	NA	1	1,000,000	0.24	0.25	0

customer is willing to pay for the derivative requested. If customer order j is a limit order to sell a derivative ($b_j = -1$), then w_j represents the minimum price the customer is willing to receive for selling the derivative requested.

The CPI example: To illustrate, once again let the auction underlying U be the upcoming monthly percentage change in CPI with $E = 3$ option strikes of $k_1 = 0.2$, $k_2 = 0.3$, and $k_3 = 0.4$. During the auction, customers submit $J = 6$ customer orders, all of which are buy orders. As discussed in Chapter 2, a parimutuel derivatives auction does not require *any* sells for customer orders to be filled. The first six columns of Table 5.4 display the details of these customer orders. The first three customer orders are for digital options, the next two orders are for vanilla options, and the last order is for a range forward.

5.2.2   Filling customer orders in a parimutuel derivatives auction

This section describes the limit-order logic, which restricts customer fills in a parimutuel derivatives auction. For notation, let x_j denote the number of filled contracts for customer order j, and let π_j denote the market price of the derivative requested in customer order j. Assume for the moment that customer order j is a buy order ($b_j = 1$) for a derivative with payout function d_j. If the customer's limit price w_j is below the market price π_j, then the customer's bid is below the market, and the customer's order receives no fill, so $x_j = 0$. If the customer's limit price w_j is exactly equal to the market price π_j, then the customer's bid is at the market, and the customer's order may receive a fill, so $0 \le x_j \le r_j$.[21] If the customer's limit price w_j is above the market price π_j, then the customer's bid is above the market, and the customer's bid is fully filled, so $x_j = r_j$.

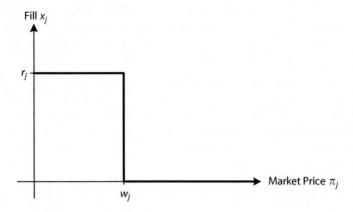

Figure 5.10 Limit order logic restrictions for customer order j in a parimutuel derivatives auction

Mathematically, the logic for a buy order is as follows:

$$\begin{cases} w_j < \pi_j & \Rightarrow \quad x_j = 0, \\ w_j = \pi_j & \Rightarrow \quad 0 \le x_j \le r_j, \\ w_j > \pi_j & \Rightarrow \quad x_j = r_j, \end{cases} \qquad (5.15)$$

where "$\Rightarrow$" denotes implies. Figure 5.10 shows this logic graphically for a buy order.

Similar logic applies for a sell order ($b_j = -1$):

$$\begin{cases} w_j > \pi_j & \Rightarrow \quad x_j = 0, \\ w_j = \pi_j & \Rightarrow \quad 0 \le x_j \le r_j, \\ w_j < \pi_j & \Rightarrow \quad x_j = r_j. \end{cases} \qquad (5.16)$$

Equations (5.15) and (5.16) can be combined together for buy and sell orders as follows:

$$\left. \begin{array}{l} b_j w_j < b_j \pi_j \quad \Rightarrow \quad x_j = 0 \\ b_j w_j = b_j \pi_j \quad \Rightarrow \quad 0 \le x_j \le r_j \\ b_j w_j > b_j \pi_j \quad \Rightarrow \quad x_j = r_j \end{array} \right\} \quad j = 1, 2, \ldots, J. \qquad (5.17)$$

Equation (5.17) represents the first mathematical principle of the PEP, namely

PEP principle 1: In a parimutuel derivatives auction, customer fills obey standard limit-order logic.

Note that π_j, the price of the derivative requested in customer order j, is *not* necessarily equal to w_j, the customer's limit price. In a parimutuel derivatives auction, every buy order with a limit price at or above the market price is filled at that market price. Similarly, every sell order with a limit price at or below the market price is filled at that market price. A parimutuel derivatives auction is an example of a "uniform-price auction," which is also sometimes called a "Dutch auction." Thus, in a parimutuel derivatives auction, a customer order may get filled at a price better than his/her limit price. The fact that all customers pay the same price for the same derivative encourages customers to submit more aggressive limit prices than in a discriminatory auction.[22]

If a customer submits a buy (resp., sell) order on an option with a limit price equal to the option's maximum (resp., minimum) payout, then that order will be fully filled and at a price that is better than the customer's limit price. Similarly, if a customer submits a buy (resp., sell) order on a range forward with a limit price equal to k_E (resp., k_1), then that order will also be fully filled and at a price that is better than the customer's limit price. Mathematically, then, for such an order, x_j equals r_j and price improvement occurs, so $b_j w_j$ is greater than $b_j \pi_j$.[23] This logic is used to create market orders in a parimutuel derivatives auction.

The customer fills $x_1, x_2, \ldots, x_6$ in column eight of Table 5.4 satisfy the logical conditions of Equation (5.17). For instance, the limit price w_5 for the fifth customer order equals 0.16, which is above the market price π_5 of 0.15. The fifth customer order receives a fill of x_5 equals 1,500,000, which equals r_5, and so this order is fully filled. Using symbols, we write that $b_5 w_5 > b_5 \pi_5 \Rightarrow x_5 = r_5$. The customer receives price improvement, paying 0.15 instead of his/her limit price of 0.16.

5.3   THE STATE CLAIMS

The section discusses the state claims (first introduced in Section 2.1), which represent the fundamental building blocks for a parimutuel derivatives auction. Section 5.3.1 defines the state claims, which are made up of a specific digital call, a specific digital put, and a specific set of digital ranges. Section 5.3.2 describes the main properties of the state claims. Section 5.3.3 shows how different derivative strategies can be replicated using the state claims.

5.3.1   The state claims and their payouts

Based on the tick size ρ, the lowest strike or floor k_1, and the highest strike or cap k_E, the sample space of U can be divided into S mutually exclusive and collectively exhaustive states where[24]

$$S = \frac{k_E - k_1}{\rho} + 2. \tag{5.18}$$

Define the S states as follows.[25] In the first state, U is strictly less than k_1. Because k_1 and the elements of Ω are all multiples of ρ, this means that in the first state, U can equal $k_1 - \rho, k_1 - 2\rho, k_1 - 3\rho$, and so on. The next $S - 2$ states have values of U that are one tick apart: in the second state, $U = k_1$; in the third state $U = k_1 + \rho; \dots$; in the $S-$ 1st state, $U = k_E - \rho$. Finally, in the Sth state, U is greater than or equal to k_E. Because k_E and all the elements of Ω are multiples of ρ, this implies that U can equal $k_E, k_E + \rho, k_E + 2\rho$, and so on. For additional notation, define the quantity s_e based on the eth strike in the auction as follows:

$$s_e \equiv \frac{k_e - k_1}{\rho} + 2 \quad e = 1, 2, \dots, E. \tag{5.19}$$

Here, s_e corresponds to the state in which $U = k_e$, that is, s_e corresponds to the state in which the underlying is exactly equal to the eth strike. The second column of Table 5.5 lists the S states.

Each state can be associated with a different state claim. As in Chapter 2, define the sth state claim to pay out one dollar if the sth state occurs for $s = 1, 2, \dots, S$. Columns three and four of Table 5.5 list

Table 5.5 States and state claims for a parimutuel derivatives auction

State and state-claim number	State values	State-claim strategy	State-claim strike(s)
1	$U < k_1$	Digital put	k_1
2	$U = k_1$	Digital range	k_1 and $k_1 + \rho$
3	$U = k_1 + \rho$	Digital range	$k_1 + \rho$ and $k_1 + 2\rho$
⋮	⋮	⋮	⋮
s_e	$U = k_e$	Digital range	k_e and $k_e + \rho$
$s_e + 1$	$U = k_e + \rho$	Digital range	$k_e + \rho$ and $k_e + 2\rho$
⋮	⋮	⋮	⋮
$S - 2$	$U = k_E - 2\rho$	Digital range	$k_E - 2\rho$ and $k_E - \rho$
$S - 1$	$U = k_E - \rho$	Digital range	$k_E - \rho$ and k_E
S	$U \geq k_E$	Digital call	k_E

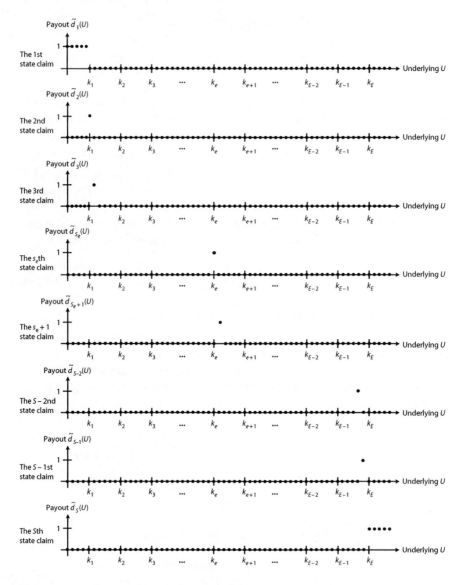

Figure 5.11 The payouts on the state claims

the strategies and strikes, respectively, for the state claims. For example, the first state claim, which pays out one dollar if U is strictly less than k_1, is a digital put struck at k_1. The second state claim, which pays out one dollar if $U = k_1$, is a digital range with strikes of k_1 and $k_1 + \rho$.[26] Figure 5.11 displays the payouts of these various state claims.

To define the payouts on the S state claims, let $\tilde{d}_s(U)$ denote the payout on the sth state claim for $s = 1, 2, \ldots, S$.[27] Consequently, Ω is the domain of $\widetilde{d}_s$. The first state claim is a digital put struck at k_1 and its payout function is

$$\widetilde{d}_1(U) = \begin{cases} 1 & \text{if } U < k_1, \\ 0 & \text{if } k_1 \leq U. \end{cases} \tag{5.20}$$

For $s = 2, 3, \ldots S - 1$, the sth state claim is a digital range with strikes of $k_1 + (s - 2)\rho$ and $k_1 + (s - 1)\rho$. Its payout function is

$$\widetilde{d}_s(U) = \begin{cases} 1 & \text{if } U = k_1 + (s - 2)\rho, \\ 0 & \text{if } U \neq k_1 + (s - 2)\rho. \end{cases} \tag{5.21}$$

For example, the payout function for the second state claim is

$$\widetilde{d}_2(U) = \begin{cases} 1 & \text{if } U = k_1, \\ 0 & \text{if } U \neq k_1. \end{cases} \tag{5.22}$$

The Sth state claim is a digital call struck at k_E with payout function[28]

$$\widetilde{d}_S(U) = \begin{cases} 0 & \text{if } U < k_E, \\ 1 & \text{if } k_E \leq U. \end{cases} \tag{5.23}$$

The CPI example: Let us return to the auction where the underlying U is the upcoming monthly percentage change in CPI with option strikes of $k_1 = 0.2, k_2 = 0.3$, and $k_3 = 0.4$. This auction has $E= 3$ strikes and $S = 4$ state claims. Table 5.6 presents information on the state claims, and Figure 5.12 graphs the payouts of these state claims.[29]

5.3.2   The properties of the state claims

Having described the payouts of the state claims in the previous section, this section describes their main properties. Each of the S state claims

Table 5.6 State-claim information for the parimutuel derivatives auction on CPI

State-claim number	State	Strategy for state claim	State-claim strike(s)
1	$U < 0.2$	Digital put	0.2
2	$U = 0.2$	Digital range	0.2 and 0.3
3	$U = 0.3$	Digital range	0.3 and 0.4
4	$U \geq 0.4$	Digital call	0.4

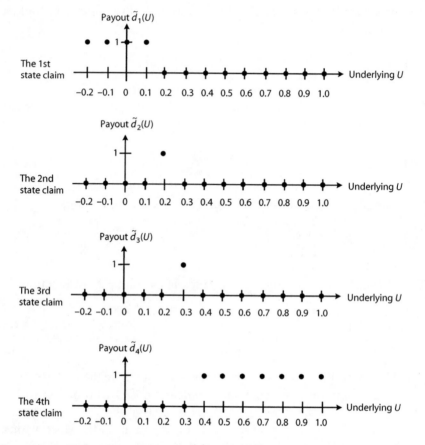

Figure 5.12 The payouts on the state claims for CPI example

pays out solely based on the value of the underlying at expiration and not on the path of the underlying over the life of the option. Consequently, the state claims are European-style exercise. By Equations (5.20)–(5.23), the payouts on all state claims are fixed when either U is strictly less than k_1 or when U is equal to or greater than k_E. Mathematically, then,

$$\tilde{d}_s(k_1 - \rho) = \tilde{d}_s(k_1 - 2\rho) = \tilde{d}_s(k_1 - 3\rho) = \cdots \quad s = 1, 2, \ldots, S,$$
(5.24)

$$\tilde{d}_s(k_E) = \tilde{d}_s(k_E + \rho) = \tilde{d}_s(k_E + 2\rho) = \cdots \quad s = 1, 2, \ldots, S.$$
(5.25)

It is natural that these two conditions hold since the derivatives that customers can trade in a parimutuel derivatives auction satisfy these properties as well, as we assumed in Equations (5.3) and (5.4).

Note that each state claim is a digital option that has a minimum payout of zero and a maximum payout of one, that is,

$$\min[\widetilde{d}_s(u): u \in \Omega] = 0 \quad s = 1, 2, \ldots, S, \tag{5.26}$$

$$\max[\widetilde{d}_s(u): u \in \Omega] = 1 \quad s = 1, 2, \ldots, S. \tag{5.27}$$

Further, note that regardless of the value of U on expiration, exactly one state claim expires in-the-money. In addition,

$$\sum_{s=1}^{S} \widetilde{d}_s(u) = 1 \quad \forall u \in \Omega. \tag{5.28}$$

Thus, regardless of the outcome of U, the portfolio of state claims pays out one dollar. Equations (5.26), (5.27), and (5.28) help enforce no-arbitrage pricing in parimutuel derivatives auctions, as discussed further in Section 6.2. Table 5.7 summarizes the properties of the state claims.

5.3.3 Replicating derivatives using the state claims

This section shows that every derivative in a parimutuel derivatives auction can be replicated with a portfolio of state claims, where this portfolio

Table 5.7 Properties of the state claims in a parimutuel derivatives auction

Attribute	Property of the state claims
Number of state claims	$S = \frac{k_E - k_1}{\rho} + 2$
Settlement	Cash settlement
Exercise style	European-style
Derivative type	Digital option
Payouts when $U < k_1$	$\widetilde{d}_s(k_1 - \rho) = \widetilde{d}_s(k_1 - 2\rho) = \widetilde{d}_s(k_1 - 3\rho)$ $= \cdots \quad s = 1, 2, \ldots, S$
Payouts when $U \geq k_E$	$\widetilde{d}_s(k_E) = \widetilde{d}_s(k_E + \rho) = \widetilde{d}_s(k_E + 2\rho) = \cdots$ $s = 1, 2, \ldots, S$
Minimum payout	$\min[\widetilde{d}_s(u): u \in \Omega] = 0 \quad s = 1, 2, \ldots, S$
Maximum payout	$\max[\widetilde{d}_s(u): u \in \Omega] = 1 \quad s = 1, 2, \ldots, S$
Number of state claims that expire in-the-money	Exactly one state claim expires in-the-money for all values of U
Payout across all state claims	$\sum_{s=1}^{S} \widetilde{d}_s(u) = 1 \quad \forall u \in \Omega$

pays out the same amount as the derivative regardless of the value of the underlying at expiration. First, however, some additional notation is required. Define u_s as follows:

$$u_s \equiv k_1 + (s - 2)\rho \quad s = 1, 2, \ldots, S. \tag{5.29}$$

For example, $u_1 = k_1 - \rho, u_2 = k_1$, and one can check using Equations (5.18) and (5.29) that $u_S = k_E$. Consequently, u_s is an element of the sth state for $s = 1, 2, \ldots, S$, and u_s is the only element of the sth state for $s = 2, 3, \ldots, S - 1$. For the derivative requested in the jth customer order, let $a_{j,s}$ represent the number of contracts of state claim s used for replication for $j = 1, 2, \ldots, J$ and $s = 1, 2, \ldots, S$.[30] The vector $[a_{j,1}, a_{j,2}, \ldots, a_{j,S}]$ is called the "replication weights" for the derivative requested in customer order j. The replication weights depend on the derivative's payout function d, but this notation suppresses that dependence for simplicity. The following theorem provides a straightforward approach for calculating replication weights.

Theorem 5.1- The State Claim Replication Theorem: If d_j represents the payout function for the derivative requested in the jth customer order, and that derivative satisfies the assumptions in Table 5.2, then the payout function can be written as

$$d_j(u) = \sum_{s=1}^{S} a_{j,s} \tilde{d}_s(u) \quad \forall u \in \Omega, \tag{5.30}$$

where

$$a_{j,s} = d_j(u_s) \quad s = 1, 2, \ldots, S. \tag{5.31}$$

This theorem is proven in Appendix 5A. This theorem shows that the sth replication weight is simply the derivative's payout in the sth state, and so $a_{j,s}$ equals $d_j(u_s)$.[31]

Because of this theorem, we can state the second mathematical principle of the PEP, namely

PEP principle 2: All tradable derivatives in a parimutuel derivatives auction are replicated using the state claims.

Because of this replication approach, the state claims represent the fundamental building blocks for all derivatives in a parimutuel derivatives auction. As described in Duffie (1988) and LeRoy and Werner (2001), this type of approach, often called the "state space approach," is at the foundation of financial theory. Replicating every derivative in a parimutuel derivatives auction using a portfolio of state claims allows *all* customer orders to be aggregated into *one* common pool of liquidity. This is a powerful approach for liquidity aggregation, as two options can help to increase each other's fills even if the options have different strikes.[32] Further, the state space approach helps facilitate arbitrage-free pricing in parimutuel derivatives auctions, as described in Chapter 6.

Using the payout functions in Equations (5.5), (5.6), and (5.7), Theorem 5.1 can be used to calculate the replication weights for digital options. If the jth customer order is for a digital call with a strike of k_e, then the replication weights are

$$a_{j,s} = \begin{cases} 0 & \text{if } s = 1, 2, \ldots, s_e - 1, \\ 1 & \text{if } s = s_e, s_e + 1, \ldots, S. \end{cases} \tag{5.32}$$

If the jth customer order is for a digital put with a strike of k_e, then the replication weights are

$$a_{j,s} = \begin{cases} 1 & \text{if } s = 1, 2, \ldots, s_e - 1, \\ 0 & \text{if } s = s_e, s_e + 1, \ldots, S. \end{cases} \tag{5.33}$$

If the jth customer order is for a digital range with strikes k_e and $k_{\tilde{e}}$ where k_e is strictly less than $k_{\tilde{e}}$, then the replication weights are

$$a_{j,s} = \begin{cases} 0 & \text{if } s = 1, 2, \ldots, s_e - 1, \\ 1 & \text{if } s = s_e, s_e + 1, \ldots, s_{\tilde{e}} - 1, \\ 0 & \text{if } s = s_{\tilde{e}}, s_{\tilde{e}} + 1, \ldots, S, \end{cases} \tag{5.34}$$

where

$$s_{\tilde{e}} \equiv \frac{k_{\tilde{e}} - k_1}{\rho} + 2. \tag{5.35}$$

Theorem 5.1 can be used to calculate the replication weights for vanilla capped calls, vanilla floored puts, and the range forward using Equations (5.10), (5.11), and (5.12), respectively. If the jth customer order is for a vanilla capped call with a strike of k_e, then the replication weights are

$$a_{j,s} = \begin{cases} 0 & \text{if } s = 1, 2, \ldots, s_e, \\ u_s - k_e & \text{if } s = s_e + 1, s_e + 2, \ldots, S. \end{cases} \tag{5.36}$$

If the jth customer order is for a vanilla floored put with a strike of k_e, then the replication weights are

$$a_{j,s} = \begin{cases} k_e - k_1 & \text{if } s = 1, \\ k_e - u_s & \text{if } s = 2, 3, \ldots, s_e - 1, \\ 0 & \text{if } s = s_e, s_e + 1, \ldots, S. \end{cases} \tag{5.37}$$

Table 5.8 Payouts and replication weights for the customer orders in the parimutuel derivatives auction on CPI

Customer order j	Derivative strategy	Strike(s)	$d_j(u_1)$ or $a_{j,1}$	$d_j(u_2)$ or $a_{j,2}$	$d_j(u_3)$ or $a_{j,3}$	$d_j(u_4)$ or $a_{j,4}$
1	Digital call	0.3	0.0	0.0	1.0	1.0
2	Digital put	0.2	1.0	0.0	0.0	0.0
3	Digital range	0.2 and 0.3	0.0	1.0	0.0	0.0
4	Vanilla capped call	0.2	0.0	0.0	0.1	0.2
5	Vanilla floored put	0.4	0.2	0.2	0.1	0.0
6	Range forward	NA	$0.2 - \pi^{rf}$	$0.2 - \pi^{rf}$	$0.3 - \pi^{rf}$	$0.4 - \pi^{rf}$

If the jth customer order is for a range forward, then, the replication weights are

$$
a_{j,s} = \begin{cases} k_1 - \pi^{rf} & \text{if } s = 1, \\ u_s - \pi^{rf} & \text{if } s = 2, 3, \ldots, S. \end{cases} \tag{5.38}
$$

The CPI example: Derivatives in the CPI example can be replicated using the four state claims shown in Table 5.6. Equation (5.29) implies that $u_1 = 0.1, u_2 = 0.2, u_3 = 0.3,$ and $u_4 = 0.4$. Table 5.8 shows the payouts and the replication weights for the six customer orders in the CPI auction using the formulas above.

APPENDIX 5A: PROOF OF THEOREM 5.1

Consider the case that $U = u_s$ where u_s is selected arbitrarily from among $u_1, u_2, \ldots, u_S$, which were defined in Equation (5.29). In this case,

$$
\sum_{t=1}^{S} a_{j,t} \tilde{d}_t(u_s) = a_{j,s} \tilde{d}_s(u_s)
$$

$$
= a_{j,s}
$$

$$
= d_j(u_s), \tag{5A.1}
$$

where the first equality follows from the fact that only the sth state claim pays out when $U = u_s$ by definition of u_s and the state claims, where the second equality follows from the formulas for the payouts of the state claims from Section 5.3.1, and where the third equality is simply the definition of $a_{j,s}$ in Equation (5.31). Therefore, Equation (5.30) holds for u_s. The fact that u_s was chosen arbitrarily implies that Equation (5.30) holds for $u_1, u_2, \ldots, u_S$, which implies further that Equation (5.30) holds for all possible values of the underlying.

CHAPTER 6

The Parimutuel Equilibrium

The Parimutuel Equilibrium Problem (PEP) represents a flexible approach for trading derivatives using parimutuel methods. Chapter 5 introduced the first two mathematical principles of the PEP, and this chapter presents the three remaining mathematical principles of the PEP. We proceed as follows. Section 6.1 describes the opening orders, which have several uses in a parimutuel derivatives auction. Section 6.2 presents the third, fourth, and fifth mathematical principles of the PEP. The third principle is that the PEP prices are arbitrage-free. The fourth principle is that the prices and fills are "self-hedging," which means that the net premiums collected fund the net payouts, regardless of the value of the underlying at expiration.[1] The fifth principle is that the PEP maximizes a measure of auction volume called "market exposure." Based on the five PEP principles, we can present the complete mathematical specification of the PEP, which is done in Table 6.7 and in shorthand form in Equation (6.28). Section 6.3 describes in more detail the features of the PEP. Throughout this chapter, we once again illustrate the material using an example based on the US Consumer Price Index (CPI) as an underlying.[2]

6.1 OPENING ORDERS IN A PARIMUTUEL DERIVATIVES AUCTION

Recall from Chapter 3 that the "auction organizer" handles a number of aspects of the auction, including determining the auction timing and the option strikes. In addition to the auction organizer, the "initial-liquidity provider" plays an important role.[3] At the start of each auction, the initial-liquidity provider, who may be a broker-dealer, enters what are called "opening orders" for each of the S state claims. The initial-liquidity provider enters the opening orders in premium terms (see Section 1.1 for an introduction to premium), so let θ_s denote the opening-order premium for the sth state claim for $s = 1, 2, \ldots, S$. The PEP requires that

$$\theta_s > 0 \quad s = 1, 2, \ldots, S. \tag{6.1}$$

Though the opening-order premium has to be positive for each state claim, each opening order's premium amount can be small. Opening orders expose the initial-liquidity provider to a small amount of risk, but opening orders perform three important functions. First, they help generate initial prices on *all* derivatives in the auction.[4] Second, opening orders ensure that the parimutuel derivatives prices are unique,[5] an important mathematical property. Third, they help guarantee that all state prices are positive, an important no-arbitrage condition (as described below).[6]

It is worth contrasting opening orders with customer orders, since they have several fundamental differences. The initial-liquidity provider submits opening orders at the start of the auction, while customers submit orders any time during the auction. The initial-liquidity provider submits opening orders to buy the state claims, while customers submit orders to buy or sell any tradable digital option, vanilla option, or the range forward. Opening orders do not have limit prices and are effectively market orders (since all opening-order premium is invested), while customers can submit market orders or limit orders. While opening orders and customers' market orders are always fully filled, customers' limit orders may be fully filled, partially filled, or unfilled. Opening orders may not be cancelled, but customer orders can be cancelled at any time while the auction is open. Table 6.1 summarizes these differences.

The CPI example: Recall from Section 5.3.1 that the CPI example has four states and four state claims. The first four columns of Table 6.2 show information on these state claims. We assume that the initial-liquidity provider enters opening orders with $600 in total premium, and column five of Table 6.2 displays the premium amounts of the opening orders.[7]

6.2 THE MATHEMATICAL PRINCIPLES OF THE PARIMUTUEL EQUILIBRIUM

Having described the opening orders in Section 6.1, this section introduces the third, fourth, and fifth mathematical principles of the PEP. Using these principles and the two mathematical principles from Chapter 5, we present the complete mathematical specification of the PEP in Section 6.2.5.

Table 6.1 Differences between opening orders and customer orders

Attribute	Opening orders	Customer orders
Submitted by	Initial-liquidity provider	Customers
Time that order is submitted	At the open of the auction	Any time while the auction is open
Derivative strategy	State claim	Digital option, vanilla option, or range forward
Order side	Buy	Buy or sell
Requested amount	In terms of premium	In terms of contracts
Order type	Market order	Market order or limit order
Flexibility	Can not be cancelled	Can be cancelled at any time while the auction is open

Table 6.2 State-claim and opening-order information for the parimutuel derivatives auction on CPI

State claim s	State	Strategy for state claim	Strike(s)	Opening-order premium θ_s in $	State-claim price p_s
1	$U < 0.2$	Digital put	0.2	100	0.20
2	$U = 0.2$	Digital range	0.2 and 0.3	200	0.40
3	$U = 0.3$	Digital range	0.3 and 0.4	200	0.30
4	$U \geq 0.4$	Digital call	0.4	100	0.10

6.2.1   No-arbitrage pricing

Let p_s denote the price of the sth state claim for $s = 1, 2, \ldots, S$.[8] The price of each state claim is required to be positive and the prices of the state claims must sum in total to one.[9] Mathematically, this means that

$$p_s > 0 \quad s = 1, 2, \ldots, S, \tag{6.2}$$

$$\sum_{s=1}^{S} p_s = 1. \tag{6.3}$$

These two no-arbitrage conditions were introduced in Section 2.1 in Equations (2.4) and (2.5). In the parimutuel framework in Section 2.1, customers only traded state claims, and no additional arbitrage-pricing restrictions were necessary. In the PEP framework described here, customers can trade derivatives that pay out in more than one state, and we require a third no-arbitrage condition to restrict the prices of such derivatives. For notation, let π_j denote the price of the derivative requested in the jth customer order. The price π_j is restricted to be

$$\pi_j \equiv \begin{cases} \sum\limits_{s=1}^{S} a_{j,s} p_s & \text{if customer order } j \text{ is for an option} \\[2mm] u_2 p_1 + \sum\limits_{s=2}^{S} u_s p_s & \text{if customer order } j \text{ is for a range forward} \end{cases}$$

$$j = 1, 2, \ldots, J. \tag{6.4}$$

This third no-arbitrage condition states that each option price is a weighted sum of the prices of the state claims, where the weights are the option's replication weights. Appendix 6B shows that the formula for the price of a range forward is set so that it has a value of zero at the time it is created. Further, Appendix 6B shows that the range forward price satisfies put-call parity, an important condition in option-pricing theory. Based on Equations (6.2), (6.3), and (6.4), the derivative prices in a parimutuel derivatives auction can be shown to be arbitrage-free in the sense that it is impossible to combine the derivatives in such a way so as to have the possibility of a profit without any risk.[10] Thus, Equations (6.2), (6.3), and (6.4) represent principle 3, the no-arbitrage principle of the PEP.

PEP principle 3: All derivatives in a parimutuel derivatives auction are priced using no-arbitrage conditions.

We now show how Equation (6.4) can be used to express the prices of various derivatives discussed in Chapter 5 in terms of the prices of the state claims. Recall from Equation (5.19) that the s_eth state is the state in which $U = k_e$. If the jth customer order is for a digital call struck at k_e, then

$$\pi_j = \sum_{s=s_e}^{S} p_s \tag{6.5}$$

by using Equations (5.32) and (6.4). If the jth customer order is for a digital put struck at k_e, then Equations (5.33) and (6.4) imply that

$$\pi_j = \sum_{s=1}^{s_e-1} p_s. \tag{6.6}$$

If the jth customer order is for a digital range with strikes of k_e and $k_{\tilde{e}}$ where k_e is strictly less than $k_{\tilde{e}}$, then

$$\pi_j = \sum_{s=s_e}^{s_{\tilde{e}}-1} p_s \tag{6.7}$$

by applying Equations (5.34) and (6.4), where $s_{\tilde{e}}$ is defined in Equation (5.35). If the jth customer order is for a vanilla capped call struck at k_e, then Equations (5.36) and (6.4) imply that

$$\pi_j = \sum_{s=s_e+1}^{S} (u_s - k_e)p_s. \tag{6.8}$$

Finally, if the jth customer order is for a vanilla floored put struck at k_e, then

$$\pi_j = (k_e - k_1)p_1 + \sum_{s=2}^{s_e-1} (k_e - u_s)p_s \tag{6.9}$$

based on Equations (5.37) and (6.4).

The CPI example: Column six of Table 6.2 shows the equilibrium state prices for the CPI example. Note that the prices of all the state claims are positive and sum to one, and so the state prices satisfy Equations (6.2) and (6.3), respectively. Table 6.3 shows information on the six customer orders in the CPI auction. Columns two, three, and four of Table 6.3 show the customers' derivative strategies, strikes, and sides, respectively. Columns five through eight show the replication weights for these strategies in each of the four states, and column nine shows the market prices for these customer orders. One can check that the market prices in column nine are related to each derivative's replication weights and the prices of the state claims as specified in Equations (6.4) through (6.9). Consider, for example, calculating the price of the derivative requested in the first customer order, the digital call struck at 0.3. Here, we use

Table 6.3 The customer orders for the parimutuel derivatives auction on CPI

Customer order j	Derivative strategy	Strike(s)	Side b_j	$d_j(u_1)$ or $a_{j,1}$	$d_j(u_2)$ or $a_{j,2}$	$d_j(u_3)$ or $a_{j,3}$	$d_j(u_4)$ or $a_{j,4}$	Derivative price π_j	Customer fill x_j	Customer premium paid $x_j\lambda_j$ in $
1	Digital call	0.3	1	0.0	0.0	1.0	1.0	0.40	100,000	40,000
2	Digital put	0.2	1	1.0	0.0	0.0	0.0	0.20	99,833	19,967
3	Digital range	0.2 and 0.3	1	0.0	1.0	0.0	0.0	0.40	99,833	39,933
4	Vanilla capped call	0.2	1	0.0	0.0	0.1	0.2	0.05	1,496,667	74,833
5	Vanilla floored put	0.4	1	0.2	0.2	0.1	0.0	0.15	1,500,000	225,000
6	Range forward	NA	1	$0.2-\pi^{rf}$	$0.2-\pi^{rf}$	$0.3-\pi^{rf}$	$0.4-\pi^{rf}$	0.25	0	0

Equation (6.5) with $s_e = 3$ and $j = 1$:

$$\pi_1 = \sum_{s=s_e}^{S} p_s$$

$$= \sum_{s=3}^{4} p_s$$

$$= 0.30 + 0.10$$

$$= 0.40. \tag{6.10}$$

In this way, we can check that the market prices of all the customer orders in Table 6.3 satisfy the third no-arbitrage restriction.

6.2.2   Premium in a Parimutuel Derivatives Auction

Before describing the fourth mathematical principle of the PEP, we need to introduce formulas for the premium of a customer order and the net premium in an auction. To that end, let λ_j be defined as follows:

$$\lambda_j \equiv \begin{cases} b_j \pi_j & \text{if customer order } j \text{ is for an option} \\ 0 & \text{if customer order } j \text{ is for a range forward} \end{cases}$$

$$j = 1, 2, \ldots, J. \tag{6.11}$$

One can interpret λ_j as the premium for a one contract trade of the derivative requested in the jth customer order with a side of b_j. Thus, $x_j \lambda_j$ represents the premium associated with the jth customer order based on the fill of x_j:

1. If customer order j receives at least some fill ($x_j > 0$) and is a buy of an option ($b_j = 1$), then $x_j \lambda_j$ is positive and equals the amount of premium that the customer *pays* for the buy of x_j contracts.

2. If customer order j receives at least some fill ($x_j > 0$) and is a sell of an option ($b_j = -1$), then $x_j \lambda_j$ is negative and $-x_j \lambda_j$ (which is positive) equals the amount of premium that the customer *receives* for the sell of x_j contracts.

3. If customer order j is for a range forward, then $x_j \lambda_j$ equals zero, which is the amount of premium exchanged with a range forward trade.

Thus, $x_j \lambda_j$ is positive (resp., negative) if the customer pays (resp., receives) premium.

Let M denote the net amount of premium paid in the auction, which is the sum of the opening - order premium amounts and the sum of the customer premiums. Therefore,

$$M = \sum_{s=1}^{S} \theta_s + \sum_{j=1}^{J} x_j \lambda_j. \tag{6.12}$$

Note if the customer orders are all buy orders, then M is greater than zero. If some of the filled customer orders are sells of options and so certain values of $x_j \lambda_j$ may be negative, then M may be negative as well.

The CPI example: The next to last column of Table 6.3 shows the customer fills x_j for the six customer orders. These fills were discussed in some detail in Section 5.2. The final column of Table 6.3 shows the premium $x_j \lambda_j$ for the six customer orders in the CPI auction. For the first five customer orders, Equation (6.11) implies that $x_j \lambda_j$ is the product of each order's side b_j, each order's fill x_j, and each order's option's price π_j. The first five customer orders, which are orders to buy options, all receive at least some fill, and so the premiums for these orders are all positive. For example, the premium for the first customer order equals

$$\begin{aligned} x_1 \lambda_1 &= b_1 x_1 \pi_1 \\ &= 1 \times 100,000 \times 0.40 \\ &= 40,000. \end{aligned} \tag{6.13}$$

The sixth customer order is for a range forward and has no fill, so this order's premium $x_6 \lambda_6$ equals zero. The net premium M, which is the sum of the opening-order premium amounts (the fifth column of Table 6.2) and the sum of the customer premiums paid (the final column of Table 6.3), equals \$400,333. Since all filled orders in the auction are buys of options, the net premium collected is a positive amount.

6.2.3 The self-hedging property

If customer order j is a buy order, then the customer receives a payout of $d_j(U)x_j$ upon expiration. If customer order j is a sell order, then the customer receives a payout of $-d_j(U)x_j$ upon expiration (or equivalently the customer makes a payout of $d_j(U)x_j$). Consequently, for a buy or a sell, customer order j receives a payout of $b_j d_j(U)x_j$ upon expiration. For notation, let u be an element of the sample space Ω. Then, the self-hedging equation can be written as

$$\sum_{s=1}^{S} \tilde{d}_s(u)(\theta_s/p_s) + \sum_{j=1}^{J} b_j d_j(u)x_j = M \quad \forall u \in \Omega, \tag{6.14}$$

where $\tilde{d}_s$ is the payout function of the sth state claim.[11] The first summation on the left-hand side is the total amount of payouts that have to be made to the initial-liquidity provider (the owner of the opening orders), since the quantity θ_s/p_s is the payout to the holder of the sth opening order if the sth state occurs. The second summation on the left-hand side equals the net payouts due to the J customer orders. Thus, the left-hand side of Equation (6.14) represents the net payouts that the auction organizer makes based on u.[12] The right-hand side of Equation (6.14) is the net premium collected by the auction organizer. Consequently, in a parimutuel derivatives auction, the amount of premium collected is exactly equal to the amount needed to fund the payouts for every value of the underlying. In this sense, the filled orders in a parimutuel derivatives auction form a zero-risk portfolio and are self-hedging. This represents the fourth PEP principle:

PEP principle 4: Prices and fills in a parimutuel derivatives auction are self-hedging.

Note that the left-hand side of Equation (6.14) depends on the value of the underlying while the right-hand side does not: thus, the total payouts required in a parimutuel derivatives auction are constant regardless of the value of the underlying. The net premium M and the customer payouts are based on all order types in the auction, including buy and sells of digital options, vanilla options, and the range forward. Equation (6.14) shows that the parimutuel equilibrium combines all these order types together into a single pool of liquidity, a powerful approach for aggregating liquidity.

Equation (6.14) holds for all values of the underlying. Since the underlying can take on any value in the sample space Ω and Ω may contain a countably infinite number of elements, Equation (6.14) may represent an infinite number of constraints. To solve for prices and fills numerically (which is done in Chapter 7), it is helpful to reduce the number of constraints from the number of elements of Ω to S, the number of state claims (which is always finite). To do so, let y_s denote the net amount of payouts to be made to filled customer orders if the sth state occurs for

$s = 1, 2, \ldots, S$. We can calculate y_s as

$$y_s \equiv \sum_{j=1}^{J} b_j d_j(u_s) x_j \quad s = 1, 2, \ldots, S,$$

$$= \sum_{j=1}^{J} a_{j,s} b_j x_j \quad s = 1, 2, \ldots, S, \tag{6.15}$$

where the second equality follows from Theorem 5.1 (the State Claim Replication Theorem) of Section 5.3. If y_s is positive (resp., negative), then the net amount of payouts to customers is positive (resp., negative) if state s occurs and the sth state claim expires in-the-money, which is the case if the filled orders are predominately buy (resp., sell) orders. Based on the definition of y_s in Equation (6.15) and the definition of $\tilde{d}_s$ in Section 5.3.1, one can show that Equation (6.14) is equivalent to

$$\frac{\theta_s}{p_s} + y_s = M \quad s = 1, 2, \ldots, S. \tag{6.16}$$

Equation (6.16) expresses the self-hedging restrictions as a set of S constraints, and it will be used in the solution algorithm described in Chapter 7.[13] Recall from Section 2.1 that one of the two mathematical principles of the parimutuel wagering framework was the self-hedging constraint of Equation (2.6). Equation (6.16) closely resembles Equation (2.6) from Chapter 2, with the difference being that opening orders are a part of the PEP framework discussed here.

The CPI example: Table 6.4 provides information that allows us to confirm that the prices and fills for the CPI example satisfy the self-hedging property of Equation (6.16): column two shows the opening order amounts (reproduced from column five of Table 6.2); column three shows the state prices (reproduced from column six of Table 6.2); column four shows the opening order payout amounts; column five displays the net customer payouts y_1, y_2, y_3, and y_4; and column six shows the opening order payouts plus the net customer payouts, state-by-state. To verify that the principle of self-hedging holds, we now check that the opening order payouts plus the customer payouts if the first state claim expires in-the-money (i.e., if CPI is below 0.2%) equals \$400,333 by evaluating Equation (6.16) for $s = 1$. If the first state occurs, then the initial-liquidity provider (i.e., the holder of the opening orders) receives a payout of

$$\frac{\theta_1}{p_1} = 500. \tag{6.17}$$

Table 6.4 State information for the parimutuel derivatives auction on CPI

State claim s	Opening-order premium θ_s in $	State-claim price p_s	Payout to the sth opening order if the sth state claim expires in-the-money θ_s/p_s in $	Net customer payouts if the sth state claim expires in-the-money y_s in $	Opening order payouts and customer payouts if the sth state claim expires in-the-money $\theta_s/p_s + y_s$ in $	State premium m_s in $
1	100	0.20	500	399,833	400,333	80,063
2	200	0.40	500	399,833	400,333	160,126
3	200	0.30	667	399,667	400,333	120,108
4	100	0.10	1,000	399,333	400,333	40,036

Further, note that

$$y_1 = \sum_{j=1}^{J} b_j d_j(u_1) x_j$$

$$= \sum_{j=1}^{6} b_j d_j(0.1) x_j$$

$$= b_2 d_2(0.1) x_2 + b_5 d_5(0.1) x_5$$

$$= 1 \times 1.0 \times 99,833 + 1 \times 0.2 \times 1,500,000$$

$$= 99,833 + 300,000$$

$$= 399,833, \tag{6.18}$$

where the third equality follows from the fact that only the second and fifth customer orders have non-zero payouts if the first state claim expires in-the-money, and the remaining equations follow by substitution and simplification. Therefore, the total customer payouts if state claim one expires in-the-money are \$399,833, implying that

$$\frac{\theta_1}{p_1} + y_1 = 500 + 399,833$$

$$= 400,333$$

$$= M. \tag{6.19}$$

In every state, the payouts equal \$400,333, which also equals M, and so the net premium collected exactly offsets the payouts required, verifying the self-hedging conditions of Equation (6.16). Recall that the net premium M and the customer payouts are based on both digital and vanilla orders, which are combined together into one pool of liquidity in a parimutuel derivatives auction.

6.2.4   The PEP objective function

For a given set of orders in a parimutuel derivatives auction, there may be instances when there are multiple sets of customer fills that satisfy the four principles described above.[14] Therefore, it is important to set an appropriate objective function (which we will maximize) in order to help determine the fills in a parimutuel equilibrium. In our view, an appropriate objective function satisfies two criteria. First, and most importantly,

Criterion 1: The objective function is an increasing function of the customer fills $x_1, x_2, \ldots, x_J$.

An objective function that satisfies criterion 1 is likely to keep aggregate measures of customer satisfaction high.

Based on this first criterion, Duffie and Jackson (1989) model financial exchanges as volume-maximizing agents.[15] Following that approach, one might set the objective to maximize the total number of filled customer contracts in the auction, that is,

$$\max_{x_1, x_2, \ldots, x_J} \sum_{j=1}^{J} x_j. \tag{6.20}$$

This objective function satisfies the first criterion and may be a very useful objective function in cases where customers are trading either digital options, or vanilla options, but not both. In the case of parimutuel derivatives auctions, customers can trade both digital options and vanilla options. In such a case, the size of the payout of an in-the-money digital contract can differ significantly from the size of the payout of an in-the-money vanilla contract, and so one may not want to equally weight fills for all derivatives, as is done in Equation (6.20). Instead, it makes sense to give greater weight toward derivatives that have larger in-the-money payouts, or equivalently a larger contract size. We now introduce criterion 2 to handle this.

To define the second criterion, we now introduce the "profit and loss" (P&L) profile of a customer order, which is simply the profit or loss of an order as a function of U. Let f_j be the function denoting the P&L profile for customer order j, which can be calculated as

$$f_j(U) = \begin{cases} (b_j d_j(U) - \lambda_j)x_j & \text{if customer order } j \text{ is for an option} \\ b_j d_j(U)x_j & \text{if customer order } j \text{ is for a range forward} \end{cases}$$
$$j = 1, 2, \ldots, J. \tag{6.21}$$

If customer order j is a buy of an option and so $b_j = 1$, then the P&L profile is the payout the customer receives, $d_j(U)x_j$, minus the premium the customer pays $x_j\lambda_j$. If the jth customer order is a buy of a range forward and so once again $b_j = 1$, then the P&L profile is simply the payout on the range forward or $d_j(U)x_j$, since the customer pays zero premium up front. Based on this, our second criterion is that

Criterion 2: The objective function is solely a function of the P&L profiles of the opening orders and the customer orders.

This second criterion assures customers that regardless of how they request a P&L profile (whether as a buy or sell of a digital option, a vanilla option, or a range forward), they will receive a fill with the same P&L profile, that is, the derivative in which they use to express their view (insofar as it does not affect their P&L profile) does not affect their fill.

This second criterion can have important implications when digital options and vanilla options have significantly different sizes in the same auction. Consider the following three hypothetical orders from our CPI example with strikes of 0.2, 0.3, and 0.4:

Order A: A buy of one contract of a digital put struck at 0.3;

Order B: A sell of one contract of a digital call struck at 0.3; and

Order C: A buy of ten contracts of a vanilla floored put struck at 0.3.

It is not hard to check that these orders all have P&L profiles as follows:[16]

$$f(U) = \begin{cases} 1 - p_1 - p_2 & \text{if } U < 0.3, \\ -p_1 - p_2 & \text{if } U \geq 0.3. \end{cases} \tag{6.22}$$

Though these orders are on different derivatives, they have the same P&L profile.[17] Criterion 2 implies that orders A, B, and C should contribute equally to the objective function, and so whether the customer submits the order as a buy of a digital put, a sell of a digital call, or a buy of a vanilla floored put, the customer will receive the same fill.

Criteria 1 and 2 can be used to evaluate different objective functions. The objective function in Equation (6.20) weights fills on all derivatives equally regardless of their P&L profile, and so it does not satisfy the second criterion. For example, the buy of one contract of a digital put struck at 0.3 (order A) and the sell of one contract of a digital call struck at 0.3 (order B) both have one tenth the impact on this objective function as the buy of ten contracts of a vanilla floored put struck at 0.3 (order C). Thus, using this objective function, a customer has incentive to express such a bearish view as a buy of ten contracts of a vanilla floored put, as this derivative will get a fill that is equal to or greater than the fill the customer would receive if the order is submitted as either a buy of a digital put or a sell of a digital call.

Next, consider the objective to maximize the net amount of premium M in the auction, that is,

$$\max_{x_1, x_2, \ldots, x_J} M = \max_{x_1, x_2, \ldots, x_J} \left(\sum_{s=1}^{S} \theta_s + \sum_{j=1}^{J} x_j \lambda_j \right). \tag{6.23}$$

Maximizing net premium does not satisfy criterion 1, as this objective function is not affected by fills on the range forward, since the range forward has zero net premium. Worse, this objective function decreases as fills for sell orders of options increase, since such sell orders decrease the net premium M. One possible way to address the problem with sells of options in the objective in Equation (6.23) would be to maximize the sum of the absolute value of the premium associated with the orders in the auction, that is,[18]

$$\max_{x_1,\, x_2,\, \ldots,\, x_J} \left(\sum_{s=1}^{S} \theta_s + \sum_{j=1}^{J} x_j \left| \lambda_j \right| \right). \tag{6.24}$$

Although this objective function has better properties than net premium, this objective function is not affected by fills on range forward orders. Consequently, Equation (6.24) does not satisfy criterion 1. Further, neither maximizing net premium nor maximizing the sum of absolute premium satisfies criterion 2. Thus, we conclude that the functions in Equations (6.23) and (6.24) are not appropriate objective functions.

To develop an appropriate objective function, we now define the market exposure of an order, which is an order's worst possible loss. To calculate the market exposure, let $\overline{d}_j$ denote the maximum payout per contract for the derivative specified in customer order j. Table 5.3 displayed the maximum payouts for different derivatives. Now, define $\tilde{\lambda}_j$ as

$$\tilde{\lambda}_j \equiv \begin{cases} \pi_j & \text{if customer order } j \text{ is a buy of an option,} \\ \pi_j - k_1 & \text{if customer order } j \text{ is a buy of a range forward,} \\ \overline{d}_j - \pi_j & \text{if customer order } j \text{ is a sell of an option,} \\ k_E - \pi_j & \text{if customer order } j \text{ is a sell of a range forward,} \end{cases}$$

$$j = 1, 2, \ldots, J \quad (6.25)$$

Here, $\tilde{\lambda}_j$ is the worst loss for a one contract position in the derivative requested in customer order j incorporating the side of the customer order. If customer order j is the buy of an option, then the market exposure per contract is the premium paid per contract. For a sell of an option, the market exposure per contract is the maximum payout that the customer may have to make minus the premium the customer receives for selling

Table 6.5 Market exposure or worst possible loss for tradable derivatives in a parimutuel derivatives auction

Derivative strategy	Strike(s)	Market exposure $x_j\tilde{\lambda}_j$ if customer order j is a buy order ($b_j = 1$)	Market exposure $x_j\tilde{\lambda}_j$ if customer order j is a sell order ($b_j = -1$)
Digital call	k_e	$x_j\pi_j$	$x_j(1 - \pi_j)$
Digital put	k_e	$x_j\pi_j$	$x_j(1 - \pi_j)$
Digital range	k_e and $k_{\tilde{e}}$	$x_j\pi_j$	$x_j(1 - \pi_j)$
Vanilla capped call	k_e	$x_j\pi_j$	$x_j(k_E - k_e - \pi_j)$
Vanilla floored put	k_e	$x_j\pi_j$	$x_j(k_e - k_1 - \pi_j)$
Range forward	NA	$x_j(\pi_j - k_1)$	$x_j(k_E - \pi_j)$

one contract. One can check that the market exposure per contract $\tilde{\lambda}_j$ is always positive.

The worst loss or market exposure for the jth customer order is simply $x_j\tilde{\lambda}_j$. Table 6.5 displays the market exposures or worst possible losses for various types of derivatives that are tradable in a parimutuel derivatives auction. It is not hard to check that if customer order j is a buy of a digital call, digital put, digital range, a vanilla capped call, or a vanilla floored put, then Equation (6.25) implies that the market exposure $x_j\tilde{\lambda}_j$ is equal to the premium paid $x_j\lambda_j$. Relating to criterion 1, one can check easily in Table 6.5 that the market exposure is a linearly increasing function of the fills of all orders. Relating to criterion 2, one can show that market exposure is solely a function of the P&L profile of an order, so orders with the same P&L profile have the same market exposure. For example, orders A, B, and C all have the same market exposure, which is equal to $p_1 + p_2$.

For the auction as a whole, define the market exposure $\tilde{M}$ as

$$\tilde{M} = \sum_{s=1}^{S} \theta_s + \sum_{j=1}^{J} x_j\tilde{\lambda}_j \tag{6.26}$$

and set as the objective to maximize market exposure[19]

$$\max_{x_1, x_2, \dots, x_J} \tilde{M} = \max_{x_1, x_2, \dots, x_J} \left(\sum_{s=1}^{S} \theta_s + \sum_{j=1}^{J} x_j\tilde{\lambda}_j \right). \tag{6.27}$$

Based on this, we choose the following as the fifth PEP mathematical principle:

PEP principle 5: A parimutuel derivatives auction maximizes market exposure subject to the constraints from the other four principles.

Maximizing market exposure helps to increase fills on all order types, including fills on sells and on range forward orders, since market exposure is an increasing function of the fills of all derivatives. Consequently, maximizing market exposure satisfies criterion 1. In addition, the market exposure is the same for orders with the same P&L profile, and so market exposure satisfies criterion 2.[20]

We now make two observations regarding the objective in Equation (6.27). First, note that the maximum in Equation (6.27) is taken over the customer fills $x_1, x_2, \ldots, x_J$, and it is not taken over other unknown variables, such as the state prices. Why is that? As it turns out, once the customer fills are known, all other unknown PEP variables can be determined (this result is discussed in more detail in Chapters 7 and 8). Thus, taking the maximum over the customer fills is an appropriate way to specify the objective. Second, note that included in the definition of the market exposure is the sum of the opening-order premium amounts. Since the opening order amounts are constants, this summation has no impact on the selection of the customer fills in Equation (6.27). We include the opening-order premium amounts in the definition of market exposure (and in the objective function) so that market exposure $\tilde{M}$ is more closely related to the net premium M in the auction (which depends on the opening order amounts). In fact, in certain cases, such as the CPI example below, net premium and market exposure are equal.

The CPI example: Since all five filled customer orders are buy orders of options, it is straightforward to check that the premium paid $x_j \lambda_j$ equals the market exposure $x_j \tilde{\lambda}_j$ for each of the filled orders. Therefore, the market exposure $\tilde{M}$ is equal to \$400,333, the net premium M. Though it is hard to verify here, Section 9.4 will confirm that the customer fills described above and listed in column ten of Table 6.3 are the market exposure maximizing fills based on the opening orders and customer orders described above.[21]

6.2.5 Summary of the mathematical principles and the equilibrium equations

Table 6.6 lists the five mathematical principles of the parimutuel equilibrium. Note that of the five PEP principles, the one that is easiest for customers to verify is the first principle, since it is straightforward for a

Table 6.6 The five mathematical principles of the PEP

Principle number	Principle description
1	Customer fills obey standard limit-order logic
2	All tradable derivatives are replicated using the state claims
3	Derivative prices satisfy no-arbitrage conditions
4	Prices and fills satisfy the self-hedging conditions
5	Customer fills are chosen to maximize the total amount of market exposure while satisfying the first four principles

customer to check that the limit-order logic is satisfied for each of his/her orders. Customers cannot verify the other principles without knowledge of amounts of the opening orders, the submitted customer orders, and the state prices.

Table 6.7 presents all the restrictions and definitions described in this chapter and in Chapter 5, providing a useful reference for this material. One can compare Tables 6.6 and 6.7 to Table 2.3, which presented the principles and equations in the parimutuel wagering framework of Chapter 2.

Equation (6.28) shows a subset of the equations from Table 6.7. We use Equation (6.28) in later chapters as a shorthand way of representing the totality of the PEP equations from Table 6.7. Equation (6.28) is presented in a standard mathematical programming format with the objective listed first.

$$
\begin{aligned}
&\max_{x_1, x_2, \dots, x_J} \quad \widetilde{M} \quad \text{subject to} \\
&\left. \begin{array}{l}
b_j w_j < b_j \pi_j \Rightarrow x_j = 0 \\
b_j w_j = b_j \pi_j \Rightarrow 0 \le x_j \le r_j \\
b_j w_j > b_j \pi_j \Rightarrow x_j = r_j
\end{array} \right\} \quad j = 1, 2, \dots, J \\
&p_s > 0 \hspace{4cm} s = 1, 2, \dots, S \\
&\sum_{s=1}^{S} p_s = 1 \\
&\frac{\theta_s}{p_s} + y_s = M \hspace{2.5cm} s = 1, 2, \dots, S.
\end{aligned}
\tag{6.28}
$$

Table 6.8 displays the known variables in the equations from Table 6.7, and Table 6.9 shows the variables that are unknown and need to be solved for.[22]

Table 6.7 The mathematical specification of the PEP

Principle 1: limit-order logic	Main equation	$$\left. \begin{aligned} b_j w_j &< b_j \pi_j \Rightarrow x_j = 0 \\ b_j w_j &= b_j \pi_j \Rightarrow 0 \le x_j \le r_j \\ b_j w_j &> b_j \pi_j \Rightarrow x_j = r_j \end{aligned} \right\} \quad j = 1, 2, \ldots, J$$
	Related definition	$$b_j \equiv \begin{cases} 1 & \text{if customer order } j \text{ is a buy order} \\ -1 & \text{if customer order } j \text{ is a sell order} \end{cases} \quad j = 1, 2, \ldots, J$$
Principle 2: replication using state claims	Main equation	$$a_{j,s} = d_j(u_s) \quad j = 1, 2, \ldots, J \text{ and } s = 1, 2, \ldots, S$$
Principle 3: no-arbitrage pricing	Main equations	$$p_s > 0 \quad s = 1, 2, \ldots, S$$ $$\sum_{s=1}^{S} p_s = 1$$ $$\pi_j \equiv \begin{cases} \sum_{s=1}^{S} a_{j,s} p_s & \text{if customer order } j \text{ is for an option} \\ u_2 p_1 + \sum_{s=2}^{S} u_s p_s & \text{if customer order } j \text{ is for a range forward} \end{cases} \quad j = 1, 2, \ldots, J$$
	Related equation	$$\theta_s > 0 \quad s = 1, 2, \ldots, S$$
Principle 4: self-hedging	Main equation	$$\frac{\theta_s}{p_s} + y_s = M \quad s = 1, 2, \ldots, S$$
	Related definition and equations	$$\lambda_j \equiv \begin{cases} b_j \pi_j & \text{if customer order } j \text{ is for an option} \\ 0 & \text{if customer order } j \text{ is for a range forward} \end{cases} \quad j = 1, 2, \ldots, J$$ $$M = \sum_{s=1}^{S} \theta_s + \sum_{j=1}^{J} x_j \lambda_j$$ $$y_s = \sum_{j=1}^{J} a_{j,s} b_j x_j \quad s = 1, 2, \ldots, S$$
Principle 5: maximize market exposure	Main equation	$$\max_{x_1, x_2, \ldots, x_J} \tilde{M}$$
	Related definition and equation	$$\tilde{\lambda}_j \equiv \begin{cases} \pi_j & \text{if customer order } j \text{ is a buy of an option} \\ \pi_j - k_1 & \text{if customer order } j \text{ is a buy of a range forward} \\ \bar{d}_j - \pi_j & \text{if customer order } j \text{ is a sell of an option} \\ k_E - \pi_j & \text{if customer order } j \text{ is a sell of a range forward} \end{cases} \quad j = 1, 2, \ldots, J$$ $$\tilde{M} = \sum_{s=1}^{S} \theta_s + \sum_{j=1}^{J} x_j \tilde{\lambda}_j$$

Table 6.8 Known variables in the PEP

Variable	Index (if any)	Description
$a_{j,s}$	$j = 1, 2, \ldots, J,$ $s = 1, 2, \ldots, S$	Replication weight for customer order j for the sth state
b_j	$j = 1, 2, \ldots, J$	Buy or sell side for customer order j
d_j	$j = 1, 2, \ldots, J$	Payout function for customer order j
E	None	Number of strikes
J	None	Number of customer orders
k_e	$e = 1, 2, \ldots, E$	The eth strike
r_j	$j = 1, 2, \ldots, J$	Requested number of contracts for customer order j
S	None	Number of state claims
u_s	$s = 1, 2, \ldots, S$	Possible value of U if the sth state occurs
w_j	$j = 1, 2, \ldots, J$	Limit price for customer order j
θ_s	$s = 1, 2, \ldots, S$	Premium amount for the opening order on the sth state

Table 6.9 Unknown variables in the PEP

Variable	Index (if any)	Description
M	None	Net auction premium
$\tilde{M}$	None	Market exposure
p_s	$s = 1, 2, \ldots, S$	Price for the sth state
x_j	$j = 1, 2, \ldots, J$	Filled amount of contracts for customer order j
y_s	$s = 1, 2, \ldots, S$	Net customer payouts for the sth state
λ_j	$j = 1, 2, \ldots, J$	Premium per contract for customer order j
$\tilde{\lambda}_j$	$j = 1, 2, \ldots, J$	Market exposure per contract for customer order j
π_j	$j = 1, 2, \ldots, J$	Price of the derivative requested in customer order j

6.3 PROPERTIES OF THE PARIMUTUEL EQUILIBRIUM

This section describes several properties of the PEP. In particular, Section 6.3.1 begins by presenting the concept of state premium, and Section 6.3.2 shows that the state premiums relate to the state prices through the principle of relative demand. Section 6.3.3 argues that PEP prices can be interpreted as market-driven measures of implied probabilities or expected values. Section 6.3.4 examines how the PEP aggregates liquidity across different derivatives. Section 6.3.5 explains how the no-arbitrage restrictions impact the PEP prices. Finally, Section 6.3.6

concludes by analyzing the risk to the initial-liquidity provider in a parimutuel derivatives auction.[23]

6.3.1 The state premium

Section 2.1 introduced m_s, the total premium invested in the sth state. Since the wagering framework in Section 2.1 allowed customers to only trade state claims and since customer orders were submitted in terms of the amount of premium requested, the state premium was fairly straightforward to calculate. In the PEP framework, customers can trade derivatives that pay out in multiple states, and customer orders are submitted in terms of the number of contracts requested (instead of premium). Consequently, in this framework, the state premium m_s or equivalently the net amount of premium invested in the sth state claim can be calculated as

$$m_s = \theta_s + p_s y_s \quad s = 1, 2, \ldots, S \tag{6.29}$$

Thus, the net premium for the sth state claim equals θ_s, the amount invested by the initial-liquidity provider in the sth state claim, plus $p_s y_s$, the price of the sth state claim multiplied by the net customer payouts if the sth state occurs. This second term on the right-hand side represents the net amount of customer premium invested in the sth state claim. Equation (6.29) is equivalent to Equation (2.3), except that Equation (6.29) includes the opening-order premium, which did not exist in the framework in Section 2.1. The state premium m_s invested in the sth state claim is based on *every* filled order in the auction, regardless of whether the filled order is for a digital option, a vanilla option, or a range forward,[24] and regardless of whether that filled order is a buy or a sell. We interpret m_s as a measure of *demand* for the sth state claim in the auction.

Appendix 6C shows that M, which was defined in Equation (6.12), can be written in terms of the state premiums as follows:

$$M = \sum_{s=1}^{S} m_s. \tag{6.30}$$

Therefore, the net premium M is the sum of the net premium invested in each state claim. Equation (6.30) is identical to Equation (2.2). However, in the PEP framework, M represents a net premium amount (as m_s can be negative), not a total premium amount as it did in Section 2.1.

The CPI example: Column seven of Table 6.4 presents the state premium for each of the four states in the CPI example based on

Equation (6.29). Using Equation (6.30), we can calculate the net premium M as the sum of the premium invested in each state claim. It is straightforward to check that the net premium based on this calculation (the sum of the values in column seven of Table 6.4) equals \$400,333, which is also the net premium calculated using Equation (6.12).

6.3.2 Relative-demand pricing

If M is non-zero, then state prices and state premiums in a parimutuel derivatives auction satisfy the following equation:[25]

$$p_s = \frac{m_s}{M} \quad s = 1, 2, \ldots, S. \tag{6.31}$$

Thus, the greater the net amount of premium invested in a particular state relative to the net premium in the auction, the greater the price of that state claim. Since the premium amount m_s is based on *all* filled orders, Equation (6.31) means that the prices of state claims are determined based on all filled orders in the auction. Recall that Equation (6.4) implies that the price of every derivative is based on the prices of the state claims. Consequently, Equations (6.4) and (6.31) imply that the prices of all derivatives in a parimutuel derivatives auction are determined based on *all* filled orders in the auction. This is in stark contrast to bilateral matching, where each derivative has its own separate pool of liquidity. In addition, if M is non-zero, the following relationship holds:

$$\frac{m_s}{m_{\tilde{s}}} = \frac{p_s}{p_{\tilde{s}}} \quad s, \tilde{s} = 1, 2, \ldots, S. \tag{6.32}$$

Thus, the greater the net amount of premium invested in a particular state relative to the net premium invested in another state, the higher the price of that first state claim versus the price of the other state claim.[26] Following earlier terminology, we continue to refer to Equation (6.32) as the relative-demand feature of a parimutuel derivatives auction. Equations (6.31) and (6.32) are identical to Equations (2.7) and (2.8), respectively, except that demand m_s (and $m_{\tilde{s}}$) is based on *net* premium in the equations here.

If no-arbitrage conditions hold and M is non-zero, Appendix 6D proves that the self-hedging conditions of Equation (6.16) and the relative-demand pricing of Equation (6.32) are equivalent. Of these two equivalent formulas, the self-hedging version in Equation (6.16) is likely to be most appealing to the auction organizer, since it means that the auction organizer takes on no market risk in running the auction. On the other hand, the relative-demand version in Equation (6.32) is likely to be most appealing to customers, since it implies that prices are driven by customer demand in an intuitive way.

The CPI example: For the CPI example, we verify Equation (6.31), namely that a state price equals the net premium invested in that state divided by the net premium in the auction. For instance, for the first state $s = 1$,

$$p_1 = 0.2$$
$$\cong \frac{80,063}{400,333}$$
$$= \frac{m_1}{M}. \tag{6.33}$$

One can confirm Equation (6.31) for the other three states as well. Next, we verify the relative-demand pricing of Equation (6.32) for state $s = 1$ and $\tilde{s} = 4$. As shown in column seven of Table 6.4, the amount of premium invested in the first state claim is $m_1 = \$80,063$, which is almost exactly twice $m_4 = \$40,036$, the amount of premium invested in the fourth state claim. Note that the price of the first state claim, which is $p_1 = 0.20$, is twice the price of the fourth state claim, which is $p_4 = 0.10$. Therefore,

$$\frac{m_1}{m_4} = \frac{80,063}{40,036}$$
$$\cong \frac{0.20}{0.10}$$
$$= \frac{p_1}{p_4}. \tag{6.34}$$

Consequently, these state prices are based on relative demand for these two states claims. We can verify this relationship holds for other state claims as well.

6.3.3 Prices, implied probabilities, and market forecasts

Whether traded in a parimutuel derivatives auction or by bilateral matching, the price of any digital option has a simple interpretation as the implied probability that the digital option expires in-the-money, as discussed in Ingersoll (2000, p. 70) and Hull (2006, p. 535). Since each state claim is a digital option, p_s can be interpreted as the implied probability that the sth state claim expires in-the-money, or equivalently that the sth state occurs. As discussed in Section 6.3.2, each state price depends on all filled orders in the auction, so the implied probability is also based on all the filled orders in the auction. When s equals $2, 3, \ldots,$ or $S - 1$, p_s

is the implied probability that U equals u_s, and so a parimutuel derivatives auction measures the "state-price density," an important quantity for academic researchers.[27]

Further, the price of each option, whether it is a digital or vanilla option, can be interpreted as the expected payout of that option, where the probabilities used to calculate the expected value are equal to the state prices. Similarly, one can interpret the price of the range forward as the expected value of $\widetilde{U}$ where

$$\widetilde{U} = \begin{cases} k_1 & \text{if } U < k_1, \\ U & \text{if } k_1 \le U < k_E, \\ k_E & \text{if } U \ge k_E. \end{cases} \tag{6.35}$$

If the floor strike k_1 and the cap strike k_E are far away from the likely range of possible values for U, then $\widetilde{U}$ is likely to equal U and the price of the range forward can be interpreted as the expected value of U based on the filled orders in the auction. Thus, the price of the range forward can be thought of as a market-driven consensus measure of the expected outcome for U based on the filled orders in the auction. In contrast to bilateral matching, the price of the range forward is based on *all* filled orders in the auction, not just on orders on the range forward.[28]

As shown in the study by Gürkaynak and Wolfers (2006), the implied probabilities from a parimutuel derivatives auction provide fairly accurate measures of the probabilities of different outcomes for economic statistics. Further, Gürkaynak and Wolfers (2006) show empirically that the market consensus forecast from a parimutuel derivatives auction is more accurate than the median from a survey of economists (which is often used to measure the market consensus). These results by Gürkaynak and Wolfers (2006) add to a general body of research which shows that forecasts made when real money is at stake are more accurate than forecasts based on surveys.

The CPI example: The state prices measure the probabilities of the different CPI outcomes based on all filled orders in the auction. For example, the first state price is 0.20, which means that the filled orders in the CPI auction imply that the probability that the first state occurs (or equivalently that CPI is less than 0.2) is 20%. The price of the range forward, which in this case equals 0.25, can be thought of as the market's consensus forecast for CPI based on all the filled orders in the auction. In this auction, there is a unique price for the range forward, even though there are no filled orders on the range forward. This differs from bilateral matching where the price of a derivative is typically determined only when a trade occurs on that derivative.

6.3.4 Liquidity aggregation

The five filled orders in the CPI example are five buys of five different options. These orders would not be filled using bilateral matching, since there are no buys and sells for the same derivative. Consequently, this CPI example nicely illustrates a parimutuel derivatives auction's ability to aggregate liquidity.[29]

Section 2.3.2 provided an example of how parimutuel matching, in its wagering embodiment, can aggregate liquidity across different types of derivatives. It is worth examining how customer orders in the more flexible format of a parimutuel derivatives auction can complement each other and increase executed volume. To illustrate this, examine the derivatives specified in the fourth and fifth customer orders, the 0.2 vanilla capped call and the 0.4 vanilla floored put, respectively. Let us increase the requested amount on the fifth customer order from 1,500,000 contracts to 2,000,000 contracts, while leaving the requested amounts of the other customer orders unchanged. Table 6.10 shows how increasing the requested amount on the fifth customer order impacts the customer fills and the other auction statistics. Note that the fills on the fourth and fifth customer orders both increase by 500,000 based on this additional requested amount, while the fills on the remaining customer orders do not change. Thus, increasing the requested amount for the vanilla capped call increases

Table 6.10 Changes in auction statistics from increasing the fifth customer's order requested amount from 1,500,000 contracts to 2,000,000 contracts for the parimutuel derivatives auction on CPI

Customer order j	Change in requested amount r_j	Change in price π_j	Change in customer fill x_j	Change in customer premium paid $x_j\lambda_j$ in $
1	0	0	0	0
2	0	0	0	0
3	0	0	0	0
4	0	0	500,000	25,000
5	500,000	0	500,000	75,000
6	0	0	0	0

the fill for that order and for the vanilla floored put, illustrating how a parimutuel derivatives auction aggregates liquidity across various types of derivatives. Next, let us examine why these two orders complement each other. Columns five through eight of Table 6.3 display the payouts of these options. One can check that a portfolio of one contract of the 0.2 vanilla capped call and one contract of the 0.4 vanilla floored put will pay out 0.2 for all values of U. Therefore, a portfolio of one contract of the vanilla capped call struck at 0.2 and one contract of the vanilla floored put struck at 0.4 form a risk-free portfolio. In a parimutuel derivatives auction, orders that can be combined together to form a risk-free portfolio can help increase fills for one another.[30]

6.3.5   No-arbitrage pricing

The no-arbitrage restrictions of Equations (6.2), (6.3), and (6.4) impact the prices that customers pay for derivatives.[31] Once again, consider a portfolio of one contract of the 0.2 vanilla capped call and one contract of the 0.4 vanilla floored put (the derivatives requested in the fourth and fifth customer orders, respectively). This portfolio pays out 0.2 for all values of the underlying. The no-arbitrage restrictions of Equations (6.3) and (6.4) imply that the cost of the portfolio must be 0.2, or equivalently that the price of the 0.2 vanilla capped call plus the price of the 0.4 vanilla floored put equals 0.2. We confirm this by noting in column nine of Table 6.3 that the price of the vanilla capped call is 0.05 and the price of the vanilla floored put is 0.15. Note that the customers' limit prices for these two orders are 0.05 and 0.16, respectively, showing that customers are willing to pay 0.21 for the portfolio of these two options. Since the no-arbitrage restrictions imply that the portfolio must cost 0.2, at least one of the orders receives an improved price. In this case, the customer who requests the vanilla floored put pays 0.15, instead of 0.16. Thus, the no-arbitrage restrictions can lead to price improvement for some customers.

6.3.6   Risk to the initial-liquidity provider

Let us now examine the initial-liquidity provider's risk associated with the opening orders. Column two of Table 6.11 shows the payout on the opening orders (reproduced from column four of Table 6.4). Column three shows the profit or loss to the initial-liquidity provider in each state, which is simply the payout on that opening order minus the $600 in premium invested by the initial-liquidity provider. Although the initial-liquidity provider invested a total of $600 in premium at the start of the auction,

Table 6.11 Opening order payouts and the initial-liquidity provider's P&L for the parimutuel derivatives auction on CPI

State claim s	Opening order payout if the sth state claim expires in-the-money θ_s/p_s in $	P&L to the initial-liquidity provider if the sth state claim expires in-the-money $\frac{\theta_s}{p_s} - \left(\sum_{t=1}^{S} \theta_t\right)$ in $
1	500	−100
2	500	−100
3	667	67
4	1,000	400

based on the market prices at the close of the auction, his/her worst loss is only $100.[32] This risk helps support filled customers orders with approximately $400,000 in premium. Consequently, the initial-liquidity provider takes on a small amount of risk from the opening orders while helping to fill a large amount of customer orders. Based on the magnitude of the risk to the initial-liquidity provider, it is unlikely that the initial-liquidity provider will find economic benefit out of hedging his/her risk to CPI. Thus, customers are able to trade different derivatives in a parimutuel derivatives auction without significant risk to the initial-liquidity provider, limiting the need for a tradable underlying for delta hedging. In this regard, a parimutuel derivatives auction can help create liquidity in derivatives markets where there is no actively traded underlying.[33]

Table 6.11 shows that the risk to the initial-liquidity provider is fairly small in this CPI example. As discussed in Section 6.1, opening orders perform three important functions in a parimutuel derivatives auction. However, one might sensibly ask, why wouldn't the initial-liquidity provider invest a penny in each state to limit his/her risk even further? As discussed in more detail in Section 7.1.3, as the opening orders amounts are reduced, the amount of time to compute the parimutuel prices and fills generally increases. Customers appreciate having indicative prices update quickly during an auction as new orders arrive (or as existing orders are modified or canceled). Therefore, the initial-liquidity provider must set the size of the opening orders based on the tradeoff between keeping his/her opening-order risk low versus accommodating customers.

Summary: The small-scale CPI example illustrates several features of a parimutuel derivatives auction. State prices are determined based on the relative amount of premium invested in the state claims, which is the principle of relative demand. All derivative prices are based on all filled orders in the auction, leading to market-driven measures for the probabilities of different outcomes (based on the state prices) and a market consensus forecast for the underlying (based on the price of the range forward). A parimutuel derivatives auction can aggregate liquidity across different derivatives without matching buyers and sellers, a unique approach for liquidity aggregation. Prices in a parimutuel derivatives auction are arbitrage-free, which leads to improved prices for certain customers. Finally, parimutuel derivatives auctions allow a significant amount of customer trades to be executed with only a limited amount of risk for the initial-liquidity provider.

APPENDIX 6A: THE PARIMUTUEL EQUILIBRIUM WITH A DISCOUNT FACTOR

In the main text of this chapter, we derived the parimutuel equilibrium conditions assuming that the interest rate between the dates that premiums are collected and payouts are made is zero, or assuming that premiums and payouts are exchanged on the same date. We now consider the case where the premium settlement date may be before the payout settlement date and the risk-free dollar interest rate between those two dates is greater than or equal to zero. To that end, let z denote the discount factor based on the risk-free dollar interest rate between the premium settlement date and the payout settlement date at the close of a parimutuel derivatives auction. With a non-negative interest rate, the range of the discount factor is

$$0 < z \leq 1. \tag{6A.1}$$

To incorporate the time value of money and to avoid arbitrage, we require that the sum of the state-claim prices equals the discount factor. Otherwise, a customer in a parimutuel derivatives auction could borrow or lend at a profit. Mathematically, we modify Equation (6.3) as follows:

$$\sum_{s=1}^{S} p_s = z. \tag{6A.2}$$

In this case, p_s can be interpreted as the discounted implied probability of state s occurring for $s = 1, 2, \ldots, S$. If customer order j is for an option, the option price is still calculated using Equation (6.4), or any of Equations (6.5), (6.6), (6.7), (6.8), and (6.9) as is relevant. However, if customer order j is for a range forward, the price of the range forward now satisfies

$$z\pi_j = u_2 p_1 + \sum_{s=2}^{S} u_s p_s. \tag{6A.3}$$

Further, we modify the self-hedging condition of Equation (6.16) as follows:

$$\frac{\theta_s}{p_s} + y_s = \frac{M}{z} \quad s = 1, 2, \ldots, S. \tag{6A.4}$$

On the right-hand side of this equation, we divide net premium M by z to reflect that premiums will be lent if $M > 0$ (resp., borrowed if $M < 0$) from the premium settlement date to the payout settlement date and will grow to M/z. The amount M/z will be exactly enough to make the net payouts required on the payout settlement date. Equations other than those corresponding to (6A.2), (6A.3), and (6A.4) in Table 6.7 require no alteration when a discount factor is incorporated. In addition, the relative-demand pricing of Equation (6.32) holds without any change. Following the derivation in Appendix 6B, we can show that

$$\pi^{\text{vcc}} - \pi^{\text{vfp}} = z(\pi^{\text{rf}} - k_e), \tag{6A.5}$$

where π^{vcc} denotes the price of a vanilla capped call struck at k_e, π^{vfp} denotes the price of a vanilla floored put struck at k_e, and π^{rf} denotes the price of the range forward. This equation closely resembles the standard version of put-call parity, described in Hull (2006, pp. 212–215).

APPENDIX 6B: THE PRICE OF A RANGE FORWARD AND PUT-CALL PARITY

This appendix derives two properties of the range forward. First, we check that the price of the range forward satisfies Equation (6.4). This is done by using the payout function for the range forward and the fact that it has a value of zero at the close of the auction. Second, we confirm that the price of the range forward satisfies a modified version of put-call parity, a well-known formula in option-pricing theory. As shown in Hull (2006, pp. 212–215), put-call parity in its standard form relates the price of a vanilla call at a particular strike and the price of a vanilla put at the same strike to the forward price. We show that a modified version of put-call parity holds in a parimutuel derivatives auction, where the modified version relates the price of the vanilla capped call at a particular strike and the price of the vanilla floored put at the same strike to the price of the range forward.[34]

The price of a range forward: The price of the range forward is set so that it has a value (based on the state prices) of zero at the close of the auction. Equivalently, the expected payout of a range forward equals zero, when the expected payout is calculated using the state prices as probabilities. Let d^{rf} denote the payout function for a range forward. It satisfies

$$0 = \sum_{s=1}^{S} d^{\text{rf}}(u_s)p_s. \tag{6B.1}$$

Letting π^{rf} denote the price of a range forward and applying Equation (5.38) implies that

$$0 = (k_1 - \pi^{\text{rf}})p_1 + \sum_{s=2}^{S}(u_s - \pi^{\text{rf}})p_s \tag{6B.2}$$

which implies that

$$0 = k_1 p_1 + \sum_{s=2}^{S} u_s p_s - \sum_{s=1}^{S} \pi^{\text{rf}} p_s. \tag{6B.3}$$

Since the sum of the state-claim prices equals one (Equation (6.3)), we have that

$$0 = k_1 p_1 + \left(\sum_{s=2}^{S} u_s p_s\right) - \pi^{\text{rf}}. \tag{6B.4}$$

Therefore,

$$\pi^{\text{rf}} = k_1 p_1 + \sum_{s=2}^{S} u_s p_s$$

$$= u_2 p_1 + \sum_{s=2}^{S} u_s p_s, \tag{6B.5}$$

where the second equality follows from Equation (5.29).

Put-call parity in a parimutuel derivatives auction: We now derive a modified version of put-call parity for a parimutuel derivatives auction.

Let π^{vcc} denote the price of a vanilla capped call struck at k_e. Equation (6.8) implies that

$$\pi^{\text{vcc}} \equiv \sum_{s=s_e+1}^{S} (u_s - k_e)p_s$$

$$= \sum_{s=s_e}^{S} (u_s - k_e)p_s, \tag{6B.6}$$

where the second step follows from the fact that u_{s_e} equals k_e and so $(u_{s_e} - k_e)p_{s_e}$ equals zero.

Let π^{vfp} denote the price for a vanilla floored put struck at k_e, which is given in Equation (6.9), and is reproduced here for convenience:

$$\pi^{\text{vfp}} = (k_e - k_1)p_1 + \sum_{s=2}^{s_e-1} (k_e - u_s)p_s. \tag{6B.7}$$

Subtracting Equation (6B.7) from Equation (6B.6) gives that

$$\pi^{\text{vcc}} - \pi^{\text{vfp}}$$

$$= \sum_{s=s_e}^{S} (u_s - k_e)p_s - \left((k_e - k_1)p_1 + \sum_{s=2}^{s_e-1} (k_e - u_s)p_s \right)$$

$$= \sum_{s=s_e}^{S} (u_s - k_e)p_s - (k_e - k_1)p_1 - \sum_{s=2}^{s_e-1} (k_e - u_s)p_s$$

$$= \sum_{s=s_e}^{S} u_s p_s - k_e \sum_{s=s_e}^{S} p_s - k_e p_1 + k_1 p_1 - k_e \sum_{s=2}^{s_e-1} p_s + \sum_{s=2}^{s_e-1} u_s p_s$$

$$= \sum_{s=s_e}^{S} u_s p_s - k_e \sum_{s=1}^{S} p_s + k_1 p_1 + \sum_{s=2}^{s_e-1} u_s p_s$$

$$= \sum_{s=2}^{S} u_s p_s - k_e + k_1 p_1$$

$$= \sum_{s=2}^{S} u_s p_s - k_e + u_2 p_1, \tag{6B.8}$$

where the fifth equality follows from Equation (6.3), and where the sixth equality follows from Equation (5.29). Substituting π^{rf} from

Equation (6B.5) into (6B.8) implies that

$$\pi^{\text{vcc}} - \pi^{\text{vfp}} = \pi^{\text{rf}} - k_e. \tag{6B.9}$$

Equation (6B.9) represents the parimutuel derivatives auction version of put-call parity.[35]

APPENDIX 6C: EQUIVALENT FORMULAS FOR THE NET AUCTION PREMIUM

The auction premium M is defined in Equation (6.12) as the sum of the opening orders and the sum of the customer premiums paid. We reproduce that equation here for convenience:

$$M = \sum_{s=1}^{S} \theta_s + \sum_{j=1}^{J} x_j \lambda_j. \tag{6C.1}$$

Equation (6.30) expresses M as a sum of the state premiums, also reproduced here for convenience:

$$M = \sum_{s=1}^{S} m_s. \tag{6C.2}$$

This appendix shows that these two equations are equivalent formulas for M.

If customer order j is for an option strategy, then

$$
\begin{aligned}
x_j \lambda_j &= b_j x_j \pi_j \\
&= b_j x_j \left(\sum_{s=1}^{S} a_{j,s} p_s \right),
\end{aligned}
\tag{6C.3}
$$

where the second equality follows from the definition of π_j in Equation (6.4). If customer order j is for a range forward, then

$$
\begin{aligned}
\sum_{s=1}^{S} a_{j,s} p_s &= (u_2 - \pi_j) p_1 + \sum_{s=2}^{S} (u_s - \pi_j) p_s \\
&= u_2 p_1 + \sum_{s=2}^{S} u_s p_s - \pi_j \\
&= 0,
\end{aligned}
\tag{6C.4}
$$

where the first equality follows from the definition of the replication weights for a range forward in Equation (5.38), where the second equality follows from Equation (6.3), and where the third equality follows from the definition of the range forward price in Equation (6.4). Therefore, for the range forward,

$$0 = x_j \lambda_j$$

$$= b_j x_j \left(\sum_{s=1}^{S} a_{j,s} p_s \right). \tag{6C.5}$$

Thus, if customer order j is for an option or a range forward, Equations (6C.3) and (6C.5) imply that

$$x_j \lambda_j = b_j x_j \left(\sum_{s=1}^{S} a_{j,s} p_s \right). \tag{6C.6}$$

Therefore, Equation (6C.1) can be written as

$$M = \sum_{s=1}^{S} \theta_s + \sum_{j=1}^{J} x_j \lambda_j$$

$$= \sum_{s=1}^{S} \theta_s + \sum_{j=1}^{J} b_j x_j \left(\sum_{s=1}^{S} a_{j,s} p_s \right)$$

$$= \sum_{s=1}^{S} \theta_s + \sum_{s=1}^{S} p_s \left(\sum_{j=1}^{J} a_{j,s} b_j x_j \right)$$

$$= \sum_{s=1}^{S} \theta_s + \sum_{s=1}^{S} p_s y_s$$

$$= \sum_{s=1}^{S} (\theta_s + p_s y_s)$$

$$= \sum_{s=1}^{S} m_s, \tag{6C.7}$$

where the second equality follows from Equation (6C.6), where the third equality comes from rearranging the order of the summations in the second expression on the right-hand side, where the fourth equality follows from the definition of y_s in Equation (6.15), and the sixth equality follows from the definition of m_s in Equation (6.29). Consequently, Equations (6C.1) and (6C.2) are equivalent.

APPENDIX 6D: SELF-HEDGING AND RELATIVE-DEMAND PRICING ARE EQUIVALENT

Theorem: Consider the following three conditions:

$$p_s > 0 \quad s = 1, 2, \ldots, S, \tag{6D.1}$$

$$\sum_{s=1}^{S} p_s = 1, \tag{6D.2}$$

$$M \neq 0. \tag{6D.3}$$

Under these three conditions

$$\frac{\theta_s}{p_s} + y_s = M \quad s = 1, 2, \ldots, S \tag{6D.4}$$

holds if and only if

$$\frac{m_s}{m_{\tilde{s}}} = \frac{p_s}{p_{\tilde{s}}} \quad s, \tilde{s} = 1, 2, \ldots, S. \tag{6D.5}$$

Proof of theorem:
$\Rightarrow$ We first show that Equation (6D.4) implies Equation (6D.5). Recall Equation (6.29):

$$m_s = \theta_s + p_s y_s \quad s = 1, 2, \ldots, S. \tag{6D.6}$$

We can divide both sides of this equation by p_s since $p_s \neq 0$ for $s=1, 2, \ldots, S$ by Equation (6D.1). Therefore,

$$\frac{m_s}{p_s} = \frac{\theta_s}{p_s} + y_s \quad s = 1, 2, \ldots, S. \tag{6D.7}$$

Combining Equations (6D.4) and (6D.7) gives that

$$\frac{m_s}{p_s} = M \quad s = 1, 2, \ldots, S \tag{6D.8}$$

which implies that

$$\frac{m_s}{p_s} = \frac{m_{\tilde{s}}}{p_{\tilde{s}}} \quad s, \tilde{s} = 1, 2, \ldots, S. \tag{6D.9}$$

Now, $M \neq 0$ (Equation (6D.3)) coupled with Equation (6D.8) implies that $m_{\tilde{s}} \neq 0$ for $\tilde{s} = 1, 2, \ldots, S$. Therefore, we can multiply both sides of Equation (6D.9) by $(p_s/m_{\tilde{s}})$, which implies that

$$\frac{m_s}{m_{\tilde{s}}} = \frac{p_s}{p_{\tilde{s}}} \quad s, \tilde{s} = 1, 2, \ldots, S. \tag{6D.10}$$

Thus, Equation (6D.4) implies Equation (6D.5).

$\Leftarrow$ Next, we show that Equation (6D.5) implies Equation (6D.4). Since $p_s > 0$ for $s = 1, 2, \ldots, S$ (Equation (6D.1)), multiply both sides of Equation (6D.5) by $(m_{\tilde{s}} p_{\tilde{s}}/p_s)$. This yields

$$\frac{m_s p_{\tilde{s}}}{p_s} = m_{\tilde{s}} \quad s, \tilde{s} = 1, 2, \ldots, S. \tag{6D.11}$$

Summing both sides of this equation over $\tilde{s} = 1, 2, \ldots, S$ yields

$$\sum_{\tilde{s}=1}^{S} \frac{m_s p_{\tilde{s}}}{p_s} = \sum_{\tilde{s}=1}^{S} m_{\tilde{s}} \quad s = 1, 2, \ldots, S. \tag{6D.12}$$

The left-hand side of Equation (6D.12) simplifies as follows:

$$\sum_{\tilde{s}=1}^{S} \frac{m_s p_{\tilde{s}}}{p_s} = \frac{m_s}{p_s} \left(\sum_{\tilde{s}=1}^{S} p_{\tilde{s}} \right) \quad s = 1, 2, \ldots, S$$

$$= \frac{m_s}{p_s} \quad s = 1, 2, \ldots, S$$

$$= \frac{\theta_s}{p_s} + y_s \quad s = 1, 2, \ldots, S, \tag{6D.13}$$

where the second equality follows from Equation (6D.2), and where the third equality follows from the formula for m_s in Equation (6D.6). The right-hand side of Equation (6D.12) equals M by Equation (6.30). Thus,

$$\frac{\theta_s}{p_s} + y_s = M \quad s = 1, 2, \ldots, S \tag{6D.14}$$

which is Equation (6D.4). Consequently, Equation (6D.5) implies Equation (6D.4). This concludes the proof.

CHAPTER 7

The Solution Algorithm for the Parimutuel Equilibrium Problem

In the parimutuel wagering framework described in Chapter 2, the equilibrium prices can be calculated easily using arithmetic. As discussed in the more recent chapters, a parimutuel derivatives auction has considerably more flexibility than the parimutuel wagering framework. Computing the equilibrium prices and fills is significantly harder in this framework, primarily due to the presence of limit orders. This chapter is devoted to numerically solving this more difficult problem, which we call the Parimutuel Equilibrium Problem (PEP). The numerical algorithm presented in this chapter has two parts. Part one solves for the equilibrium state prices and the equilibrium derivative strategy prices using an iterative and nonlinear algorithm. Part two uses the equilibrium prices from part one and a linear program (LP) to solve for the customer fills that maximize the market exposure, a measure of auction volume. After the LP determines the customer fills, the remaining unknown variables can be solved for in a straightforward fashion. Table 7.1 summarizes the properties of the two parts of the solution algorithm.[1]

This chapter proceeds as follows. Section 7.1 presents part one of the algorithm. Section 7.2 checks that once the prices are known, the objective function and the constraints are linear. Section 7.3 introduces the concept of complementary orders and shows how complementary orders can increase the market exposure in the auction. Throughout this chapter,

Table 7.1 The two parts of the PEP solution algorithm

Part	Nature of solution technique	Variables solved for
Part one	Nonlinear	State prices: $p_1, p_2, \dots, p_S$
		Derivative strategy prices: $\pi_1, \pi_2, \dots, \pi_J$
		Premiums per contract: $\lambda_1, \lambda_2, \dots, \lambda_J$
		Market exposures per contract: $\tilde{\lambda}_1, \tilde{\lambda}_2, \dots, \tilde{\lambda}_J$
Part two	Linear	Customer fills: $x_1, x_2, \dots, x_J$
		Auction premium: M
		Total market exposure: $\widetilde{M}$
		Net customer payouts: $y_1, y_2, \dots, y_S$

we illustrate the general discussion with a specific auction example based on the US Consumer Price Index (CPI).

7.1   PART ONE OF THE SOLUTION ALGORITHM

This section describes part one of the solution algorithm. The main work in this part involves determining the equilibrium state prices $p_1, p_2, \dots, p_S$. Once the state prices are known, it will be straightforward to determine the equilibrium derivative strategy prices $\pi_1, \pi_2, \dots, \pi_J$, the equilibrium premiums per contract $\lambda_1, \lambda_2, \dots, \lambda_J$, and the market exposures per contract $\tilde{\lambda}_1, \tilde{\lambda}_2, \dots, \tilde{\lambda}_J$. Section 7.1.1 reviews the setup for the problem. Section 7.1.2 discusses how to initialize the variables in part one and the steps that are taken in each iteration. Section 7.1.3 makes some observations about this part of the algorithm. Section 7.1.4 illustrates these techniques with an example auction using US CPI. Section 7.1.5 relates this algorithm to techniques from the field of optimization.

It is worth discussing the notation relating to part one of the algorithm. In previous chapters, we have used M, p_s, x_j, y_s, and π_j to denote the values of variables in equilibrium. In the context of part one of this algorithm, we use M, p_s, x_j, y_s, and π_j to denote values of the variables on different iterations in part one, and not necessarily in equilibrium. In addition, we allow the variables v_j, V, and δ_j (which are defined below) to vary depending on the iteration of the algorithm in part one. To keep the notation simple, we do not label (either with a subscript or superscript) any of these variables with the iteration number.

7.1.1 Setup

The PEP constraints: Recall from Equation (6.28) that the prices and customer fills of the PEP satisfy the following four constraints:

$$\left.\begin{array}{l} b_j w_j < b_j \pi_j \;\Rightarrow\; x_j = 0 \\ b_j w_j = b_j \pi_j \;\Rightarrow\; 0 \le x_j \le r_j \\ b_j w_j > b_j \pi_j \;\Rightarrow\; x_j = r_j \end{array}\right\} \quad j = 1, 2, \ldots, J, \tag{7.1}$$

$$p_s > 0 \quad s = 1, 2, \ldots, S, \tag{7.2}$$

$$\sum_{s=1}^{S} p_s = 1, \tag{7.3}$$

$$\frac{\theta_s}{p_s} + y_s = M \quad s = 1, 2, \ldots, S. \tag{7.4}$$

Equation (7.1) relates the customer fills to the requested amounts, the order sides, the limit prices, and the derivative strategy prices. We refer to Equation (7.1) as the "limit-order conditions." Equations (7.2) and (7.3) are no-arbitrage conditions that restrict the state prices to be positive and to sum to one.[2] Equation (7.4) ensures that in every state the net customer payouts equal the net premium collected, and we once again refer to these conditions as the "self-hedging conditions."[3]

Measuring the limit-order violations: Within each iteration in part one of the algorithm, the PEP variables satisfy Equations (7.2), (7.3), and (7.4). While the PEP variables satisfy the limit-order restrictions of Equation (7.1) on the *final* iteration of the algorithm in part one, the variables do not all satisfy this equation on *earlier* iterations. At each iteration, we adjust the customer fills so that Equation (7.1) is closer to being satisfied, where we now make the concept of "closer" precise. To quantify the progress of the algorithm at each iteration, we use the variable v_j to measure the degree to which customer order j violates the limit-order conditions in Equation (7.1). For a buy order ($b_j = 1$), v_j is defined as

$$v_j \equiv \begin{cases} (\pi_j - w_j)x_j & \text{if } w_j < \pi_j \\ 0 & \text{if } w_j = \pi_j \\ (w_j - \pi_j)(r_j - x_j) & \text{if } w_j > \pi_j \end{cases} \quad j = 1, 2, \ldots, J. \tag{7.5}$$

Based on this definition, we now check that if customer order j satisfies the limit-order constraints of Equation (7.1), then v_j equals zero by considering the three "if" conditions in Equation (7.5).

1. If customer order j's limit price is below the market price ($w_j < \pi_j$) and customer order j has no fill ($x_j = 0$), then Equation (7.1) is satisfied, and v_j equals zero.

2. If customer order j's limit price equals the market price ($w_j = \pi_j$), then v_j equals zero.

3. If customer order j's limit price is above the market price ($w_j > \pi_j$) and customer order j is fully filled ($x_j = r_j$), then Equation (7.1) is satisfied, and v_j equals zero.

In a similar way, we now confirm that if the limit-order constraints are violated for customer order j, then v_j is strictly positive. First, note that the stepping approach used below in Equation (7.12) implies that x_j is always greater than or equal to zero and less than or equal to r_j.

1. If customer order j's limit price is below the market price ($w_j < \pi_j$) and customer order j has a fill ($x_j > 0$), then Equation (7.1) is violated, and v_j is positive.

2. If customer order j's limit price equals the market price ($w_j = \pi_j$), Equation (7.1) is never violated.

3. If customer order j's limit price is above the market price ($w_j > \pi_j$) and customer order j is less than fully filled ($x_j < r_j$), then Equation (7.1) is violated, and v_j is positive.

We can interpret v_j for a buy order as follows. If the jth customer order were to receive a fill of x_j at a price π_j greater than w_j (case (1) immediately above), then v_j is the amount of dollars that the customer would overpay above his/her limit price for the fill of x_j contracts. If the jth customer order were to receive a fill of x_j at a price π_j less than w_j (case (3) immediately above), then v_j is the amount of additional dollars the customer would have been willing to pay for $r_j - x_j$ contracts, the unfilled portion of the order. In either case, the larger v_j is, the larger the violation of Equation (7.1) for the jth customer order.

Similar to Equation (7.5), the variable v_j can also be defined for a sell order ($b_j = -1$):

$$v_j \equiv \begin{cases} (w_j - \pi_j)x_j & \text{if } w_j > \pi_j \\ 0 & \text{if } w_j = \pi_j \quad j = 1, 2, \ldots, J. \\ (\pi_j - w_j)(r_j - x_j) & \text{if } w_j < \pi_j \end{cases} \qquad (7.6)$$

For a general formula for v_j that encompasses either a buy order or a sell order, we write that

$$
v_j \equiv \begin{cases} (b_j \pi_j - b_j w_j) x_j & \text{if } b_j w_j < b_j \pi_j \\ 0 & \text{if } b_j w_j = b_j \pi_j \quad j = 1, 2, \ldots, J. \\ (b_j w_j - b_j \pi_j)(r_j - x_j) & \text{if } b_j w_j > b_j \pi_j \end{cases}
$$

(7.7)

To measure in total how far away the limit-order conditions are from being satisfied across all J customer orders, define V as follows:

$$
V \equiv \sum_{j=1}^{J} v_j.
$$

(7.8)

If V equals zero, then the variables satisfy the limit-order conditions for all J customer orders, while if V is positive, then at least one of the limit-order conditions is violated.

Brief algorithm overview: Part one of the algorithm solves for the unique equilibrium state prices and the unique equilibrium derivative strategy prices that satisfy the four constraints (7.1), (7.2), (7.3), and (7.4).[4] As an objective, we choose to minimize the limit-order violations V. Within each iteration, we adjust the customer fills to reduce the limit-order violations V, while still satisfying Equations (7.2), (7.3), and (7.4).[5] The final iteration is the one in which we eliminate all the limit-order violations and V is minimized. Since V is non-negative and equals zero when the limit-order conditions are met, minimizing V is equivalent to setting it to zero. The state and strategy prices from that final iteration are the equilibrium prices.[6]

7.1.2　The initialization and the steps of the algorithm

We now explain how the variables are initialized, and the seven steps that comprise each iteration of part one of the algorithm. Figure 7.1 provides a flow diagram of this algorithm.

Initialize the variables: At initialization, we set $x_1, x_2, \ldots, x_J$ to be equal to zero. Without any filled customer orders, the sth state price p_s is simply the proportion of the opening orders allocated to the sth state claim, i.e., $p_s = \theta_s / \sum_{t=1}^{S} \theta_t$ for $s = 1, 2, \ldots, S$. Equation (6.4)

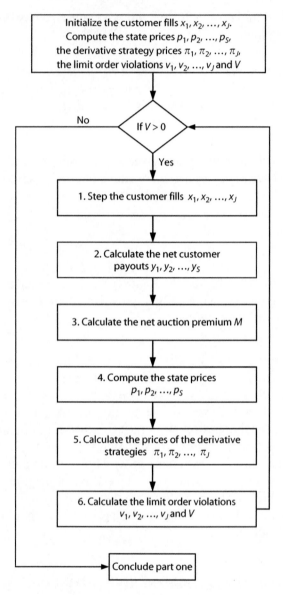

Figure 7.1 Steps in part one of the solution algorithm

defines π_j as

$$\pi_j \equiv \begin{cases} \sum_{s=1}^{S} a_{j,s}\, p_s & \text{if customer order } j \text{ is for an option} \\ u_2 p_1 + \sum_{s=2}^{S} u_s\, p_s & \text{if customer order } j \text{ is for a range forward} \end{cases}$$

$$j = 1, 2, \ldots, J, \tag{7.9}$$

where the $a_{j,s}$'s were defined in Equation (5.31) and the u_s's were defined in Equation (5.29). Using Equation (7.9) and the initial state prices $p_1, p_2, \ldots, p_S$, we can calculate the initial derivative strategy prices $\pi_1, \pi_2, \ldots, \pi_J$. Based on these values, we use Equation (7.7) to calculate $v_1, v_2, \ldots, v_J$, and we use Equation (7.8) to calculate V. If V is positive, then we proceed to step 1 and start iterating. If V equals zero, then this completes part one and the initial prices are the equilibrium prices.

Step 1- Adjust the customer fills: The algorithm adjusts the fills on multiple customer orders within a single iteration as follows. For $j = 1, 2, \ldots, J$, let δ_j be a positive number that denotes the "step size," or equivalently the number of contracts that x_j may change by on a particular iteration. We allow δ_j to vary based on the iteration number, though we suppress this in our notation. Section 7.1.5 will describe how δ_j is determined. We adjust the customer fill x_j if the jth customer order is a buy order as follows:

$$x_j \leftarrow \begin{cases} \max[x_j - \delta_j, 0] & \text{if } w_j < \pi_j \\ x_j & \text{if } w_j = \pi_j \\ \min[x_j + \delta_j, r_j] & \text{if } w_j > \pi_j \end{cases} \quad j = 1, 2, \ldots, J. \quad (7.10)$$

Here the notation "$x_j \leftarrow$" means that we modify the variable x_j on this iteration according to the expression following the arrow. If customer order j's limit price is below the market price ($w_j < \pi_j$), then we decrease x_j by δ_j contracts as long as that reduction does not decrease x_j below zero. If customer order j's limit price is equal to the market price ($w_j = \pi_j$), then we leave x_j unchanged. Finally, if customer order j's limit price is greater than the market price ($w_j > \pi_j$), then we increase x_j by δ_j contracts as long as that addition does not increase x_j above the customer's requested contract amount r_j. For a sell order, we step x_j according to similar logic:

$$x_j \leftarrow \begin{cases} \max[x_j - \delta_j, 0] & \text{if } w_j > \pi_j \\ x_j & \text{if } w_j = \pi_j \\ \min[x_j + \delta_j, r_j] & \text{if } w_j < \pi_j \end{cases} \quad j = 1, 2, \ldots, J. \quad (7.11)$$

We combine Equations (7.10) and (7.11) to handle both buy and sell orders in one equation as follows:

$$x_j \leftarrow \begin{cases} \max[x_j - \delta_j, 0] & \text{if } b_j w_j < b_j \pi_j \\ x_j & \text{if } b_j w_j = b_j \pi_j \\ \min[x_j + \delta_j, r_j] & \text{if } b_j w_j > b_j \pi_j \end{cases} \quad j = 1, 2, \ldots, J. \quad (7.12)$$

The step size δ_j is always positive, and we adjust it in different iterations to reduce v_j and V more quickly than can generally be accomplished with a static step size. Doing so keeps the total time to solve for the equilibrium prices lower than it would be otherwise.

Step 2- Calculate the net customer payouts: Based on the values for $x_1, x_2, \ldots, x_J$ from step 1, we calculate $y_1, y_2, \ldots, y_S$ using Equation (6.15)

$$y_s = \sum_{j=1}^{J} a_{j,s} b_j x_j \quad s = 1, 2, \ldots, S. \tag{7.13}$$

Note that if customer order j is for an option strategy, then the $a_{j,s}$'s are constants. However, if customer order j is for the range forward, then the $a_{j,s}$'s depend upon the price of the range forward. To handle such a dependency for the range forward, we calculate the $a_{j,s}$'s for Equation (7.13) based on the price for the range forward from the previous iteration.

Step 3- Compute the net auction premium: Using the values of $y_1, y_2, \ldots, y_S$ from step 2, we compute the net auction premium M using "Newton's method," as detailed in Appendix 7A.

Step 4- Calculate the state prices: Using the values of $y_1, y_2, \ldots, y_S$ from step 2 and M from step 3, we calculate $p_1, p_2, \ldots, p_S$ by rearranging Equation (7.4) as follows:

$$p_s = \frac{\theta_s}{M - y_s} \quad s = 1, 2, \ldots, S. \tag{7.14}$$

Because we calculate the state prices in this way, it is easy to see that these values of $p_1, p_2, \ldots, p_S, y_1, y_2, \ldots, y_S$, and M satisfy the self-hedging conditions of Equation (7.4). Further, one can check that $p_1, p_2, \ldots, p_S$ are all positive (Equation (7.2)) and sum to one (Equation (7.3)).[7]

Step 5- Calculate the prices of the derivative strategies: Using Equation (7.9) and the state prices $p_1, p_2, \ldots, p_S$ from step 4, we calculate the derivative strategy prices $\pi_1, \pi_2, \ldots, \pi_J$.

Step 6- Calculate the limit-order violations: Based on $x_1, x_2, \ldots, x_J$ from step 1 and $\pi_1, \pi_2, \ldots, \pi_J$ from step 5, we use Equation (7.7) to calculate $v_1, v_2, \ldots, v_J$, and we use Equation (7.8) to calculate V.

Step 7- Return to step 1 or conclude part one: If V is positive, then we return to step 1 and continue iterating. If V equals zero, then this completes part one and the prices from this iteration are the equilibrium prices.[8] Based on those prices, we can use Equation (6.11) to determine the equilibrium premiums per contract $\lambda_1, \lambda_2, \ldots, \lambda_J$, and we can use Equation (6.25) to determine the market exposures per contract $\tilde{\lambda}_1, \tilde{\lambda}_2, \ldots, \tilde{\lambda}_J$.

7.1.3 Comments on the steps in part one

As mentioned above, at step 4 of every iteration, the two restrictions on the state prices (Equations (7.2) and (7.3)) are met, and the variables satisfy the self-hedging conditions of Equation (7.4). However, in step 6, we see that the current prices and customer fills may violate the limit-order restrictions of Equation (7.1), and correspondingly, V may be positive. Customer fills are modified on each iteration so that the limit-order restrictions are closer to being satisfied, or equivalently, so that V is closer to reaching its minimum of zero. When we have eliminated all limit-order violations and V is minimized and equals zero, all PEP conditions – Equations (7.1), (7.2), (7.3), and (7.4) – are met and part one is completed.

It is worth analyzing in some detail how modifying the customer fills in each iteration based on Equation (7.12) helps to reduce V. For this analysis, assume that the jth customer order is a buy order ($b_j = 1$) for a digital option, which implies that the replication weights $a_{j,s}$ equal zero or one for $s = 1, 2, \ldots, S$. Further, assume that the jth customer order is the only customer order of the J customer orders that violates the limit-order conditions of Equation (7.1). If this customer order's limit price is above the market price in the current iteration ($w_j > \pi_j$) but this order is not fully filled ($x_j < r_j$), then we increase the customer's fill x_j based on Equation (7.10), where we assume that the step size δ_j is small enough so that increasing x_j by δ_j keeps the market price below customer order j's limit price. How does increasing x_j impact π_j?

1. Equation (7.13) implies that increasing x_j increases y_s if $a_{j,s}$ equals one, and leaves y_s unchanged if $a_{j,s}$ equals zero;

2. Then, the definition of m_s (Equation (6.29)) implies that m_s increases if $a_{j,s}$ equals one, or remains unchanged if $a_{j,s}$ equals zero;

3. Then, relative-demand pricing (Equation (6.32)) implies that p_s, the price of the sth state claim, increases if $a_{j,s}$ equals one, or decreases if $a_{j,s}$ equals zero;

4. Then, the formula for pricing derivative strategies (Equation (7.9)) implies that π_j increases.

Thus, increasing the customer fill x_j increases π_j, and therefore decreases $w_j - \pi_j$.[9,10] Recall that v_j is the product of $w_j - \pi_j$ and $r_j - x_j$, and since both terms are positive and decrease on the next iteration, then v_j will decrease on the next iteration as well. A similar effect takes place if the jth customer order's limit price is below the market price ($w_j < \pi_j$) and has some fill. Here, x_j is reduced based on Equation (7.12), which will reduce π_j and v_j as well.[11] Making changes in customer fills according to Equation (7.12) changes state and derivative strategy prices, which in turn reduces V. Consequently, stepping customer fills using Equation (7.12) is a natural approach to minimize V.

It is worth noting the impact that the size of the opening orders has on the stepping distance and the number of iterations in part one of the algorithm. If the opening-order amounts are large, then prices are not very sensitive to changes in customer fills (see Equation (7.14)),[12] and so we can step the customer fills a relatively large distance at a time. In such a case, a limited number of iterations are required to converge to the equilibrium prices. As the opening-order amounts become small, the prices become more sensitive to changes in customer fills. Therefore, we need to step the customer fills smaller amounts, and a larger number of iterations are required to converge. As a general rule, the smaller the size of the opening orders, the greater the number of iterations and the longer the algorithm in part one takes to converge.

7.1.4   Example with US CPI as an underlying

This section illustrates part one of the PEP solution algorithm using an example based on the upcoming monthly percentage change in US CPI. This example was discussed most recently in Section 6.3.

Auction setup: This auction has $E = 3$ option strikes of $k_1 = 0.2, k_2 = 0.3$, and $k_3 = 0.4$. There are $S = 4$ state claims. The opening orders total \$600 in premium, and they are allocated as follows: $\theta_1 = 100, \theta_2 = 200, \theta_3 = 200$, and $\theta_4 = 100$. There are $J = 6$ customer orders in this auction, all of which are buy orders. The first six columns of Table 7.2 display the details of these customer orders, and the remaining columns of Table 7.2 show the replication weights for these orders. We now discuss the first part of the algorithm as applied to this auction.

Table 7.3 shows the values of the main PEP variables upon initialization, at the first iteration, at the second iteration, and then at the final iteration.[13] In particular, this table displays the customer fills $x_1, x_2, \ldots, x_6$;[14] the net customer payouts y_1, y_2, y_3, and y_4; the net premium M; the state prices p_1, p_2, p_3, and p_4; the derivative strategy prices $\pi_1, \pi_2, \ldots, \pi_6$;[15] the limit-order violations $v_1, v_2, \ldots, v_6$; and the total

Table 7.2 The customer orders and replication weights for the parimutuel derivatives auction on CPI

Customer order j	Derivative strategy	Strike(s)	Side b_j	Requested number of contracts r_j	Limit price w_j	$d_j(u_1)$ or $a_{j,1}$	$d_j(u_2)$ or $a_{j,2}$	$d_j(u_3)$ or $a_{j,3}$	$d_j(u_4)$ or $a_{j,4}$
1	Digital call	0.3	1	100,000	0.40	0.0	0.0	1.0	1.0
2	Digital put	0.2	1	150,000	0.20	1.0	0.0	0.0	0.0
3	Digital range	0.2 and 0.3	1	200,000	0.40	0.0	1.0	0.0	0.0
4	Vanilla capped call	0.2	1	2,000,000	0.05	0.0	0.0	0.1	0.2
5	Vanilla floored put	0.4	1	1,500,000	0.16	0.2	0.2	0.1	0.0
6	Range forward	NA	1	1,000,000	0.24	$0.2-\pi_6$	$0.2-\pi_6$	$0.3-\pi_6$	$0.4-\pi_6$

Table 7.3 The value of variables on initialization and different iterations in part one of the PEP solution algorithm

Variable	Initialization	Iteration 1	Iteration 2		Final iteration
x_1	0.00	0.00	0.00	...	175.63
x_2	0.00	1.00	2.00	...	8.90
x_3	0.00	1.00	2.00	...	8.90
x_4	0.00	0.00	0.00	...	1,496,666.77
x_5	0.00	1.00	2.00	...	1,500,000.00
x_6	0.00	0.00	0.00	...	0.00
y_1	0.00	1.20	2.40	...	300,008.90
y_2	0.00	1.20	2.40	...	300,008.90
y_3	0.00	0.10	0.20	...	299,842.31
y_4	0.00	0.00	0.00	...	299,508.98
M	600.00	600.63	601.27	...	300,508.92
—	—	—	—	—	—
p_1	0.1667	0.1668	0.1670	...	0.2000
p_2	0.3333	0.3336	0.3340	...	0.4000
p_3	0.3333	0.3330	0.3327	...	0.3000
p_4	0.1667	0.1665	0.1663	...	0.1000
π_1	0.5000	0.4995	0.4991	...	0.4000
π_2	0.1667	0.1668	0.1670	...	0.2000
π_3	0.3333	0.3336	0.3340	...	0.4000
π_4	0.0667	0.0666	0.0665	...	0.0500
π_5	0.1333	0.1334	0.1335	...	0.1500
π_6	0.2667	0.2666	0.2665	...	0.2500
—	—	—	—	—	—
v_1	0	0	0	...	0
v_2	4,995	4,980	4,950	...	0
v_3	13,340	13,280	13,200	...	0
v_4	0	0	0	...	0
v_5	40,050	39,900	39,750	...	0
v_6	0	0	0	...	0
V	58,385	58,160	57,900	...	0

limit-order violations V.[16] We now describe how these variables are determined.

Initialization: Column two of Table 7.3 shows the initial values of the variables. Following the description in Section 7.1.2, the algorithm sets $x_1, x_2, \ldots, x_6$ equal to zero. In this case, the net premium M is simply the amount of opening orders, or \$600. The state prices are then proportional to the opening orders, and the derivative strategy prices are based on Equation (7.9). Note that the state prices are positive (Equation (7.2)) and sum to one (Equation (7.3)). Further, it can be shown that these variables satisfy the self-hedging conditions of Equation (7.4). To illustrate how to calculate the limit-order violations, consider the second customer order: it is a buy order so $b_2 = 1$; it has a limit price of $w_2 = 0.2$; and it has a requested amount of $r_2 = 150,000$. Upon initialization, this customer order receives no fill, that is, $x_2 = 0$, and the initial market price π_2 equals 0.1667. Since this order's limit price is above the market price $(0.2 > 0.1667)$, this represents a violation of the limit-order condition (7.1) for $j = 2$. Using Equation (7.7), we calculate v_2 as

$$
\begin{aligned}
v_2 &= (b_2 w_2 - b_2 \pi_2)(r_2 - x_2) \\
&= (0.2 - 0.1667)(150,000 - 0) \\
&= 4,995.
\end{aligned}
\tag{7.15}
$$

Calculating the violations for the remaining customer orders, we determine that the limit-order conditions are also violated for the third and fifth customer orders. Note that V equals \$58,385 upon initialization. Since these variables do not satisfy the limit-order conditions, we begin iterating.

Iteration 1: The third column of Table 7.3 shows the variables at the first iteration. Following Equation (7.12), we increase the fills on the second, third, and fifth customer orders since these customer orders have limit prices greater than their respective market prices and are not fully filled. We set $\delta_2 = \delta_3 = \delta_5 = 1$ and increase the fills on these orders by one contract.[17] Based on these customer fills, we calculate y_1, y_2, y_3, and y_4 using Equation (7.13). We compute M using the approach from Appendix 7A, and we calculate p_1, p_2, p_3, and p_4 using Equation (7.14). Based on these values, we can confirm that the state prices are positive and sum to one (to within rounding error). Note that π_2, π_3, and π_5 are greater than their initial values $(0.1668 > 0.1667, 0.3336 > 0.3333$, and $0.1334 > 0.1333$, respectively). This is due to the fact that the fills for the second, third, and fifth customer orders increased (since they had limit prices greater than their market prices and were not fully filled on this iteration). The limit-order violation v_2 for the second customer order is

$$
\begin{aligned}
v_2 &= (b_2 w_2 - b_2 \pi_2)(r_2 - x_2) \\
&= (0.2 - 0.1668)(150,000 - 1) \\
&= 4,980.
\end{aligned}
\tag{7.16}
$$

Thus, the limit-order violation v_2 dropped by \$15 from \$4995 to \$4980 between the initialization and the first iteration. This drop is due to the fact that both $w_2 - \pi_2$ and $r_2 - x_2$ decreased. The total limit-order violations V drop between the initialization and the first iteration by \$225, from \$58,385 to \$58,160.

Iteration 2: The fourth column of Table 7.3 shows the variables at the second iteration. Once again following Equation (7.12), we increase the fills on the second, third, and fifth customer orders (once again by one contract) since these orders have limit prices above their respective market prices and are not fully filled. We calculate the other variables following the steps described in Section 7.1.2. Note that π_2, π_3, and π_5 are greater than their values at the first iteration ($0.1670 > 0.1668$, $0.3340 > 0.3336$, and $0.1335 > 0.1334$, respectively). Once again, these changes are due to the fact that we increased fills on the second, third, and fifth customer orders. Note that

$$
\begin{aligned}
v_2 &= (b_2 w_2 - b_2 \pi_2)(r_2 - x_2) \\
&= (0.2 - 0.1670)(150,000 - 2) \\
&= 4,950.
\end{aligned}
\tag{7.17}
$$

Consequently, v_2 drops by an additional \$30 to \$4,950. On this iteration, V drops, this time by \$260, going from \$58,160 to \$57,900.

Final iteration: The last column of Table 7.3 shows the values of the variables on the final iteration. The first five customer orders all end up with at least some fill at the final iteration. In comparison, note that only customer orders two, three, and five received fills on the second iteration. How do customer orders one and four receive fills between the second iteration and the final iteration of part one?

Fills for the fourth customer order: By examining the replication weights in Table 7.2, it is not hard to check that a portfolio containing one contract of the derivative requested in the fourth customer order (the vanilla capped call struck at 0.2) and one contract of the derivative requested in the fifth customer order (the vanilla floored put struck at 0.4) pays out 0.2 in all four states.[18] The no-arbitrage restrictions of the PEP imply that this portfolio must cost 0.2, or equivalently, that π_4 plus π_5 must equal 0.2. This can be confirmed by examining the values of these variables in Table 7.3 at each iteration. Since v_5 is greater than zero and customer order five's limit price is below the market price for each of these early iterations, we increase x_5 (Equation (7.12)), which increases π_5 and decreases π_4. For instance, between initialization and iteration number two, x_5 increases from 0 to 2, π_5 increases from 0.1333 to 0.1335, and π_4 drops from 0.0667 to 0.0665. For several iterations greater than two, v_5 is greater than zero and customer order five's limit price is below the market price. As we continue to increase x_5, the market price π_5 continues to increase, while π_4 continues to decreases. At a certain point (when π_4 is below 0.0500), the algorithm based on Equation (7.12) starts increasing the customer fills x_4. So, this stepping approach leads to fills for the fourth customer order.

Thus, filling the fifth customer order increases π_5, which decreases π_4, and which eventually leads to fills for the fourth customer order. In a similar way, the stepping algorithm leads to fills for the first customer order.[19] On this final iteration, note that $v_1, v_2, \ldots, v_6$ are all equal to zero, and so the customer fills satisfy the limit-order conditions of Equation (7.1). These variables satisfy Equations (7.2), (7.3), and (7.4), and the state and derivative strategy prices represent the PEP equilibrium prices.

7.1.5   Relationship to other nonlinear techniques

This section relates the algorithm for part one to standard optimization techniques. In the PEP, the constraints in Equation (7.1) are particularly difficult to satisfy given their behavior when customer orders are close to being at the market. Rather than leave Equation (7.1) as a set of constraints, we introduce the variable V to measure how far away the constraints in Equation (7.1) are from being satisfied, and we then set as our objective to minimize V. Incorporating constraints into an objective function is a well-known and widely used technique in mathematical programming problems (see Chapter 12 of Luenberger (2005)). Such an approach is called a "penalty method," because the objective function is penalized based on how far away the constraints are from being satisfied.

The stepping method of Equation (7.12) is called a "primal method," which means that the variables that are being stepped (the customer fills) remain in the "feasible region" (i.e., x_j is between zero and r_j for $j = 1, 2, \ldots, J$) at every iteration. In general, primal methods have good global convergence properties. Luenberger (2005, Chapter 11) points out that primal methods often have difficulties associated with keeping variables in the feasible region, but the algorithm in part one avoids those difficulties because of the simplicity of the feasible region and the simplicity of the formula for stepping in Equation (7.12).[20]

Equation (7.12) steps customer fills in a direction to reduce V, as described above. The direction used for stepping the customer fills in part one resembles the direction used in the "gradient projection method."[21] The gradient projection method steps the customer fills along the negative gradient, where the gradient is the vector of derivatives of V with respect to the customer fills. Although the stepping direction used in Equation (7.12) is similar to the gradient projection method, the stepping distance used in part one can be significantly different than that dictated by the gradient projection method. The gradient projection method steps the customer fills the distance along the negative gradient that reduces the violations V by *as much as possible* on every iteration. Finding that optimal distance generally requires an iterative "line search." Such a search is somewhat problematic in the PEP because calculating V for different sets of customer fills under consideration requires applying Newton's method (described in Appendix 7A), another iterative technique. Thus, solving the PEP using the gradient projection method requires iterations inside of iterations, and is computationally very expensive. Instead of using the intelligence and the corresponding computational expense of the gradient projection method, we step more naively and with fewer calculations than the gradient projection method. Although this approach generally leads to smaller stepping distances than the gradient projection method,[22] we find that it leads overall to faster algorithm times.

Peters, So, and Ye (2006) consider a closely related problem to the PEP, which they call the Convex Parimutuel Call Auction Mechanism (CPCAM). They show that the CPCAM is a "convex program," a very useful formulation for numerical solution purposes.[23] Peters, So, and Ye (2006) show that the state prices from the CPCAM equal the state prices from the PEP. Consequently, using Peters, So, and Ye's (2006) results, one could use a convex program to solve the CPCAM for the PEP state prices.

7.2 PART TWO OF THE SOLUTION ALGORITHM

Part one of the algorithm determines the equilibrium prices. However, the customer fills from part one do not (necessarily) maximize market exposure as required by the objective from Equation (6.28). Based on the equilibrium state and derivative strategy prices, part two determines the customer fills that maximize market exposure, which then allows us to calculate the remaining variables of the PEP. Section 7.2.1 shows that once prices are known, the objective function is linear in the customer fills, and *all* PEP constraints can be represented as linear equality or linear inequality constraints of the customer fills. These properties make the LP an appropriate maximization tool.[24] Section 7.2.2 illustrates this analysis using our example based on US CPI.

7.2.1   The linear nature of the PEP when prices are known

To confirm that we can use an LP *after* the state prices and derivative strategy prices have been determined, we now relate $x_1, x_2, \ldots, x_J$ to the following: the objective function, the limit-order constraints of Equation (7.1), the net customer payouts and the net premium, and the self-hedging constraints of Equation (7.4).[25] For terminology, we refer to customer order j as being "worse than the market" if $b_j w_j < b_j \pi_j$, "at the market" if $b_j w_j = b_j \pi_j$, or "better than the market" if $b_j w_j > b_j \pi_j$.

The objective function is a linear function of $x_1, x_2, \ldots, x_J$: Recall that our objective is to maximize market exposure $\widetilde{M}$, where

$$\widetilde{M} = \sum_{s=1}^{S} \theta_s + \sum_{j=1}^{J} x_j \tilde{\lambda}_j. \tag{7.18}$$

Note that $\theta_1, \theta_2, \ldots, \theta_S$ are fixed at the start of the auction, and so they are constants. Recall Equation (6.25)

$$\tilde{\lambda}_j \equiv \begin{cases} \pi_j & \text{if customer order } j \text{ is a buy of an option} \\ \pi_j - k_1 & \text{if customer order } j \text{ is a buy of a range forward} \\ \overline{d}_j - \pi_j & \text{if customer order } j \text{ is a sell of an option} \\ k_E - \pi_j & \text{if customer order } j \text{ is a sell of a range forward} \end{cases}$$

$$j = 1, 2, \ldots, J. \tag{7.19}$$

Since the market exposures per contract, $\tilde{\lambda}_1, \tilde{\lambda}_2, \ldots, \tilde{\lambda}_J$, are constant once prices are known, and since the total market exposure is a linear function of $x_1, x_2, \ldots, x_J$, we conclude that the objective function is a linear function of $x_1, x_2, \ldots, x_J$.

The limit-order constraints are linear functions of $x_1, x_2, \ldots, x_J$: If the prices are unknown, then the limit-order constraints are nonlinear functions of $x_1, x_2, \ldots, x_J$, as can be seen by inspecting Equation (7.1). However, once the prices of the derivative strategies are known, it is easy to check whether a particular order is worse than the market, at the market, or better than the market. Because of this, once the prices of the derivative strategies are known, we can easily represent the limit-order restrictions as linear equality constraints (i.e., $x_j = 0$ if the jth customer order is worse than the market, or $x_j = r_j$ if the jth customer order is better than the market) and linear inequality constraints (i.e., $0 \le x_j \le r_j$ if the jth customer order is at the market).

The net customer payouts and the net premium are linear functions of $x_1, x_2, \ldots, x_J$: Recall Equation (7.13), which shows that $y_1, y_2, \ldots, y_S$

are linear functions of $x_1, x_2, \ldots, x_J$. Further, one can show that (see the next to last step in deriving Equation (6C.7))

$$M = \sum_{s=1}^{S} \theta_s + \sum_{s=1}^{S} p_s y_s. \qquad (7.20)$$

Therefore, M is a linear function of $y_1, y_2, \ldots, y_S$. Since M is a linear function of $y_1, y_2, \ldots, y_S$, and since $y_1, y_2, \ldots, y_S$ are linear functions of $x_1, x_2, \ldots, x_J$, we conclude that M is a linear function of $x_1, x_2, \ldots, x_J$, once prices are known.

The self-hedging constraints are linear functions of $x_1, x_2, \ldots, x_J$:
Recall the self-hedging constraints of Equation (7.4)

$$\frac{\theta_s}{p_s} + y_s = M \quad s = 1, 2, \ldots, S. \qquad (7.21)$$

Of course, $\theta_1, \theta_2, \ldots, \theta_S$ are fixed and $p_1, p_2, \ldots, p_S$ are known from part one. Since $y_1, y_2, \ldots, y_S$, and M are linear functions of $x_1, x_2, \ldots, x_J$, the self-hedging constraints are linear functions of $x_1, x_2, \ldots, x_J$, once state prices are known.

Since the objective function is a linear function of the customer fills, and since all the constraints are linear equality and linear inequality constraints once prices are known, part two uses an LP to solve for the customer fills that maximize market exposure. In the LP, there are J limit-order constraints, S equations that relate the net customer payouts to the customer fills, one equation that relates net premium to the customer fills, and S self-hedging constraints. Thus, there are a total of $J + 2S + 1$ constraints in the LP. Of these $J + 2S + 1$ constraints, the number that are inequality constraints is equal to the number of customer orders that are at the market. The remaining constraints are equality constraints.

7.2.2   CPI example

We now return to the CPI example from Section 7.1.4. Using the prices from part one of the solution algorithm, we confirm that the objective function and the constraints are linear in $x_1, x_2, \ldots, x_6$.

The objective function and the constraints: The objective is to maximize market exposure, which equals

$$\tilde{M} = \sum_{s=1}^{S} \theta_s + \sum_{j=1}^{J} x_j \tilde{\lambda}_j$$

$$= 600 + \sum_{j=1}^{6} x_j \tilde{\lambda}_j$$

$$= 600 + 0.4x_1 + 0.2x_2 + 0.4x_3 + 0.05x_4 + 0.15x_5 + 0.05x_6, \tag{7.22}$$

where the exposures for the customer orders are calculated based on Equation (7.19). Consequently, the objective function is a linear function of $x_1, x_2, \ldots, x_6$.[26] The first row of Table 7.4 shows the objective function.

Table 7.4 shows the six limit-order constraints for the six customer orders. The first four customer orders are at the market since each limit price equals the corresponding market price. Consequently, the first four limit-order restrictions are inequality constraints. Since customer orders five and six are away from the market, the fifth and sixth restrictions are equality constraints.

We can relate y_1, y_2, y_3, y_4, and M to $x_1, x_2, \ldots, x_6$. We use y_1 to illustrate:

$$y_1 = \sum_{j=1}^{6} a_{j,1} b_j x_j$$

$$= x_2 + 0.2x_5 - 0.05x_6, \tag{7.23}$$

where the second equality is based on the replication weights in column seven of Table 7.2. Further, note that Equation (7.20) implies that

$$M = \sum_{s=1}^{4} \theta_s + \sum_{s=1}^{4} p_s y_s$$

$$= 600 + 0.2y_1 + 0.4y_2 + 0.3y_3 + 0.1y_4. \tag{7.24}$$

Table 7.4 shows the constraints for y_1, y_2, y_3, y_4, and M.

Based on the opening-order contracts from column four of Table 6.4 (which equal θ_s/p_s for states $s = 1, 2, 3,$ and 4), we can write out the $S = 4$ self-hedging constraints from Equation (7.4) for this example. We display these equations in the bottom four rows of Table 7.4. The PEP

Table 7.4 The equations for the LP of part two of the PEP solution algorithm

Equation type	Description
Objective	Maximize $\widetilde{M} = 600 + 0.4x_1 + 0.2x_2 + 0.4x_3 + 0.05x_4 + 0.15x_5 + 0.05x_6$
Limit-order constraint for $j = 1$	$0 \le x_1 \le 100,000$
Limit-order constraint for $j = 2$	$0 \le x_2 \le 150,000$
Limit-order constraint for $j = 3$	$0 \le x_3 \le 200,000$
Limit-order constraint for $j = 4$	$0 \le x_4 \le 2,000,000$
Limit-order constraint for $j = 5$	$x_5 = 1,500,000$
Limit-order constraint for $j = 6$	$x_6 = 0$
Equation for y_1	$y_1 = x_2 + 0.2x_5 - 0.05x_6$
Equation for y_2	$y_2 = x_3 + 0.2x_5 - 0.05x_6$
Equation for y_3	$y_3 = x_1 + 0.1x_4 + 0.1x_5 + 0.05x_6$
Equation for y_4	$y_4 = x_1 + 0.2x_4 + 0.15x_6$
Equation for M	$M = 600 + 0.2y_1 + 0.4y_2 + 0.3y_3 + 0.1y_4$
Self-hedging condition for state $s = 1$	$500 + y_1 = M$
Self-hedging condition for state $s = 2$	$500 + y_2 = M$
Self-hedging condition for state $s = 3$	$(200/0.3) + y_3 = M$
Self-hedging condition for state $s = 4$	$1,000 + y_4 = M$

seeks to maximize the market exposure subject to: the $J = 6$ limit-order constraints; the $S = 4$ equations relating $y_1, y_2, y_3,$ and y_4 to $x_1, x_2, \ldots, x_6$; the single equation relating M to $y_1, y_2, y_3,$ and y_4; and the $S = 4$ self-hedging constraints. Thus, there are 15 constraints ($J + 2S + 1 = 6 + 2 \times 4 + 1 = 15$) and 4 are inequality constraints.

7.3 COMPLEMENTARY ORDERS AND PART TWO OF THE SOLUTION ALGORITHM

This section develops the conditions under which the LP of part two increases auction market exposure. This material is not necessary to understand the mechanics of the solution algorithm, and the reader who is primarily interested in algorithm implementation may skip this material and instead examine the results from the LP, which are displayed in Table 7.5.

This section defines the concept of "complementary orders," connoting orders that help contribute liquidity to the auction. As a simple example, one might consider a bid and an offer for the same derivative as

Table 7.5 Changes in variables between part one and part
two of the PEP solution algorithm

Variable	Part one value	Part two value	Change from part one to part two
x_1	175.63	100, 000.00	99, 824.37
x_2	8.90	99, 833.27	99, 824.37
x_3	8.90	99, 833.27	99, 824.37
x_4	1, 496, 666.77	1, 496, 666.77	0.00
x_5	1, 500, 000.00	1, 500, 000.00	0.00
x_6	0.00	0.00	0.00
y_1	300, 008.90	399, 833.27	99, 824.37
y_2	300, 008.90	399, 833.27	99, 824.37
y_3	299, 842.31	399, 666.68	99, 824.37
y_4	299, 508.98	399, 333.35	99, 824.37
M	300, 508.92	400, 333.29	99, 824.37
$\tilde{M}$	300, 508.92	400, 333.29	99, 824.37

complementary orders, as they can help fill each other. Our definition of
complementary orders includes this simple situation as a special case.
However, since orders on one derivative can contribute liquidity to other
derivatives in a parimutuel derivatives auctions, we generalize the concept of complementary orders to capture this. Section 7.3.3 will relate
the existence of complementary orders in an auction to the LP's ability
to increase an auction's market exposure.[27]

7.3.1 Definition of complementary orders

We now create a portfolio (of complementary orders) based on the customers' orders in an auction. Let $\mathbf{C}$ denote the non-empty subset of the
J customer orders which are used to create the portfolio. For example, if
$\mathbf{C} = \{1, 2\}$, then the portfolio is based on the first and second customer
orders. For a set of constants $c_1, c_2, \ldots, c_J$, we construct the portfolio
as follows:

1. The portfolio is long c_j contracts of the derivative requested in the
    jth customer order if $b_j c_j > 0$;

2. The portfolio has no contracts of the derivative requested in the jth
    customer order if $b_j c_j = 0$; and

3. The portfolio is short c_j contracts of the derivative requested in the jth customer order if $b_jc_j < 0$.

For example, if the first customer order is a buy ($b_1 = 1$) of a digital call and $c_1 = 3$, then the portfolio is long three contracts of that digital call. Alternatively, if the second customer order is a sell ($b_2 = -1$) of a digital call and $c_2 = 4$, then the portfolio is short four contracts of that digital call. Consequently, c_j equals the number of contracts in the portfolio of the derivative strategy requested in the jth customer order based on the side b_j for $j = 1, 2, \ldots, J$. Note that the portfolio's composition depends on the derivative strategies requested and the sides of the customer orders in $\mathbf{C}$, but not on the customers' requested amounts or limit prices.

For the definition of complementary orders, we require that

$$
\begin{cases}
c_j > 0 & \text{if } j \in \mathbf{C} \\
c_j = 0 & \text{if } j \notin \mathbf{C}
\end{cases}
\quad j = 1, 2, \ldots, J. \tag{7.25}
$$

Thus, c_j is positive if and only if j is an element of $\mathbf{C}$. For example, if $\mathbf{C} = \{1, 2\}$, then let $c_1 = c_2 = 1$, and let $c_3 = c_4 = \cdots = c_J = 0$. Thus, $c_1, c_2, \ldots, c_J$ satisfy Equation (7.25). If the first and second customer orders are buy orders (b_1 and b_2 both equal one), then the portfolio is long one contract of the derivative strategy requested in the first customer order and long one contract of the derivative strategy requested in the second customer order. If the first and second customer orders are sell orders (b_1 and b_2 both equal negative one), then the portfolio is short one contract of the derivative strategy requested in the first customer order and short one contract of the derivative strategy requested in the second customer order.

Next, let κ be a constant, and consider the following equation:

$$
\sum_{j=1}^{J} a_{j,s}b_jc_j = \kappa \quad s = 1, 2, \ldots, S. \tag{7.26}
$$

If Equations (7.25) and (7.26) hold, then a portfolio of the customer orders in $\mathbf{C}$ with contract amounts of $c_1, c_2, \ldots, c_J$ pays out the same net amount κ in every state, and so it represents a risk-free portfolio.[28] There are no restrictions placed on κ in Equation (7.26), so κ may be positive, negative, or zero.[29] We say that the customer orders in $\mathbf{C}$ are complementary if there exist contract amounts $c_1, c_2, \ldots, c_J$ and a constant κ that satisfy Equations (7.25) and (7.26). For a portfolio of complementary orders $\mathbf{C}$, there exists a set of contract amounts $c_1, c_2, \ldots, c_J$ that makes the portfolio risk-free.[30] Given J customer orders, there may be no such portfolio of complementary orders, there may be exactly one such portfolio, or there may be more than one such portfolio of complementary orders.

7.3.2 Examples of complementary orders

To better understand when customer orders complement one another, we now examine three examples. If the first and second customer orders request the same derivatives strategy but with opposite sides, then

$$a_{1,s} = a_{2,s} \quad s = 1, 2, \ldots, S \tag{7.27}$$

and

$$b_1 + b_2 = 0 \tag{7.28}$$

which implies that

$$a_{1,s}b_1 + a_{2,s}b_2 = 0 \quad s = 1, 2, \ldots, S. \tag{7.29}$$

Let $C = \{1, 2\}$, let $c_1 = c_2 = 1$, and let $c_3 = c_4 = \cdots = c_J = 0$. Thus, $c_1, c_2, \ldots, c_J$ satisfy Equation (7.25) and

$$a_{1,s}b_1c_1 + a_{2,s}b_2c_2 = 0 \quad s = 1, 2, \ldots, S \tag{7.30}$$

which implies that

$$\sum_{j=1}^{J} a_{j,s}b_jc_j = 0 \quad s = 1, 2, \ldots, S. \tag{7.31}$$

Therefore, $c_1, c_2, \ldots, c_J$ satisfy Equation (7.26) with $\kappa = 0$, and so the first and second customer orders complement one another. As this example shows, an order to buy a derivative and an order to sell the same derivative are complementary orders. Thus, our definition of complementary orders handles this special case in a natural way.

Next, consider the case where the first customer order is a buy of a digital call at a particular strike, and the second customer order is a buy of a digital put at the same strike. Equations (5.32) and (5.33) imply that

$$a_{1,s} + a_{2,s} = 1 \quad s = 1, 2, \ldots, S \tag{7.32}$$

and

$$b_1 = b_2 = 1. \tag{7.33}$$

As in the previous example, let $\mathbf{C} = \{1,2\}$, let $c_1 = c_2 = 1$, and let $c_3 = c_4 = \cdots = c_J = 0$. Consequently, $c_1, c_2, \ldots, c_J$ satisfy Equation (7.25) and

$$a_{1,s}b_1c_1 + a_{2,s}b_2c_2 = 1 \quad s = 1, 2, \ldots, S \tag{7.34}$$

which implies that

$$\sum_{j=1}^{J} a_{j,s}b_jc_j = 1 \quad s = 1, 2, \ldots, S. \tag{7.35}$$

Therefore, $c_1, c_2, \ldots, c_J$ satisfy Equation (7.26) with $\kappa = 1$. Thus, an order to buy a digital call and an order to buy a digital put with the same strike are complementary orders.

These two examples illustrate the case in which *two* orders complement one another. As we now show with the CPI example, *three* or more customer orders can also be complementary. Based on the replication weights from Table 7.2, we can check that

$$a_{1,s} + a_{2,s} + a_{3,s} = 1 \quad s = 1, 2, 3, 4. \tag{7.36}$$

Since these first three customer orders are buy orders, then

$$a_{1,s}b_1 + a_{2,s}b_2 + a_{3,s}b_3 = 1 \quad s = 1, 2, 3, 4. \tag{7.37}$$

Equation (7.37) shows that one contract of each derivative strategy requested in the first three customer orders forms a risk-less portfolio. Let $\mathbf{C} = \{1, 2, 3\}$, set $c_1 = c_2 = c_3 = 1$, and set $c_4 = c_5 = c_6 = 0$. Then $c_1, c_2, \ldots, c_6$ satisfy Equation (7.25), and

$$\sum_{j=1}^{6} a_{j,s}b_jc_j = 1 \quad s = 1, 2, 3, 4. \tag{7.38}$$

Consequently, $c_1, c_2, \ldots, c_6$ satisfy Equation (7.26) with $\kappa = 1$. Thus, customer orders one, two, and three from the CPI example complement one another.[31]

7.3.3   Complementary orders and their impact on the linear program

This section presents two theorems that relate complementary orders to the LP of part two of the solution algorithm. Appendix 7B proves these theorems.

Theorem 7.1: Suppose that there exists a subset C of the customer orders in an auction such that

   Condition 1: The customer orders in C are complementary;

   Condition 2: All customer orders in C are at the market;[32]

   Condition 3: Every customer order in C is less than fully filled (i.e., the fill for every customer order in C is less than the corresponding requested amount) at the completion of part one of the algorithm.

Then the LP increases the auction's total market exposure in part two of the algorithm.

Thus, when there are a set of complementary orders in an auction that are all at the market and all less than fully filled at the end of part one, then the LP will increase market exposure. If the LP has no impact on market exposure in an auction, then there is no set of complementary orders that are all at the market and all less than fully filled at the end of part one.

   To illustrate Theorem 7.1 using the CPI example, we now verify that the three conditions hold for $C = \{1, 2, 3\}$ and for $c_1 = c_2 = c_3 = 1$ and $c_4 = c_5 = c_6 = 0$. Since the first three customer orders are complementary (as shown in Section 7.3.2), condition 1 holds. Comparing the limit prices in column six of Table 7.2 with the corresponding market prices in the final column of Table 7.3, we see that the first, second, and third customer orders are at the market. Consequently, condition 2 is also met. Further, comparing the requested amounts in column five of Table 7.2 with the corresponding fills in the final column of Table 7.3, note that none of these first three customer orders are fully filled at the end of part one. Thus, condition 3 is met. Since conditions one, two, and three are satisfied, Theorem 7.1 implies that the LP will increase market exposure for this example.

   For notation for the next theorem, let Δx_j denote the change in the jth customer fill from part one to part two.

Theorem 7.2: If the LP increases market exposure, and $\Delta x_1, \Delta x_2, \ldots, \Delta x_J$ are all non-negative, then there exists a set of complementary orders C that are at the market, less than fully filled at the end of part one, and whose contract amounts $c_1, c_2, \ldots, c_J$ are proportional to the changes in customer fills, that is, there exists a positive constant β such that $c_j = \beta \Delta x_j$ for $j = 1, 2, \ldots, J$.

Theorem 7.2 shows that under certain conditions, the contract amounts for a set of complementary orders $\mathbf{C}$ are proportional to the changes in customer fills between part one and part two, as we illustrate below. It is worth noting that there can exist multiple sets of complementary orders in an auction (see endnote 31 for the CPI example). If the LP increases market exposure and the customer fills are non-negative, Theorem 7.2 does not necessarily imply that *all* sets of complementary orders have contract amounts that are proportional to the changes in customer fills. Theorem 7.2 simply implies that there exists *at least one* set of complementary orders with that property.

For the CPI example, we submit the equations from Table 7.4 to our LP software program, and Table 7.5 displays the results from the LP.[33] The LP increases the market exposure by $99,824.37, from $300,508.92 in part one to $400,333.29 in part two. This 33% increase in market exposure is due to the presence of the complementary orders in this auction. Note that the fills on the first three customer orders increase by 99,824.37 contracts, while the fills on the last three customer orders remain unchanged. The changes in customer fills are non-negative, and these changes are given by

$$\Delta x_j = \beta c_j \quad j = 1, 2, \ldots, 6, \tag{7.39}$$

where $\beta = 99,824.37$ and as before $c_1 = c_2 = c_3 = 1$ and $c_4 = c_5 = c_6 = 0$. This result is consistent with Theorem 7.2, as the complementary orders in $\mathbf{C}$ are at the market and less than fully filled at the end of part one.

APPENDIX 7A: COMPUTING NET AUCTION PREMIUM BASED ON NET CUSTOMER PAYOUTS

This appendix describes step 3 of part one of the solution algorithm, which computes the net auction premium M using the net customer payouts $y_1, y_2, \ldots, y_S$. Section 7A.1 begins by calculating a lower bound for M, and then Section 7A.2 shows that M is determined uniquely from $y_1, y_2, \ldots, y_S$. Section 7A.3 uses Newton's method to solve for M. Finally, Section 7A.4 illustrates these techniques with our CPI example.

7A.1   Lower bound for *M*

To determine a lower bound for M, we begin by noting that Equations (7.2) and (7.3) imply that

$$0 < p_s < 1 \quad s = 1, 2, \ldots, S. \tag{7A.1}$$

Since $\theta_s > 0$ for $s = 1, 2, \ldots, S$, we can write that

$$\theta_s < \frac{\theta_s}{p_s} \quad s = 1, 2, \ldots, S. \tag{7A.2}$$

Adding y_s to both sides of Equation (7A.2) gives

$$\theta_s + y_s < \frac{\theta_s}{p_s} + y_s \quad s = 1, 2, \ldots, S. \tag{7A.3}$$

Recall the self-hedging restrictions [34]

$$\frac{\theta_s}{p_s} + y_s = M \quad s = 1, 2, \ldots, S. \tag{7A.4}$$

Substituting the expression for M from Equation (7A.4) into Equation (7A.3), we obtain that

$$\theta_s + y_s < M \quad s = 1, 2, \ldots, S. \tag{7A.5}$$

Since Equation (7A.5) holds for $s = 1, 2, \ldots, S$, we can write that

$$\max[\theta_1 + y_1, \theta_2 + y_2, \ldots, \theta_S + y_S] < M. \tag{7A.6}$$

Therefore, define $\underline{M}$ as

$$\underline{M} \equiv \max[\theta_1 + y_1, \theta_2 + y_2, \ldots, \theta_S + y_S]. \tag{7A.7}$$

We can conclude that [35]

$$\underline{M} < M. \tag{7A.8}$$

7A.2   Uniqueness of *M*

Rearranging terms in Equation (7A.4) yields that

$$p_s = \frac{\theta_s}{M - y_s} \quad s = 1, 2, \ldots, S. \tag{7A.9}$$

Since the sum of the state prices equals one (Equation (7.3)), we can write that

$$\sum_{s=1}^{S} \frac{\theta_s}{M - y_s} = 1 \tag{7A.10}$$

or equivalently that

$$-1 + \sum_{s=1}^{S} \frac{\theta_s}{M - y_s} = 0. \tag{7A.11}$$

Define the function f as

$$f(G) = -1 + \sum_{s=1}^{S} \frac{\theta_s}{G - y_s}. \tag{7A.12}$$

Note that $f(M) = 0$ by Equation (7A.11).

We now show that there exists a unique M greater than $\underline{M}$ such that $f(M) = 0$. Note that

$$f(\underline{M}) = f(\max[\theta_1 + y_1, \theta_2 + y_2, \ldots, \theta_S + y_S])$$

$$= -1 + \sum_{s=1}^{S} \frac{\theta_s}{\max[\theta_1 + y_1, \theta_2 + y_2, \ldots, \theta_S + y_S] - y_s}. \tag{7A.13}$$

It is not hard to check that every element in this summation is positive, and at least one element in the summation is one or greater. Therefore, the summation is greater than one, and so

$$f(\underline{M}) > 0. \tag{7A.14}$$

Over the range $G \in [\underline{M}, \infty)$, we can check that $f(G)$ is a continuous function that is strictly decreasing. In addition, note that $f(G)$ approaches -1 as G approaches ∞. Therefore, there is a unique M greater than $\underline{M}$ such that

$$f(M) = 0. \tag{7A.15}$$

Figure 7A.1 graphs $f(G)$ over the range $G \in [\underline{M}, \infty)$.

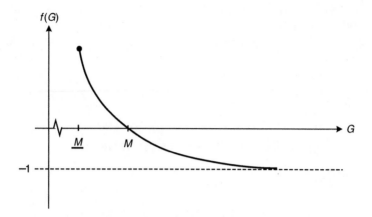

Figure 7A.1 Graph of the function f at $\underline{M}$ and above

7A.3   Using Newton's method to solve for M

Let f' denote the first derivative of f with respect to G. Note that

$$f'(G) = \frac{df}{dG}$$

$$= -\sum_{s=1}^{S} \frac{\theta_s}{(G - y_s)^2}. \tag{7A.16}$$

It is not hard to check that the first derivative of f is non-zero for all $G \in [\underline{M}, \infty)$. Based on this, we solve for M using Newton's method as follows.[36] For an initial value, we set

$$G = \underline{M}. \tag{7A.17}$$

For each iteration, set

$$G \leftarrow G - \frac{f(G)}{f'(G)}. \tag{7A.18}$$

We iterate until we find a value that sets the function f equal to zero, and we set that value equal to M.[37] As an empirical matter, M is found in seven iterations or less for most auction examples.[38]

7A.4   Computing M in the CPI example

To illustrate the techniques described in this appendix, we now compute M for the final iteration of part one of the CPI example from this chapter.

There are $S = 4$ states in this example, and the opening orders are $\theta_1 = 100, \theta_2 = 200, \theta_3 = 200$, and $\theta_4 = 100$. The final column of Table 7.3 shows y_1, y_2, y_3, and y_4. Based on these values, we calculate $\underline{M}$ using Equation (7A.7)

$$
\begin{aligned}
\underline{M} &\equiv \max[\theta_1 + y_1, \theta_2 + y_2, \theta_3 + y_3, \theta_4 + y_4] \\
&= \max[100 + 300{,}008.90, 200 + 300{,}008.90, \\
&\qquad\qquad 200 + 299{,}842.31, 100 + 299{,}508.98] \\
&= 300{,}208.90.
\end{aligned}
\tag{7A.19}
$$

Based on Equations (7A.12) and (7A.16), note that f and f' are given by

$$
\begin{aligned}
f(G) &= -1 + \frac{100}{G - 300{,}008.90} + \frac{200}{G - 300{,}008.90} \\
&\quad + \frac{200}{G - 299{,}842.31} + \frac{100}{G - 299{,}508.98},
\end{aligned}
\tag{7A.20}
$$

$$
\begin{aligned}
f'(G) &= -\frac{100}{(G - 300{,}008.90)^2} - \frac{200}{(G - 300{,}008.90)^2} \\
&\quad - \frac{200}{(G - 299{,}842.31)^2} - \frac{100}{(G - 299{,}508.98)^2}.
\end{aligned}
\tag{7A.21}
$$

Table 7A.1 shows the values of different variables as we iterate to find M.[39] We use $\underline{M} = 300{,}208.90$ as our initial value, and we iterate using Newton's method from Equation (7A.18). After five iterations, we find that $f(300{,}508.92) = 0$, and thus, for the final iteration in part one, we set $M = 300{,}508.92$.

Table 7A.1 Values of variables across different iterations of Newton's method for determining M

Variable	G	f(G)	f'(G)
Initial value	300,208.90	1.1884	−0.0092
Iteration 1	300,338.19	0.4350	−0.0037
Iteration 2	300,454.94	0.1048	−0.0022
Iteration 3	300,503.61	0.0094	−0.0018
Iteration 4	300,508.87	0.0001	−0.0018
Iteration 5	300,508.92	0.0000	−0.0017

APPENDIX 7B: PROOFS OF THEOREMS 7.1 AND 7.2

Section 7.3.3 presented Theorems 7.1 and 7.2. We now prove these two theorems.

7B.1 Proof of Theorem 7.1

Notation and setup: We use a superscript of "(1)" to denote values of variables at the completion of part one of the algorithm. Consequently, $M^{(1)}$ denotes the net amount of premium at the conclusion of part one, $\widetilde{M}^{(1)}$ denotes the market exposure at the end of part one, and $x_j^{(1)}$ denotes the fill for the jth customer order at the conclusion of part one for $j = 1, 2, \ldots, J$. Based on a set $\mathbf{C}$ of customers orders that satisfy conditions 1, 2, and 3, we now define the variable $\tilde{\kappa}$ and use that variable to construct a new set of customer fills (denoted as $\tilde{x}_1, \tilde{x}_2, \ldots, \tilde{x}_J$ below) that satisfy the PEP conditions and have a higher market exposure than $\widetilde{M}^{(1)}$.

Defining the customer fills: Define the variable $\tilde{\kappa}$ as follows:

$$\tilde{\kappa} \equiv \min_{j \in \mathbf{C}} \left[\frac{r_j - x_j^{(1)}}{c_j} \right]. \tag{7B.1}$$

We now check that $\tilde{\kappa}$ is strictly positive. If $j \in \mathbf{C}$, then the jth customer order is less than fully filled (condition 3) at the end of part one, which means that

$$x_j^{(1)} < r_j \quad \forall j \in \mathbf{C} \tag{7B.2}$$

which implies that

$$0 < r_j - x_j^{(1)} \quad \forall j \in \mathbf{C}. \tag{7B.3}$$

Further, if $j \in \mathbf{C}$, then c_j is positive (by condition 1 and Equation (7.25)). Since the numerator and the denominator of the terms inside the minimum function in Equation (7B.1) are strictly positive, this implies that $\tilde{\kappa}$ is strictly positive.
Define

$$\tilde{x}_j \equiv x_j^{(1)} + c_j \tilde{\kappa} \quad j = 1, 2, \ldots, J. \tag{7B.4}$$

We now check that: $\tilde{x}_1, \tilde{x}_2, \ldots, \tilde{x}_J$ satisfy the PEP limit-order conditions (see, e.g., Equation (7.1)); $\tilde{x}_1, \tilde{x}_2, \ldots, \tilde{x}_J$ satisfy the PEP self-hedging conditions (see, e.g., Equation (7.4)); and $\tilde{x}_1, \tilde{x}_2, \ldots, \tilde{x}_J$ have greater market exposure than $\widetilde{M}^{(1)}$.

Checking the PEP limit-order conditions: The definition of $\tilde{\kappa}$ from Equation (7B.1) implies that

$$\tilde{\kappa} \le \frac{r_j - x_j^{(1)}}{c_j} \quad \forall j \in \mathbf{C}. \tag{7B.5}$$

Multiplying both sides of this equation by c_j gives that

$$c_j \tilde{\kappa} \le r_j - x_j^{(1)} \quad \forall j \in \mathbf{C}. \tag{7B.6}$$

Adding $x_j^{(1)}$ to both sides of this equation leads to

$$x_j^{(1)} + c_j \tilde{\kappa} \le r_j \quad \forall j \in \mathbf{C}. \tag{7B.7}$$

Using the definition of $\tilde{x}_j$ from Equation (7B.4) implies that

$$\tilde{x}_j \le r_j \quad \forall j \in \mathbf{C}. \tag{7B.8}$$

Note that $x_j^{(1)}$ satisfies the PEP limit-order logic, and so it is non-negative for $j \in \mathbf{C}$. Since $c_j \tilde{\kappa}$ is non-negative for $j \in \mathbf{C}$, the definition of $\tilde{x}_j$ in Equation (7B.4) implies that $\tilde{x}_j$ is also non-negative. This result coupled with Equation (7B.8) imply that

$$0 \le \tilde{x}_j \le r_j \quad \forall j \in \mathbf{C}. \tag{7B.9}$$

If $j \in \mathbf{C}$, then customer order j is at the market, and $\tilde{x}_j$ satisfies the PEP limit-order constraints for $j \in \mathbf{C}$. If $j \notin \mathbf{C}$, then $\tilde{x}_j$ equals $x_j^{(1)}$. Since $x_j^{(1)}$ satisfies the PEP limit-order constraints, $\tilde{x}_j$ satisfies them as well for $j \notin \mathbf{C}$. Thus, $\tilde{x}_j$ satisfy the PEP limit-order constraints for $j = 1, 2, \ldots, J$.

Checking the PEP self-hedging conditions: We now check that $\tilde{x}_1, \tilde{x}_2, \ldots, \tilde{x}_J$ satisfy the PEP self-hedging restrictions. Recall that $x_1^{(1)}, x_2^{(1)}, \ldots, x_J^{(1)}$ satisfy the self-hedging restrictions, so

$$\frac{\theta_s}{p_s} + \sum_{j=1}^{J} a_{j,s} b_j x_j^{(1)} = M^{(1)} \quad s = 1, 2, \ldots, S, \tag{7B.10}$$

where we use Equation (7.13) to express the self-hedging restrictions in terms of customer fills, instead of net customer payouts.[40] Now,

$$\frac{\theta_s}{p_s} + \sum_{j=1}^{J} a_{j,s} b_j \tilde{x}_j = \frac{\theta_s}{p_s} + \sum_{j=1}^{J} a_{j,s} b_j (x_j^{(1)} + c_j \tilde{\kappa}) \quad s = 1, 2, \ldots, S$$

$$= \frac{\theta_s}{p_s} + \sum_{j=1}^{J} a_{j,s} b_j x_j^{(1)} + \sum_{j=1}^{J} a_{j,s} b_j c_j \tilde{\kappa} \quad s = 1, 2, \ldots, S$$

$$= M^{(1)} + \kappa \times \tilde{\kappa} \quad s = 1, 2, \ldots, S, \qquad (7B.11)$$

where the first equality follows from the definition of $\tilde{x}_j$ in Equation (7B.4), where the second equality is by algebraic expansion, and where the third equality follows from Equations (7B.10) and (7.26). Equation (7B.11) implies that $\tilde{x}_1, \tilde{x}_2, \ldots, \tilde{x}_J$ satisfy the PEP self-hedging restrictions.

Calculating total market exposure: Recall that total market exposure is a linear and increasing function of the customer fills. Note that Equation (7B.4) implies that

$$\begin{cases} \tilde{x}_j > x_j^{(1)} & j \in \mathbf{C}, \\ \tilde{x}_j = x_j^{(1)} & j \notin \mathbf{C}. \end{cases} \qquad (7B.12)$$

Consequently, the market exposure for $\tilde{x}_1, \tilde{x}_2, \ldots, \tilde{x}_J$ is strictly greater than $\widetilde{M}^{(1)}$, the market exposure for $x_1^{(1)}, x_2^{(1)}, \ldots, x_J^{(1)}$. The LP maximizes auction exposure, so the market exposure from the LP will be greater than or equal to the market exposure for any set of customer fills that satisfy the PEP limit-orders conditions and the PEP self-hedging restrictions. Thus, the market exposure from the LP is greater than or equal to the market exposure for $\tilde{x}_1, \tilde{x}_2, \ldots, \tilde{x}_J$, which is strictly greater than $\widetilde{M}^{(1)}$, the market exposure from part one. We conclude that the LP in part two increases market exposure relative to the market exposure from part one, and so Theorem 7.1 holds.

7B.2   Proof of Theorem 7.2

For this proof, we use a superscript of "(2)" to denote values of variables upon completion of part two of the algorithm. Therefore, $M^{(2)}$ denotes the net amount of premium at the conclusion of part two, and $x_j^{(2)}$ denotes the fill for the jth customer order at the end of part two for $j = 1, 2, \ldots, J$. To prove this theorem, we now construct $c_1, c_2, \ldots, c_J$ and $\mathbf{C}$ based on the changes in customer fills between part one and part two. Similar to Equation (7B.10), we can write for part two that

$$\frac{\theta_s}{p_s} + \sum_{j=1}^{J} a_{j,s} b_j x_j^{(2)} = M^{(2)} \quad s = 1, 2, \ldots, S. \tag{7B.13}$$

Subtracting (7B.10) from (7B.13) gives

$$\sum_{j=1}^{J} a_{j,s} b_j (x_j^{(2)} - x_j^{(1)}) = M^{(2)} - M^{(1)} \quad s = 1, 2, \ldots, S \tag{7B.14}$$

which implies that

$$\sum_{j=1}^{J} a_{j,s} b_j \Delta x_j = M^{(2)} - M^{(1)} \quad s = 1, 2, \ldots, S \tag{7B.15}$$

which we re-write as

$$\sum_{j=1}^{J} a_{j,s} b_j c_j = \kappa \quad s = 1, 2, \ldots, S, \tag{7B.16}$$

where

$$c_j \equiv \Delta x_j \quad j = 1, 2, \ldots, J \tag{7B.17}$$

and

$$\kappa \equiv M^{(2)} - M^{(1)}. \tag{7B.18}$$

Let **C** contain all customer orders whose fills change between part one and part two. Thus, $c_1, c_2, \ldots, c_J$ satisfy Equation (7.25), since no fills decrease between part one and part two. Further, $c_1, c_2, \ldots, c_J$ satisfy Equation (7.26) since Equation (7B.17) holds. If $j \in$ **C**, then the jth customer order is at the market since its fill changed between part one and part two. Further, if $j \in$ **C**, then the jth customer order must be less than fully filled at the end of part one, since the LP increased the fill on the jth customer order between part one and part two. Further,

$$c_j = \beta \Delta x_j \quad j = 1, 2, \ldots, J, \tag{7B.19}$$

where $\beta = 1$. Consequently, Theorem 7.2 holds.

APPENDIX 7C: LIMIT-PRICE RESTRICTIONS FOR COMPLEMENTARY ORDERS

In Theorem 7.1, condition 1 (the customer orders in C are complementary) and condition 2 (the customer orders in C are at the market) significantly restrict the limit prices of customer orders in C. Related to this, we now present the following theorem when the customer orders in C are also buys of options (we will prove this theorem at the end of this section).

Theorem 7C.1: Let C be a subset of the J customer orders in an auction. If the customer orders in C are (1) complementary; (2) at the market; and (3) buys of options; then

$$\sum_{j=1}^{J} c_j w_j = \kappa. \tag{7C.1}$$

Similar but more complicated restrictions than Equation (7C.1) can be derived if the customer orders in C include sells of options, buys of the range forward, and sells of the range forward. Theorem 7C.1 is also the basis for some results in Appendix 9A, which relate to "competing orders."

To illustrate Theorem 7C.1, we examine the CPI example, and note that the first three customer orders are (1) complementary with $c_1 = c_2 = c_3 = 1, c_4 = c_5 = c_6 = 0$, and $\kappa = 1$; (2) at the market; and (3) buys of options. Therefore, Theorem 7C.1 implies that

$$w_1 + w_2 + w_3 = 1. \tag{7C.2}$$

We can confirm that the limit prices of the first three customer orders sum to one $(0.4 + 0.2 + 0.4 = 1)$, by examining column six of Table 7.2, thus illustrating Theorem 7C.1.

Proof of Theorem 7C.1: Since all customer orders in C are complementary orders to buy options, then $b_j = 1$ for $j \in C$, and Equation (7.26) becomes

$$\sum_{j=1}^{J} a_{j,s} c_j = \kappa \quad s = 1, 2, \ldots, S. \tag{7C.3}$$

Multiplying both sides of this equation by p_s gives that

$$\sum_{j=1}^{J} a_{j,s} c_j p_s = \kappa p_s \quad s = 1, 2, \ldots, S. \tag{7C.4}$$

Summing both sides of this equation over the range s from 1 to S implies that

$$\sum_{s=1}^{S} \left(\sum_{j=1}^{J} a_{j,s} c_j p_s \right) = \kappa \sum_{s=1}^{S} p_s. \tag{7C.5}$$

Rearranging the order of the summations on the left-hand side and applying Equation (7.3) on the right-hand side gives that

$$\sum_{j=1}^{J} c_j \left(\sum_{s=1}^{S} a_{j,s} p_s \right) = \kappa. \tag{7C.6}$$

On the left-hand side, the inner summation is simply π_j, the price of the option requested in the jth customer order (see Equation (7.9)). Therefore,

$$\sum_{j=1}^{J} c_j \pi_j = \kappa. \tag{7C.7}$$

We now show that

$$c_j \pi_j = c_j w_j \quad j = 1, 2, \ldots, J. \tag{7C.8}$$

If $c_j > 0$, then customer order j is at the market, which implies that $\pi_j = w_j$, and so $c_j \pi_j = c_j w_j$. Alternatively, if $c_j = 0$, then $c_j \pi_j = c_j w_j$ (trivially). Consequently, Equation (7C.8) holds. Equations (7C.7) and (7C.8) imply that

$$\sum_{j=1}^{J} c_j w_j = \kappa. \tag{7C.9}$$

This concludes the proof of Theorem 7C.1.

CHAPTER 8

Mathematical Properties of Parimutuel Equilibrium Prices

This chapter describes the mathematical properties of the prices in the Parimutuel Equilibrium Problem (PEP). Specifically, for a given set of opening orders and customer orders (the "auction inputs"), this chapter shows that the PEP has a *unique* set of state prices and derivative strategy prices. The fact that prices are unique is a very strong result mathematically. In addition, it is a very desirable result pragmatically, as auction participants are likely to find comfort that a particular set of orders can only generate *one* set of prices.[1]

This chapter proceeds as follows. Section 8.1 begins by representing the self-hedging restrictions as an "eigensystem." This representation allows us to characterize certain key properties of the PEP, including its nonlinear nature. Using some well-known machinery from the eigensystem literature, we show that prices are unique when customers only submit market orders (no limit orders). Section 8.2 examines the framework in which customers can submit both market orders and limit orders. This framework has more flexibility for auction participants, but it is a more challenging problem to characterize mathematically. In this case, we observe that the PEP is a type of Box Constrained Variational Inequality Problem (BVIP), a general class of problems that have been well studied in the mathematical economics literature and in the operations research literature. Using results from those fields and certain special properties of the PEP, we prove that the PEP prices are unique. The material in this chapter relies on concepts from linear algebra, multivariate calculus, and real analysis, and references for these topics might include Strang (1988), McCallum *et al.* (2004), and Schramm (1996), respectively. We relegate the most technical material, including all proofs, to the appendices.

8.1   UNIQUE PRICES WITH MARKET ORDERS

This section analyzes a simplified version of the PEP of Equation (6.28). Namely, we study the case when customers submit only market orders and no limit orders. In Section 8.1.1, we begin by specifying this problem mathematically. Section 8.1.2 shows that the "self-hedging" conditions can be represented as an eigensystem. Section 8.1.3 uses theorems from the eigensystem literature to prove that prices are unique for this problem. Finally, Section 8.1.4 illustrates these results with a numerical example.

8.1.1   The simplified parimutuel equilibrium problem

We begin by eliminating the limit-order constraints

$$
\left.
\begin{array}{l}
b_j w_j < b_j \pi_j \;\Rightarrow\; x_j = 0 \\
b_j w_j = b_j \pi_j \;\Rightarrow\; 0 \le x_j \le r_j \\
b_j w_j > b_j \pi_j \;\Rightarrow\; x_j = r_j
\end{array}
\right\} \quad j = 1, 2, \ldots, J
\tag{8.1}
$$

and replacing these limit-order constraints with the constraints that all customer orders are market orders, and so they get fully filled, that is, [2]

$$
x_j = r_j \quad j = 1, 2, \ldots, J
\tag{8.2}
$$

Thus, we rewrite the PEP from Equation (6.28) in this simplified framework as

$$
\begin{array}{ll}
\displaystyle\max_{p_1, p_2, \ldots, p_S} \widetilde{M} \text{ subject to} & \\[2mm]
x_j = r_j & j = 1, 2, \ldots, J \\[1mm]
p_s > 0 & s = 1, 2, \ldots, S \\[1mm]
\displaystyle\sum_{s=1}^{S} p_s = 1 & \\[2mm]
\dfrac{\theta_s}{p_s} + y_s = M & s = 1, 2, \ldots, S.
\end{array}
\tag{8.3}
$$

In Equation (6.28) we maximize market exposure over the customer fills, but in Equation (8.3) we maximize market exposure over the state prices, since the customer fills are already fixed and known from Equation (8.2). We refer to this problem as the Simplified Parimutuel Equilibrium Problem (SPEP). Equations (8.2) and (7.13) imply that

$$y_s = \sum_{j=1}^{J} a_{j,s} b_j r_j \quad s = 1, 2, \ldots, S. \tag{8.4}$$

Thus, in this simplified framework, we can express y_s in terms of the customers' requested amounts.

8.1.2   The self-hedging restrictions as an eigensystem

The final restrictions listed in Equation (8.3) are the self-hedging conditions:

$$\frac{\theta_s}{p_s} + y_s = M \quad s = 1, 2, \ldots, S. \tag{8.5}$$

We now represent these self-hedging restrictions as an eigensystem.[3,4] For notation, let $\mathbf{H}$ be an S by S square matrix defined as

$$\mathbf{H} \equiv \begin{bmatrix} \theta_1 + y_1 & \theta_1 & \theta_1 & \cdots & \theta_1 \\ \theta_2 & \theta_2 + y_2 & \theta_2 & \cdots & \theta_2 \\ \theta_3 & \theta_3 & \theta_3 + y_3 & \cdots & \theta_3 \\ \vdots & \vdots & \vdots & \ddots & \vdots \\ \theta_S & \theta_S & \theta_S & \cdots & \theta_S + y_S \end{bmatrix}. \tag{8.6}$$

Let $\mathbf{p}$ be the column vector of length S of state prices, that is, the element in the sth row of $\mathbf{p}$ is p_s for $s = 1, 2, \ldots, S$. Appendix 8A proves the following theorem.

Theorem 8.1: The self-hedging restrictions of Equation (8.5) can be represented as the eigensystem

$$\mathbf{Hp} = M\mathbf{p}. \tag{8.7}$$

Equation (8.7) states that post-multiplying the matrix $\mathbf{H}$ by the vector of state prices $\mathbf{p}$ equals M, the net premium in the auction, multiplied by the vector of state prices $\mathbf{p}$. Equation (8.7) is an eigensystem, where M is an "eigenvalue" corresponding to the "eigenvector" $\mathbf{p}$.[5] Representing the self-hedging restrictions as an eigensystem allows us to observe that the PEP is inherently a nonlinear problem, like all eigensystems.[6,7]

When customers only submit market orders, Theorem 8.1 implies that the SPEP can be written as follows:

$$\begin{aligned}
&\max_{p_1, p_2, \ldots, p_S} \quad \tilde{M} \text{ subject to} \\
&\quad x_j = r_j \quad j = 1, 2, \ldots, J \\
&\quad p_s > 0 \quad s = 1, 2, \ldots, S \\
&\quad \sum_{s=1}^{S} p_s = 1 \\
&\quad \mathbf{Hp} = M\mathbf{p}.
\end{aligned} \tag{8.8}$$

Equation (8.8) is identical to Equation (8.3), except that this equation uses the eigensystem representation, instead of the self-hedging formulation. Representing the self-hedging restrictions as an eigensystem will allow us to use the well-known machinery for eigensystems to characterize the mathematical nature of the SPEP.

8.1.3 Eigensystem theorems and applications to the SPEP

We now present a theorem relating to eigensystems that has important implications for the SPEP.

Theorem 8.2: If a square matrix has all positive elements, then

Property 1: There exists a maximum unique eigenvalue of that matrix;

Property 2: Corresponding to that maximum unique eigenvalue, there exists a unique eigenvector with elements that are all greater than zero and sum to one;

Property 3: Any other eigenvector of that matrix has either at least one negative element or does not sum to one.

This theorem and close relatives to this theorem are sometimes called "Perron's Theorem," after Oskar Perron, a twentieth-century algebraist. As discussed in Horn and Johnson (1985, p. 497), the maximal eigenvalue of property 1 is called the "Perron root." Its corresponding eigenvector of property 2 has elements that are all positive and sum to one, and it is called the "Perron vector." These quantities have been widely studied by academics. See, for instance, Kolotilina (2004) and the citations therein.

Theorem 8.2 relates to a matrix that has all positive elements. How does this theorem apply to the matrix **H,** as defined in Equation (8.6)? First, note that the opening orders $\theta_1, \theta_2, \ldots, \theta_S$ are all positive (by Equation (6.1)), so all the off-diagonal elements of **H** are positive. If customers only submit orders that are buys of option strategies (and so customers do not submit sell orders or orders for the range forward), then all the diagonal elements of **H** are positive as well. In this case, **H** contains all positive elements, and Theorem 8.2 applies immediately. However, if some of the diagonals of **H** are negative, then we cannot apply Theorem 8.2 directly. Appendix 8A shows how this theorem can be modified appropriately to handle this case. Based on this work and Theorem 8.2, we can conclude the following.

Theorem 8.3: In the SPEP of Equation (8.8),

Property 1: H has a maximum unique eigenvalue M;

Property 2: Corresponding to the maximum unique eigenvalue M, there exists a unique eigenvector **p** with elements that are all greater than zero and sum to one;

Property 3: Any other eigenvector of **H** has either at least one negative element or does not sum to one.

Theorem 8.3 shows that in the absence of limit orders, there is a single net premium M, and a single state price vector **p** that contains all positive elements, sums to one, and satisfies **Hp**$= M$**p**.[8] Since prices are unique, there is only one feasible value for market exposure in the SPEP (see Equations (6.25) and (6.26)). Thus, without limit orders, there is no need to maximize market exposure, and we can restate the SPEP of Equation (8.8) equivalently as follows:

$$
\begin{array}{|l|}
\hline
\text{Solve for } \mathbf{p} \text{ such that} \\
\quad x_j = r_j \quad j = 1, 2, \ldots, J \\
\quad p_s > 0 \quad s = 1, 2, \ldots, S \\
\quad \sum_{s=1}^{S} p_s = 1 \\
\quad \mathbf{Hp} = M\mathbf{p}. \\
\hline
\end{array}
\qquad (8.9)
$$

Although the SPEP in Equations (8.3) and (8.8) appears at first to be an optimization problem since it contains an objective function, it is in fact an eigensystem problem where M is the maximal eigenvalue of $\mathbf{H}$, and $\mathbf{p}$ is the corresponding eigenvector, whose elements are all positive and sum to one. Eigensystems can be typically solved using a simple iterative technique. Appendix 7A, for example, used Newton's method to solve for M and $\mathbf{p}$. Chapter 7 of Strang (1988) discusses other solution methods.

8.1.4   An illustrative example

Chapters 5, 6, and 7 worked with a specific auction example in which the customer orders were limit orders. To illustrate the SPEP, we now introduce a new example in which the customer orders are market orders. As before, let the underlying be the monthly percentage change in the Consumer Price Index (CPI), let the tick size be $\rho = 0.1$, and let the auction strikes be 0.2, 0.3, and 0.4. Customers submit $J = 4$ orders, all of which are market orders to buy digital options. Since these four orders are market orders, they will be fully filled.[9] Table 8.1 displays information on these customer orders, including these orders' replication weights. We can check that the first three customer orders request the same three options as the first three customer orders in the example in Chapters 5, 6, and 7.

Based on the auction strikes of 0.2, 0.3, and 0.4 and the tick size of 0.1, Equation (5.18) implies that there are $S = 4$ state claims. We display information on the state claims and opening orders for this auction in the first five columns of Table 8.2. The state claims and the opening orders for this auction are the same as those in the example described in Chapters 5, 6, and 7.

Based on the opening orders and the customer orders (together, the "auction inputs"), we now solve for the state prices using the eigensystem results from above. Using Equation (8.4), we display formulas for the net customer payouts y_1, y_2, y_3, and y_4 in column two of Table 8.3. Based on the requested amounts from column six of Table 8.1, we show the values of the net customer payouts in column three of Table 8.3. Using these values, we can calculate $\mathbf{H}$:

$$
\mathbf{H} = \begin{bmatrix}
\theta_1 + y_1 & \theta_1 & \theta_1 & \theta_1 \\
\theta_2 & \theta_2 + y_2 & \theta_2 & \theta_2 \\
\theta_3 & \theta_3 & \theta_3 + y_3 & \theta_3 \\
\theta_4 & \theta_4 & \theta_4 & \theta_4 + y_4
\end{bmatrix}
$$

$$
= \begin{bmatrix}
250{,}100 & 100 & 100 & 100 \\
200 & 250{,}200 & 200 & 200 \\
200 & 200 & 100{,}200 & 200 \\
100 & 100 & 100 & 100{,}100
\end{bmatrix}. \tag{8.10}
$$

Table 8.1 The customer orders and replication weights for the parimutuel derivatives auction on CPI

Customer order j	Derivative strategy	Strike(s)	Side b_j	Order type	Requested number of contracts r_j	$d_j(u_1)$ or $a_{j,1}$	$d_j(u_2)$ or $a_{j,2}$	$d_j(u_3)$ or $a_{j,3}$	$d_j(u_4)$ or $a_{j,4}$
1	Digital call	0.3	1	Market order	100,000	0	0	1	1
2	Digital put	0.2	1	Market order	125,000	1	0	0	0
3	Digital range	0.2 and 0.3	1	Market order	125,000	0	1	0	0
4	Digital put	0.3	1	Market order	125,000	1	1	0	0

Table 8.2 Information on the state claims and opening orders for the parimutuel derivatives auction on CPI

State claim s	State	Strategy for state claim	Strike(s)	Opening-order premium θ_s in $	State price p_s
1	$U < 0.2$	Digital put	0.2	100	0.3327
2	$U = 0.2$	Digital range	0.2 and 0.3	200	0.6653
3	$U = 0.3$	Digital range	0.3 and 0.4	200	0.0013
4	$U \geq 0.4$	Digital call	0.4	100	0.0007

Table 8.3 State-payout information for the parimutuel derivatives auction on CPI

State claim s	Formula for net customer payouts y_s	Net customer payouts y_s in $	In-the-money payout to sth opening order θ_s/p_s in $	Total payouts $\theta_s/p_s + y_s$ in $
1	$r_2 + r_4$	250,000	301	250,301
2	$r_3 + r_4$	250,000	301	250,301
3	r_1	100,000	150,301	250,301
4	r_1	100,000	150,301	250,301

Based on $\mathbf{H}$, we can solve for the largest eigenvalue–eigenvector pair for the equation $\mathbf{Hp} = M\mathbf{p}$ using Newton's method. We determine that $M = 250,301$ and that

$$\mathbf{p} = \begin{bmatrix} 0.3327 \\ 0.6653 \\ 0.0013 \\ 0.0007 \end{bmatrix}. \tag{8.11}$$

It is straightforward to check that these state prices are positive and sum to one, satisfying the PEP no-arbitrage restrictions.[10] By Theorem 8.3, these state prices, which are also shown in column six of Table 8.2, are unique.

Table 8.4 Information on the customer orders for the parimutuel derivatives auction on CPI

Customer order j	Side b_j	Requested number of contracts r_j	Derivative price π_j	Filled number of contracts x_j	Premium $x_j\lambda_j$ in $
1	1	100,000	0.0020	100,000	200
2	1	125,000	0.3327	125,000	41,588
3	1	125,000	0.6653	125,000	83,163
4	1	125,000	0.9980	125,000	124,750

We now check that these values of M and $\mathbf{p}$ satisfy the self-hedging conditions.

The net customer payouts: Column four of Table 8.3 displays the payout on the sth opening order if it expires in-the-money (which equals θ_s/p_s for opening orders $s = 1, 2, 3, 4$). Column five of Table 8.3 shows the total payouts, which equal $250,301 in every state.

The net premium collected: Using Table 8.4, we now check that the total premium collected equals $250,301. The second and third columns of Table 8.4 display the side and requested amounts, respectively, for the four customer orders in the auction. The fourth column of Table 8.4 shows the equilibrium prices of the requested options, calculated based on (1) the replication weights from the last four columns of Table 8.1; (2) the state prices from column six of Table 8.2; and (3) the following equation:

$$\pi_j = \sum_{s=1}^{4} a_{j,s} p_s \quad j = 1, 2, 3, 4. \tag{8.12}$$

The fifth column of Table 8.4 shows the filled amounts for the customer orders. Since these orders are market orders, the filled amounts equal the requested amounts from column three. Column six of Table 8.4 shows the premium amounts. Since all four customer orders are buys of options and are filled, every premium amount is positive (indicating that the customers pay premium for the options). The total premium for the four customer orders equals $249,701, which can be calculated by adding up the premium amounts in column six. With the \$600 in opening orders, M, the premium in the auction, equals \$250,301.

Since the net payouts in all four states equal the net premium collected, we have confirmed the self-hedging equations for this example.

Summary: Section 8.1 introduced the SPEP, a simplified version of the parimutuel equilibrium problem in which customers only submit market orders. We showed that the SPEP is an eigensystem problem where M is the maximal eigenvalue of $\mathbf{H}$, and $\mathbf{p}$ is the unique eigenvector which (1) corresponds to the eigenvalue M; (2) has all positive elements; and (3) whose elements sum to one. For the SPEP, M and $\mathbf{p}$ are unique and can be solved for numerically in an iterative but straightforward manner.

8.2 UNIQUE PRICES WITH MARKET ORDERS AND LIMIT ORDERS

Section 8.1 showed that the PEP with only market orders, or equivalently the SPEP, is a straightforward eigensystem problem. With *both* market orders and limit orders, solving the PEP becomes more difficult because we do not know the equilibrium prices until we know which customer orders will be filled (either fully or partially), and we do not know which customer orders will be filled until we know the equilibrium prices. So, the customer orders that are filled in equilibrium are a function of the equilibrium prices, and, of course, these very equilibrium prices determine which customer orders are filled. Thus, the PEP must determine the prices and the fills jointly.

In the academic literature, such "joint determination" problems can often be represented as Variational Inequality Problems (VIPs). VIPs are found in many different areas, including engineering and economics. Ferris and Pang (1997), for example, demonstrate the pervasiveness of VIPs in these and others areas. There exists a specific subclass of VIPs which have "box" constrained variables, meaning that the variables lie between a lower and upper bound. This subclass of VIPs is called, not surprisingly, Box Constrained Variational Inequality Problems (BVIPs). The limit-order constraints of Equation (8.1) restrict customer fills to lie between zero and their requested amounts. This property helps us to represent the PEP as a BVIP. In their most general form BVIPs are difficult to study. However, we can exploit the special structure of the PEP and use the BVIP literature to show that PEP state prices are unique.

We proceed as follows. Section 8.2.1 presents very general conditions under which parimutuel prices are unique. Section 8.2.2 provides an overview of the proof of this result. Appendices 8B and 8C present the complete details of the proof.

8.2.1　Statement of the theorems and implications

Recall that we stated the PEP in Chapter 6 as follows:

$$
\begin{aligned}
& \max_{x_1, x_2, \ldots, x_J} \widetilde{M} \quad \text{subject to} \\[1ex]
& \left.\begin{aligned}
b_j w_j < b_j \pi_j &\implies x_j = 0 \\
b_j w_j = b_j \pi_j &\implies 0 \le x_j \le r_j \\
b_j w_j > b_j \pi_j &\implies x_j = r_j
\end{aligned}\right\} \quad j = 1, 2, \ldots, J \\[1ex]
& p_s > 0 \qquad\qquad\qquad\qquad\quad s = 1, 2, \ldots, S \qquad (8.13) \\[1ex]
& \sum_{s=1}^{S} p_s = 1 \\[1ex]
& \frac{\theta_s}{p_s} + y_s = M \qquad\qquad\qquad s = 1, 2, \ldots, S.
\end{aligned}
$$

Based on this specification, we can prove the following.

Theorem 8.4: For a given set of auction inputs, the PEP of Equation (8.13) has a unique set of state prices and derivative strategy prices.

Theorem 8.4 is a very strong result mathematically, and it stands in contrast to many other equilibrium problems in economics, where equilibrium prices do not exist or there exist multiple vectors of equilibrium prices.[11] In addition, Theorem 8.4 is a very desirable result pragmatically, as auction participants are likely to find comfort that a particular set of auction inputs can only generate one set of prices.

Can one set of PEP prices be the result of multiple sets of customer orders? Consider an auction where the jth customer order is a buy order in which the limit price w_j is above the equilibrium market price π_j. This customer order is above the market and so it is fully filled, that is, $x_j = r_j$. Changing the limit price w_j on this customer order does not change any prices or customer fills, as long as the customer's limit price w_j remains above the market price π_j. For example, consider the fifth customer order from the auction example from Chapters 5, 6, and 7. This order was a buy of a vanilla floored put with a limit price of $w_5 = 0.16$. Since the market price $\pi_5 = 0.15$, this order was fully filled for an amount of $x_5 = r_5 = 1,500,000$ contracts. Increasing the limit price w_5 to 0.17 or reducing the limit price w_5 to 0.155, for example, will not change any equilibrium prices or customer fills. In a similar manner, changing the limit price on an order that is below the market also does not affect any prices, so long as that new limit price remains below the market price for that derivative. Thus, one set of prices in the PEP can be the result of multiple sets of customer orders.

Consider the following problem:

$$
\begin{array}{ll}
\text{Solve for } x_1, x_2, \ldots, x_J \text{ such that} & \\
\left. \begin{array}{l}
b_j w_j < b_j \pi_j \Rightarrow x_j = 0 \\
b_j w_j = b_j \pi_j \Rightarrow 0 \le x_j \le r_j \\
b_j w_j > b_j \pi_j \Rightarrow x_j = r_j
\end{array} \right\} & j = 1, 2, \ldots, J \\[2ex]
p_s > 0 & s = 1, 2, \ldots, S \\[2ex]
\displaystyle\sum_{s=1}^{S} p_s = 1 & \\[2ex]
\dfrac{\theta_s}{p_s} + y_s = M & s = 1, 2, \ldots, S.
\end{array}
$$

(8.14)

Equation (8.14) is identical to Equation (8.13) except that Equation (8.14) does not have an objective function to maximize. Consequently, this problem is a more general problem than the PEP because solutions to Equation (8.14) include fills that do not maximize market exposure. We refer to Equation (8.14) as the Generalized Parimutuel Equilibrium Problem (GPEP). Appendices 8B and 8C prove the following theorem.

Theorem 8.5: For a given set of auction inputs, the GPEP of Equation (8.14) has a unique set of state prices and derivative strategy prices.

Theorem 8.5 implies that for any given set of auction inputs, there exists a unique set of state prices *regardless* of the objective function, a somewhat surprising result. Thus, the equilibrium state prices are the same if the objective is to *maximize* market exposure in the auction, or if the objective is to *minimize* the market exposure in the auction. As Chapter 9 will show, the choice of the objective function can impact customer fills, but the choice of the objective function does not affect state prices and the derivative strategy prices. This is a very strong property of the parimutuel framework. For example, recall that the equilibrium customer fills from Chapters 5, 6, and 7 from maximizing market exposure are $x_1 = 100,000, x_2 = x_3 = 99,833, x_4 = 1,496,667, x_5 = 1,500,000$, and $x_6 = 0$. The equilibrium fills from minimizing market exposure are $x_1 = 167, x_2 = x_3 = 0, x_4 = 1,496,667, x_5 = 1,500,000$, and $x_6 = 0$. The equilibrium state and derivative strategy prices are equal for both sets of

Table 8.5 Summary of different parimutuel equilibrium problems and their properties

Type of problem	Types of customer orders	Objective function	Properties of state prices and derivative strategy prices	Properties of customer fills
Simplified Parimutuel Equilibrium Problem (SPEP)	Market orders	Maximize market exposure	Unique	Unique
Parimutuel Equilibrium Problem (PEP)	Market orders and limit orders	Maximize market exposure	Unique	Multiple vectors of fills possible
Generalized Parimutuel Equilibrium Problem (GPEP)	Market orders and limit orders	None	Unique	Multiple vectors of fills possible

fills. It is straightforward to check that Theorem 8.5 is a stronger theorem than Theorem 8.4, that is, if the state prices and the derivative strategy prices for the GPEP are unique, then the state prices and the derivative strategy prices for the PEP are also unique.

Table 8.5 compares the properties of the SPEP, the PEP, and the GPEP. In the SPEP, customers only submit market orders, while in the PEP and the GPEP, customers submit both market orders and limit orders. The SPEP and the PEP have as their objective to maximize market exposure, while the GPEP is a more general problem and does not have an objective function.[12] State prices and derivatives strategy prices are unique for all three problems. Customer fills are unique for the SPEP, while multiple vectors of customer fills may exist for the PEP and GPEP. Chapter 9 will provide more details on the nature of those customer fills for the PEP.

8.2.2   Proving the theorems

We now provide an overview of the proof of Theorem 8.5, providing intuition behind the machinery used.[13] For ease of exposition, we break-up the description of the proof into four parts. For the complete proof, see Appendices 8B and 8C.

Part 1: The pseudo-orders

Recall that there are J customer orders in a parimutuel derivatives auction. To prove that the state prices are unique, we need to introduce S additional orders, where S is, as before, the number of states. We refer to these orders as "pseudo-orders." These pseudo-orders are not actual orders in the auction: they receive no fill, and they do not impact the equilibrium prices and fills of other orders in the GPEP.[14] Instead, these pseudo-orders are tools solely used for proving uniqueness.

The J customer orders are subscripted (as before) from 1 to J, and we subscript the pseudo-orders from $J+1$ to $J+S$. For $j = J+1, J+2, \ldots, J+S$, the jth order (or the $j - J$th pseudo-order) is a buy order (so b_j equals 1) of the $j - J$th state claim. Thus, the $J+1$st order (the first pseudo-order) is a buy of the first state claim, the $J+2$nd order (the second pseudo-order) is a buy of the second state claim, and so on. The $J+S$th order (the Sth pseudo-order) is a buy of the Sth state claim. For $j = J+1, J+2, \ldots, J+S$, the jth pseudo-order has a limit price of $w_j = 0$ and a requested quantity of $r_j = 1$.[15] We display the details of these pseudo-orders in Table 8.6. Note that for the pseudo-orders, $a_{j,s}$ equals one if $s = J+j$ or zero otherwise. Since their limit prices are all zero, and since the prices of the state claims must be positive in equilibrium, the limit-order logic implies that each of these S pseudo-orders will have zero fill in equilibrium.[16] Although they have no fill, these S pseudo-orders are a helpful device for proving that the GPEP has unique state prices, as described below.

Table 8.6 Pseudo-orders for the proof that GPEP prices are unique

Order number j	Strategy	Side b_j	Limit price w_j	Requested amount r_j	$d_j(u_1)$ or $a_{j,1}$	$d_j(u_2)$ or $a_{j,2}$	$d_j(u_3)$ or $a_{j,3}$	...	$d_j(u_{S-1})$ or $a_{j,S-1}$	$d_j(u_S)$ or $a_{j,S}$
$J+1$	First state claim	1	0	1	1	0	0	...	0	0
$J+2$	Second state claim	1	0	1	0	1	0	...	0	0
$J+3$	Third state claim	1	0	1	0	0	1	...	0	0
⋮	⋮	⋮	⋮	⋮				...		
$J+S-1$	$(S-1)$th state claim	1	0	1	0	0	0	...	1	0
$J+S$	Sth state claim	1	0	1	0	0	0	...	0	1

Part 2: Representing the GPEP as a BVIP

We now represent the GPEP as a BVIP, as doing so allows us to use the machinery from the BVIP literature. To confirm that the GPEP is a BVIP, we have to show two properties. First, we have to show that the fills lie in a "box." Second, we have to show that there exists a function F that contains the functional form of the GPEP and satisfies what is called in the optimization literature a "mixed-complementarity condition."

For notation, let $\mathbf{x}$ be the $J + S$ by 1 column vector whose element in the jth row is x_j for $j = 1, 2, \ldots, J + S$. Note that x_j is between 0 and r_j for $j = 1, 2, \ldots, J + S$. Therefore, let

$$X \equiv \left\{ \mathbf{x} \in \mathbb{R}^{J+S} \middle| 0 \leq x_j \leq r_j, j = 1, 2, \ldots, J + S \right\}. \tag{8.15}$$

Thus, the fills lie in the "box" X, and this first BVIP requirement is satisfied.

To denote the derivative strategy prices' explicit dependence on the fills, let $\pi_j(\mathbf{x})$ denote the function from $\mathbb{R}^{J+S} \to \mathbb{R}^1$ that maps the fill vector $\mathbf{x}$ to the price of the derivative strategy requested in the jth order for $j = 1, 2, \ldots, J + S$. Though the function $\pi_j(\mathbf{x})$ cannot be written analytically, it incorporates the functional information regarding:

1. How the net customer payouts are calculated from $\mathbf{x}$ using Equation (7.13);

2. How net auction premium is computed from the net customer payouts using Newton's method from Appendix 7A;

3. How the state prices are calculated from the net auction premium and the net customer payouts using Equation (7.14); and

4. How derivative strategy prices are calculated from the state prices based on Equation (7.9).

Based on these steps, the functions $\pi_1(\mathbf{x}), \pi_2(\mathbf{x}), \ldots, \pi_{J+S}(\mathbf{x})$ embed all the equilibrium conditions of the GPEP, except for the limit-order restrictions.[17]

To address the limit-order conditions of the GPEP, let $F_j : \mathbb{R}^{J+S} \to \mathbb{R}^1$ be the function defined as follows:

$$F_j(\mathbf{x}) = b_j(\pi_j(\mathbf{x}) - w_j) \quad j = 1, 2, \ldots, J + S. \tag{8.16}$$

Further, let $F : \mathbb{R}^{J+S} \rightarrow \mathbb{R}^{J+S}$ be the vector valued function whose element in the jth row is F_j for $j = 1, 2, \ldots, J + S$. Therefore,

$$
F(\mathbf{x}) = \begin{bmatrix} b_1(\pi_1(\mathbf{x}) - w_1) \\ b_2(\pi_2(\mathbf{x}) - w_2) \\ \vdots \\ b_{J+S}(\pi_{J+S}(\mathbf{x}) - w_{J+S}) \end{bmatrix}.
\tag{8.17}
$$

Based on Equation (8.1), we can relate the limit-order conditions of the GPEP to F_j as follows:

$$
\left.
\begin{array}{l}
F_j(\mathbf{x}) > 0 \;\Rightarrow\; x_j = 0 \\
F_j(\mathbf{x}) = 0 \;\Rightarrow\; 0 \leq x_j \leq r_j \\
F_j(\mathbf{x}) < 0 \;\Rightarrow\; x_j = r_j
\end{array}
\right\} \quad j = 1, 2, \ldots, J + S.
\tag{8.18}
$$

Based on the definition of $\pi_j(\mathbf{x})$ from above, we can conclude that Equation (8.18) is an equivalent representation of the GPEP of Equation (8.14). Equation (8.18) is often called a "mixed-complementarity condition" in the optimization literature. This equation represents the second requirement for representing a problem as a BVIP.

Solving the GPEP is equivalent to finding a set of fills $\mathbf{x}$ from the box X of Equation (8.15) that solve Equation (8.18) for the function F from Equation (8.17). This representation and the results of Harker and Pang (1990) and Kanzow (2000) imply that the GPEP is a BVIP, which we write as BVIP(F, X) for shorthand. Representing the GPEP as a BVIP will enable us to use a powerful theorem from the BVIP literature.

Part 3: Properties of the Jacobian of F

Let $\mathbf{D}$ denote the $J + S$ by $J + S$ matrix of first derivatives of F with respect to $\mathbf{x}$, that is,

$$
\mathbf{D} \equiv \frac{dF(\mathbf{x})}{d\mathbf{x}}
$$

$$
= \begin{bmatrix}
\dfrac{\partial F_1}{\partial x_1} & \dfrac{\partial F_1}{\partial x_2} & \dfrac{\partial F_1}{\partial x_3} & \cdots & \dfrac{\partial F_1}{\partial x_{J+S}} \\[2ex]
\dfrac{\partial F_2}{\partial x_1} & \dfrac{\partial F_2}{\partial x_2} & \dfrac{\partial F_2}{\partial x_3} & \cdots & \dfrac{\partial F_2}{\partial x_{J+S}} \\[2ex]
\dfrac{\partial F_3}{\partial x_1} & \dfrac{\partial F_3}{\partial x_2} & \dfrac{\partial F_3}{\partial x_3} & \cdots & \dfrac{\partial F_3}{\partial x_{J+S}} \\[2ex]
\vdots & \vdots & \vdots & \ddots & \vdots \\[2ex]
\dfrac{\partial F_{J+S}}{\partial x_1} & \dfrac{\partial F_{J+S}}{\partial x_2} & \dfrac{\partial F_{J+S}}{\partial x_3} & \cdots & \dfrac{\partial F_{J+S}}{\partial x_{J+S}}
\end{bmatrix}.
\tag{8.19}
$$

$\mathbf{D}$ is often called the "Jacobian" of F with respect to $\mathbf{x}$. Let "T" denote the matrix transpose operator. Appendix 8C shows that $\mathbf{D}$ is "symmetric," which means that $\mathbf{D} = \mathbf{D}^T$, and "positive semi-definite," which means that

$$\mathbf{z}^T \mathbf{D} \mathbf{z} \geq 0 \text{ for all column vectors } \mathbf{z} \text{ of length } J + S. \qquad (8.20)$$

The fact that $\mathbf{D}$ satisfies these two properties is important for proving Theorem 8.5.[18]

Part 4: Unique prices for the GPEP

The GPEP with the $J + S$ orders is a BVIP(F, X) where the Jacobian of F is continuous, symmetric, and positive semi-definite. Because of this, we can use the machinery from the BVIP literature to prove that:

1. There exists at least one solution $\mathbf{x}$ to the GPEP; and

2. Every argument $\mathbf{x}$ that solves Equation (8.18) has the same unique value of $F(\mathbf{x})$, or in other words, if $\mathbf{x}_1$ and $\mathbf{x}_2$ solve the BVIP, then $F(\mathbf{x}_1) = F(\mathbf{x}_2)$. By the definition of F from Equation (8.17), a unique value of F means that $\pi_1(\mathbf{x}), \pi_2(\mathbf{x}), \ldots, \pi_{J+S}(\mathbf{x})$ are unique (since $b_1, b_2, \ldots, b_{J+S}$ are non-zero constants and $w_1, w_2, \ldots, w_{J+S}$ are constants). Since $\pi_{J+s}(\mathbf{x}) = p_s$ for $s = 1, 2, \ldots, S$, we can also conclude that the state prices for the GPEP with pseudo-orders are unique.

Thus, the state and derivative strategy prices for the GPEP with pseudo-orders are unique.

In the GPEP with $J + S$ orders, the pseudo-orders do not receive any fills. Consequently, removing them from the auction does not change the state prices, the derivative strategy prices, or the fills of the J customer orders. Based on this, we conclude that the GPEP state and derivative strategy prices without the pseudo-orders equal the GPEP prices with the pseudo-orders, and so the GPEP state and derivative strategy prices without the pseudo-orders are also unique.

Comments on the proof and its implications

Although we have proven that the state and derivative strategy prices for the GPEP are unique, this analysis does not rule out the possibility of multiple vectors of customer fills that solve the GPEP, while leading to the same set of prices. In Chapter 9, for instance, we show that under certain conditions, there are an infinite number of vectors of customer fills that satisfy the PEP, which (of course) implies that there are cases where there are an infinite number of fills for the GPEP.

In a recent working paper, Peters, So, and Ye (2006) consider a closely related problem to the PEP, which they call the Convex Parimutuel Call Auction Mechanism (CPCAM). Their formulation has the computational advantage over the PEP that it is a convex program. Based on this fact, Peters, So, and Ye (2006) prove that the state prices from the CPCAM are unique. This result can be used to show that the PEP has unique prices. Nagurney (2002, pp. 12–13) points out that there is a close link between convex programs and BVIPs with symmetric and positive semi-definite Jacobians. Thus, the fact that the convex approach taken in Peters, So, and Ye (2006) and our BVIP approach are both fruitful approaches should not be surprising.

The fact that $\mathbf{D}$, the Jacobian of F, is positive semi-definite provides some perspective on part one of our solution algorithm from Chapter 7 for determining the equilibrium prices. Our algorithm steps the customer fills in such a way that the state prices and the derivative strategy prices change on each iteration. The fact that changes in state and derivative strategy prices due to changes in customer fills are well behaved is crucial for our solution algorithm to work. For example, consider a particular iteration of the solution algorithm of part one where the jth customer order is a buy order ($b_j = 1$) that is above the market ($w_j > \pi_j$) but it is not fully filled ($x_j < r_j$). This order's violation v_j, as defined in Equation (7.7), is greater than zero. In this case, we increase the fill x_j based on the stepping algorithm of Equation (7.12). $\mathbf{D}$ is positive semi-definite, which implies that all the diagonal elements of $\mathbf{D}$ are non-negative. Consequently, increasing the fill x_j will increase or at least not decrease the price π_j, which will decrease the violation v_j on the next iteration. Thus, as we step according to this algorithm, we reduce the violations on each iteration for buy orders. A similar argument applies for sell orders. Therefore, the fact that $\mathbf{D}$ is positive semi-definite gives us insight into the efficacy of the solution algorithm of part one.

APPENDIX 8A: PROOFS OF THEOREMS FROM SECTION 8.1

This appendix proves Theorems 8.1, 8.2, and 8.3, which were presented in Section 8.1.

Proof of Theorem 8.1: Using the definition of $\mathbf{H}$ in Equation (8.6), note that

$$
\mathbf{Hp} =
\begin{bmatrix}
\theta_1 + y_1 & \theta_1 & \theta_1 & \cdots & \theta_1 \\
\theta_2 & \theta_2 + y_2 & \theta_2 & \cdots & \theta_2 \\
\theta_3 & \theta_3 & \theta_3 + y_3 & \cdots & \theta_3 \\
\vdots & \vdots & \vdots & \ddots & \vdots \\
\theta_S & \theta_S & \theta_S & \cdots & \theta_S + y_S
\end{bmatrix}
\begin{bmatrix}
p_1 \\ p_2 \\ p_3 \\ \vdots \\ p_S
\end{bmatrix}
$$

$$
=
\begin{bmatrix}
p_1\theta_1 + p_1 y_1 + p_2\theta_1 + p_3\theta_1 + \cdots + p_S\theta_1 \\
p_1\theta_2 + p_2\theta_2 + p_2 y_2 + p_3\theta_2 + \cdots + p_S\theta_2 \\
p_1\theta_3 + p_2\theta_3 + p_3 y_3 + p_3\theta_3 + \cdots + p_S\theta_3 \\
\vdots \\
p_1\theta_S + p_2\theta_S + p_3\theta_S + \cdots + p_S\theta_S + p_S y_S
\end{bmatrix}
$$

$$
=
\begin{bmatrix}
\theta_1 \left(\sum_{s=1}^{S} p_s \right) + p_1 y_1 \\[2ex]
\theta_2 \left(\sum_{s=1}^{S} p_s \right) + p_2 y_2 \\[2ex]
\theta_3 \left(\sum_{s=1}^{S} p_s \right) + p_3 y_3 \\[2ex]
\vdots \\[1ex]
\theta_S \left(\sum_{s=1}^{S} p_s \right) + p_S y_S
\end{bmatrix}
$$

$$
=
\begin{bmatrix}
\theta_1 + p_1 y_1 \\
\theta_2 + p_2 y_2 \\
\theta_3 + p_3 y_3 \\
\vdots \\
\theta_S + p_S y_S
\end{bmatrix},
\tag{8A.1}
$$

where the last equality follows from the fact that the state prices sum to one. Next, multiplying both sides of the self-hedging Equation (8.5) by p_s gives that

$$
\theta_s + p_s y_s = M p_s \quad s = 1, 2, \ldots, S. \tag{8A.2}
$$

Writing Equation (8A.2) in vector format, we have that

$$
\begin{bmatrix}
\theta_1 + p_1 y_1 \\
\theta_2 + p_2 y_2 \\
\theta_3 + p_3 y_3 \\
\vdots \\
\theta_S + p_S y_S
\end{bmatrix}
=
\begin{bmatrix}
M p_1 \\
M p_2 \\
M p_3 \\
\vdots \\
M p_S
\end{bmatrix}
$$

$$
= M\mathbf{p}. \tag{8A.3}
$$

Consequently, Equations (8A.1) and (8A.3) imply that

$$
\mathbf{Hp} = M\mathbf{p} \tag{8A.4}
$$

and so the self-hedging conditions of Equation (8.5) can be represented as an eigensystem. This concludes the proof.

Proof of Theorem 8.2: See Chapter 8 of Horn and Johnson (1985) for properties 1 and 2, and see Theorem 1.3(b) of Berman and Plemmons (1994, p. 27) for property 3.[19]

Proof of Theorem 8.3: If $\mathbf{H}$ contains all positive elements, then Theorem 8.2 implies immediately that there is a single eigenvector $\mathbf{p}$ (the Perron vector) with all positive elements that sum to one, and there is a unique corresponding eigenvalue M (the Perron root). If $\mathbf{H}$ contains at least one element less than or equal to zero, then let $y_{(1)}$ be the minimum of the y's. That is, let

$$
y_{(1)} \equiv \min[y_1, y_2, \ldots, y_S]. \tag{8A.5}
$$

In this case, note that

$$
y_{(1)}\mathbf{Ip} = y_{(1)}\mathbf{p}. \tag{8A.6}
$$

Therefore,

$$
\mathbf{Hp} = M\mathbf{p} \tag{8A.7}
$$

holds if and only if

$$
\mathbf{Hp} - y_{(1)}\mathbf{Ip} = M\mathbf{p} - y_{(1)}\mathbf{p}, \tag{8A.8}
$$

where Equation (8A.8) is simply obtained by subtracting Equation (8A.6) from Equation (8A.7). Equation (8A.8) holds if and only if

$$
(\mathbf{H} - y_{(1)}\mathbf{I})\mathbf{p} = (M - y_{(1)})\mathbf{p}. \tag{8A.9}
$$

Thus, if $M - y_{(1)}$ and $\mathbf{p}$ are an eigenvalue and eigenvector pair of the matrix $\mathbf{H} - y_{(1)}\mathbf{I}$, then M and $\mathbf{p}$ are an eigenvalue and eigenvector pair of the matrix $\mathbf{H}$. The matrix $\mathbf{H} - y_{(1)}\mathbf{I}$ contains all positive elements. Therefore, Theorem 8.2 implies that associated with the maximum eigenvalue $M - y_{(1)}$ of the matrix $\mathbf{H} - y_{(1)}\mathbf{I}$ is a unique eigenvector $\mathbf{p}$ with all positive elements that sum to one. This implies that associated with the matrix $\mathbf{H}$ is the maximum eigenvalue M and correspondingly there is a unique $\mathbf{p}$ with all positive elements that sum to one. This concludes the proof.

APPENDIX 8B: PROOF THAT GPEP PRICES ARE UNIQUE

In this appendix, we prove Theorem 8.5, which states that the GPEP has unique state and derivative strategy prices.[20] To do so, we proceed as follows. First, Section 8B.1 defines a BVIP and presents two related theorems. Section 8B.2 begins by representing the GPEP as a BVIP. Using the properties of the GPEP (some of which are derived in Appendix 8C) and the BVIP theorems from Section 8B.1, we prove that the GPEP state and derivative strategy prices are unique.

Section 8.2.2 described the proof of Theorem 8.5 in four parts. It is worth relating those four parts to the organization of the material covered below. Creating the pseudo-orders (part 1) and representing the GPEP as a BVIP (part 2) is done in Section 8B.2. The properties of the Jacobian of F (part 3) are determined in Appendix 8C. The conclusion that GPEP prices are unique (part 4) is based on the theorems from Section 8B.1 and from material from Section 8B.2.

8B.1   Box variational inequality problems

For notation, let $\mathbf{x}$ be a column vector of length n, and let x_j be the jth element of $\mathbf{x}$ for $j = 1, 2, \ldots, n$. Further, let l_j and h_j be constants for $j = 1, 2, \ldots, n$. We now define the canonical version of the BVIP.

BVIP definition: Let X be the box defined by

$$X \equiv \left\{ \mathbf{x} \in \mathbb{R}^n \mid l_j \leq x_j \leq h_j, j = 1, 2, \ldots, n \right\}. \tag{8B.1}$$

Let F be a function that maps $\mathbb{R}^n$ to $\mathbb{R}^n$. As described in Harker and Pang (1990), the canonical box constrained variational inequality problem or BVIP is to find a vector $\mathbf{x} \in X$ such that

$$F(\mathbf{x})^{\mathrm{T}}(\mathbf{v} - \mathbf{x}) \geq 0 \quad \forall \mathbf{v} \in X \tag{8B.2}$$

In geometrical terms, the BVIP seeks an $\mathbf{x}$ such that $F(\mathbf{x})^{\mathrm{T}}$ is orthogonal to the feasible set X at the point $\mathbf{x}$. For shorthand notation, we write the problem specified in Equations (8B.1) and (8B.2) as BVIP(F, X). We now show that the BVIP has an equivalent representation as the following mixed-complementarity problem.

Theorem 8B.1: The BVIP(F, X) of Equations (8B.1) and (8B.2) is equivalent to finding a vector $\mathbf{x} \in X$ such that

$$\left. \begin{array}{ll} F_j(\mathbf{x}) > 0 & \Rightarrow \quad x_j = l_j \\ F_j(\mathbf{x}) = 0 & \Rightarrow \quad l_j \leq x_j \leq h_j \\ F_j(\mathbf{x}) < 0 & \Rightarrow \quad x_j = h_j \end{array} \right\} \quad j = 1, 2, \ldots, n, \tag{8B.3}$$

where F_j is the jth row of the function F for $j = 1, 2, \ldots, n$.

Proof: See, for example, Kanzow (2000, p. 1).

Next, let $\mathbf{D}$ denote the Jacobian of F with respect to $\mathbf{x}$, where $\mathbf{x} \in X$. We now prove a theorem regarding a BVIP(F, X) based on the properties of the Jacobian of F.

Theorem 8B.2: Let X be the box defined in Equation (8B.1). If the function F is continuously differentiable over X, and $\mathbf{D}$ is symmetric and positive semi-definite for $\mathbf{x} \in X$, then there exists at least one solution $\mathbf{x}$ to the BVIP(F, X) of Equation (8B.3). If there are multiple solutions to the BVIP(F, X), then $F(\mathbf{x})$ is the same for every $\mathbf{x}$ that is a solution to the BVIP(F, X).

Proof: We first prove that there exists at least one solution $\mathbf{x}$ to the BVIP(F, X), and then we prove that $F(\mathbf{x})$ is the same for any solution $\mathbf{x}$.

Existence: Since X satisfies Equation (8B.1), it is non-empty, "compact," and "convex."[21] Theorem 3.1 of Harker and Pang (1990, p. 170), which is based on Brouwer's Fixed-Point Theorem, implies that there exists at least one solution to the BVIP(F, X).

Uniqueness: As defined in Iusem (1998), a function G is "paramonotone" over X if and only if it is monotone[22] and

$$(G(\mathbf{w}) - G(\mathbf{v}))^{\mathrm{T}}(\mathbf{w} - \mathbf{v}) = 0 \Rightarrow G(\mathbf{w}) = G(\mathbf{v}) \quad \forall \mathbf{v}, \mathbf{w} \in X, \mathbf{v} \neq \mathbf{w}. \tag{8B.4}$$

Iusem (1998) proves (see Proposition 4.2 on page 275 and see the final remarks on page 277) that if the Jacobian of a function is well defined, continuous, symmetric, and positive semi-definite over X, then the function is paramonotone over X. Thus, by assumption, F is paramonotone over X. Next, consider two (possibly equal) solutions $\mathbf{x}_1$ and $\mathbf{x}_2$ to the BVIP(F, X). Since they are solutions, Equation (8B.2) implies that

$$F(\mathbf{x}_1)^{\mathrm{T}}(\mathbf{v} - \mathbf{x}_1) \geq 0 \quad \forall \mathbf{v} \in X, \tag{8B.5}$$

$$F(\mathbf{x}_2)^{\mathrm{T}}(\mathbf{v} - \mathbf{x}_2) \geq 0 \quad \forall \mathbf{v} \in X. \tag{8B.6}$$

Substituting $\mathbf{x}_2$ for $\mathbf{v}$ into Equation (8B.5) and substituting $\mathbf{x}_1$ for $\mathbf{v}$ into Equation (8B.6) yields

$$F(\mathbf{x}_1)^{\mathrm{T}}(\mathbf{x}_2 - \mathbf{x}_1) \geq 0, \tag{8B.7}$$

$$F(\mathbf{x}_2)^{\mathrm{T}}(\mathbf{x}_1 - \mathbf{x}_2) \geq 0. \tag{8B.8}$$

Adding Equations (8B.7) and (8B.8) together implies that

$$(F(\mathbf{x}_1) - F(\mathbf{x}_2))^{\mathrm{T}}(\mathbf{x}_2 - \mathbf{x}_1) \geq 0. \tag{8B.9}$$

Since F is paramonotone, this implies (by definition) that F is monotone, so

$$(F(\mathbf{x}_1) - F(\mathbf{x}_2))^{\mathrm{T}}(\mathbf{x}_1 - \mathbf{x}_2) \geq 0. \tag{8B.10}$$

Equations (8B.9) and (8B.10) imply that

$$(F(\mathbf{x}_1) - F(\mathbf{x}_2))^{\mathrm{T}}(\mathbf{x}_1 - \mathbf{x}_2) = 0. \tag{8B.11}$$

Therefore, Equation (8B.11) and the fact that F is paramonotone imply that

$$F(\mathbf{x}_1) = F(\mathbf{x}_2). \tag{8B.12}$$

Thus, all solutions $\mathbf{x}_1$ and $\mathbf{x}_2$ to the BVIP(F, X) have equal values of F. This concludes the proof.

Theorems 8B.1 and 8B.2 will be used in the next section.

8B.2 Representing the GPEP as a BVIP and proving uniqueness

There are J customer orders in a parimutuel derivatives auction. As described in part 1 of Section 8.2.2, to prove that the state and derivative strategy prices are unique, we include S additional orders, which we refer to as "pseudo-orders." As before, let $\mathbf{x}$ be the $J + S$ by 1 column vector whose element in the j th row is x_j for $j = 1, 2, \ldots, J+S$. Let $\mathbf{p}(\mathbf{x})$ denote the S by 1 column vector of equilibrium state prices for these $J+S$ orders. Further, let $\pi(\mathbf{x})$ denote the $J+S$ by 1 column vector of derivative prices, that is, the jth element of $\pi(\mathbf{x})$ equals $\pi_j(\mathbf{x})$ for $j = 1, 2, \ldots, J + S$. Note that the last S elements of $\pi(\mathbf{x})$ are the vector $\mathbf{p}(\mathbf{x})$, since the pseudo-orders request the state claims (see Table 8.6). Recall from part 2 of Section 8.2.2 that embedded in the function $\pi(\mathbf{x})$ are all the restrictions of the GPEP, except for the limit-order constraints.

Theorem 8B.3: The GPEP with $J + S$ orders has an equivalent representation as a BVIP.

Proof: Set $l_j = 0$ and $h_j = r_j$ for $j = 1, 2, \ldots, J + S$, and let $n = J + S$. Define X as the box in Equation (8.15). Thus, X satisfies Equation (8B.1). Next, let F be defined as the function in Equation (8.17). As argued in part 2 in Section 8.2.2, the limit-order constraints of Equation (8.1) are equivalent to Equation (8B.3). Consequently, the GPEP can be written as BVIP(F, X). This concludes the proof.

Theorem 8B.4: Let $\mathbf{D}$ denote the Jacobian of F with respect to $\mathbf{x}$, where $\mathbf{x} \in X$ is defined in Equation (8.15), and where F is defined in Equation (8.17). Then, $\mathbf{D}$ is symmetric and positive semi-definite.

Proof: See Appendix 8C.

Using the fact that the GPEP is a BVIP (Theorem 8B.3), and using the fact that the Jacobian $\mathbf{D}$ is symmetric and positive semi-definite (Theorem 8B.4), we now prove that the GPEP prices based on the $J + S$ orders are unique.

Theorem 8B.5: For the GPEP with $J + S$ orders, the derivative strategy prices $\pi(\mathbf{x})$ and the state prices $\mathbf{p}(\mathbf{x})$ are unique.

Proof: X, as defined in Equation (8.15), is a box. F, as defined in Equation (8.17), is continuously differentiable over X, and Theorem 8B.4 implies that $\mathbf{D}$, the Jacobian of F, is symmetric and positive semi-definite. Therefore, Theorem 8B.2 implies that there exists a solution to the BVIP(F, X), and for any solution $\mathbf{x}$ to the BVIP, $F(\mathbf{x})$ is unique. Since $F(\mathbf{x})$ is unique, and since the limit prices $w_1, w_2, \ldots, w_{J+S}$ and the sides $b_1, b_2, \ldots, b_{J+S}$ are fixed, there exists a single solution $\pi(\mathbf{x})$ (even though there may be multiple $\mathbf{x}$'s that are solutions) to the BVIP(F, X). For that unique $\pi(\mathbf{x})$, $\mathbf{p}(\mathbf{x})$ is simply the last S rows of the $J + S$ rows of $\pi(\mathbf{x})$. Thus, $\mathbf{p}(\mathbf{x})$ is unique as well.

Theorem 8B.6: For the GPEP with the J customer orders (and without the S pseudo-orders), the state and derivative strategy prices are unique and are equal to the state and derivative strategy prices, respectively, for the GPEP with $J + S$ customer orders.

Proof: The additional S pseudo-orders do not impact the state prices, the customer fills, or the derivative strategy prices since the S pseudo-orders are worse than the market and have zero fill. Consequently, the state and derivative strategy prices in the auction based on the J customer orders are equal to the state and derivative strategy prices in the auction based on the $J + S$ orders. Theorem 8B.5 implies that they are unique.

APPENDIX 8C: JACOBIAN PROPERTIES

This appendix proves Theorem 8B.4, namely that $\mathbf{D}$ – the Jacobian of F from Equation (8.17) – is symmetric and positive semi-definite. Appendix 8B used this result to show that the GPEP has unique state and derivative strategy prices. Our proof proceeds as follows. Section 8C.1 expresses the Jacobian of F as a function of various quantities including $\tilde{\mathbf{D}}$, the Jacobian of the state prices with respect to the net customer payouts. Section 8C.2 derives certain properties of $\tilde{\mathbf{D}}$. Section 8C.3 completes the proof by analyzing $\mathbf{D}$ using those properties of $\tilde{\mathbf{D}}$.

8C.1   Notation and related formulas

Let $\mathbf{x}, \tilde{\boldsymbol{\pi}}$, and $\tilde{\mathbf{w}}$ denote $J + S$ by 1 column vectors whose elements in the jth row are $x_j, b_j\pi_j$, and $b_j w_j$, respectively, for $j = 1, 2, \ldots, J + S$. Therefore, if the jth order is a buy order, then the jth element of $\tilde{\boldsymbol{\pi}}$ and $\tilde{\mathbf{w}}$ equal π_j and w_j, respectively. Alternatively, if the jth order is a sell order, then the jth element of $\tilde{\boldsymbol{\pi}}$ and $\tilde{\mathbf{w}}$ equal $-\pi_j$ and $-w_j$, respectively. Using this notation, Equation (8.17) can be written in vector form as

$$F(\mathbf{x}) = \tilde{\boldsymbol{\pi}} - \tilde{\mathbf{w}}. \tag{8C.1}$$

As before, let $\mathbf{D}$ denote the Jacobian matrix of F with respect to customer fills $\mathbf{x}$, as defined in Equation (8.19). Further, let $\mathbf{y}$ denote the S by 1 column vector of net customer payouts, that is, the sth element of $\mathbf{y}$

equals y_s for $s = 1, 2, \ldots, S$. Therefore,

$$
\begin{aligned}
\mathbf{D} &= \frac{dF(\mathbf{x})}{d\mathbf{x}} \\
&= \frac{d(\tilde{\pi} - \tilde{\mathbf{w}})}{d\mathbf{x}} \\
&= \frac{d\tilde{\pi}}{d\mathbf{x}} \\
&= \frac{d\tilde{\pi}}{d\mathbf{p}} \times \frac{d\mathbf{p}}{d\mathbf{y}} \times \frac{d\mathbf{y}}{d\mathbf{x}},
\end{aligned}
\tag{8C.2}
$$

where the second equality is based on Equation (8C.1), where the third equality follows from the fact that $\tilde{\mathbf{w}}$ is a vector of constants, and where the fourth equality follows from the "matrix chain rule." Let $\tilde{\mathbf{A}}$ denote the $J + S$ by S matrix with element $a_{j,s}b_j$ in the jth row and sth column for $j = 1, 2, \ldots, J + S$ and for $s = 1, 2, \ldots, S$. Therefore,

$$
\tilde{\mathbf{A}} =
\begin{bmatrix}
a_{1,1}b_1 & a_{1,2}b_1 & a_{1,3}b_1 & \cdots & a_{1,s}b_1 \\
a_{2,1}b_2 & a_{2,2}b_2 & a_{2,3}b_2 & \cdots & a_{2,s}b_2 \\
a_{3,1}b_3 & a_{3,2}b_3 & a_{3,3}b_3 & \cdots & a_{3,s}b_3 \\
\vdots & \vdots & \vdots & \ddots & \vdots \\
a_{J+S,1}b_{J+S} & a_{J+S,2}b_{J+S} & a_{J+S,3}b_{J+S} & \cdots & a_{J+S,s}b_{J+S}
\end{bmatrix}.
\tag{8C.3}
$$

To simplify Equation (8C.2), note that

$$
\tilde{\pi} = \tilde{\mathbf{A}} \times \mathbf{p}.
\tag{8C.4}
$$

This is equivalent to the matrix version of Equation (7.9).[23] Since $\tilde{\mathbf{A}}$ is a matrix of constants, Equation (8C.4) implies that

$$
\frac{d\tilde{\pi}}{d\mathbf{p}} = \tilde{\mathbf{A}}.
\tag{8C.5}
$$

Now, let $\tilde{\mathbf{D}}$ be the Jacobian of state prices with respect to net customer payouts. Therefore, $\tilde{\mathbf{D}}$ is an S by S square matrix such that

$$
\tilde{\mathbf{D}} \equiv \frac{d\mathbf{p}}{d\mathbf{y}}
$$

$$
= \begin{bmatrix}
\frac{\partial p_1}{\partial y_1} & \frac{\partial p_1}{\partial y_2} & \frac{\partial p_1}{\partial y_3} & \cdots & \frac{\partial p_1}{\partial y_S} \\[6pt]
\frac{\partial p_2}{\partial y_1} & \frac{\partial p_2}{\partial y_2} & \frac{\partial p_2}{\partial y_3} & \cdots & \frac{\partial p_2}{\partial y_S} \\[6pt]
\frac{\partial p_3}{\partial y_1} & \frac{\partial p_3}{\partial y_2} & \frac{\partial p_3}{\partial y_3} & \cdots & \frac{\partial p_3}{\partial y_S} \\[6pt]
\vdots & \vdots & \vdots & \ddots & \vdots \\[6pt]
\frac{\partial p_S}{\partial y_1} & \frac{\partial p_S}{\partial y_2} & \frac{\partial p_S}{\partial y_3} & \cdots & \frac{\partial p_S}{\partial y_S}
\end{bmatrix} .
\tag{8C.6}
$$

Further, note that

$$
\mathbf{y} = \tilde{\mathbf{A}}^{\mathrm{T}} \mathbf{x}
\tag{8C.7}
$$

This is the matrix version of Equation (7.13). Thus, we have that

$$
\frac{d\mathbf{y}}{d\mathbf{x}} = \tilde{\mathbf{A}}^{\mathrm{T}} .
\tag{8C.8}
$$

Therefore,

$$
\begin{aligned}
\mathbf{D} &= \frac{d\tilde{\pi}}{d\mathbf{p}} \times \frac{d\mathbf{p}}{d\mathbf{y}} \times \frac{d\mathbf{y}}{d\mathbf{x}} \\
&= \tilde{\mathbf{A}} \times \tilde{\mathbf{D}} \times \tilde{\mathbf{A}}^{\mathrm{T}},
\end{aligned}
\tag{8C.9}
$$

where the second equality follows by Equation (8C.5), the definition of $\tilde{\mathbf{D}}$ in Equation (8C.6), and Equation (8C.8).

To prove that $\mathbf{D}$ is symmetric and positive semi-definite, we first study the properties of $\tilde{\mathbf{D}}$.

8C.2 Properties of $\tilde{\mathbf{D}}$

We now derive three properties of $\tilde{\mathbf{D}}$, and we interpret these properties below.

Property 1: Each column of $\tilde{\mathbf{D}}$ sums to zero.

Derivation: Note that the state prices sum to one, that is,

$$\sum_{s=1}^{S} p_s = 1. \tag{8C.10}$$

Taking the partial derivative of this equation with respect to $y_{\tilde{s}}$ gives us that

$$\sum_{s=1}^{S} \frac{\partial p_s}{\partial y_{\tilde{s}}} = 0 \quad \tilde{s} = 1, 2, \ldots, S. \tag{8C.11}$$

Note that the summation on the left-hand side is the $\tilde{s}$th column of $\tilde{\mathbf{D}}$, so the sum of the $\tilde{s}$th column of $\tilde{\mathbf{D}}$ equals zero. Since $\tilde{s}$ was selected arbitrarily, property 1 holds. Since the state prices always sum to one in equilibrium regardless of the net customer payouts, the sum of state price changes due to a change in net customer payouts in a particular state must always be zero.

To help derive properties 2 and 3 below, we now develop an expression for $dp_s/dy_{\tilde{s}}$, the element in the sth row and the $\tilde{s}$th column of $\tilde{\mathbf{D}}$, where s and $\tilde{s}$ may or may not be equal. Note that the self-hedging conditions of Equation (8.5) imply that

$$p_s(M - y_s) - \theta_s = 0 \quad s = 1, 2, \ldots, S. \tag{8C.12}$$

Taking the partial derivative of both sides of Equation (8C.12) with respect to $y_{\tilde{s}}$ implies that

$$\frac{\partial (p_s(M - y_s) - \theta_s)}{\partial y_{\tilde{s}}} = 0 \quad s, \tilde{s} = 1, 2, \ldots, S. \tag{8C.13}$$

The product rule and the fact that θ_s is a constant imply that

$$\frac{\partial p_s}{\partial y_{\tilde{s}}}(M - y_s) + p_s \left(\frac{\partial M}{\partial y_{\tilde{s}}} - \frac{\partial y_s}{\partial y_{\tilde{s}}} \right) = 0 \quad s, \tilde{s} = 1, 2, \ldots, S. \tag{8C.14}$$

Note that

$$\frac{\partial y_s}{\partial y_{\tilde{s}}} = \begin{cases} 1 & \text{if } s = \tilde{s} \\ 0 & \text{if } s \neq \tilde{s} \end{cases}$$
$$= I[\tilde{s} = s], \tag{8C.15}$$

where I denotes the indicator function. Equations (8C.14) and (8C.15) imply that

$$\frac{\partial p_s}{\partial y_{\tilde{s}}}(M - y_s) + p_s \left(\frac{\partial M}{\partial y_{\tilde{s}}} - I[\tilde{s} = s] \right) = 0 \quad s, \tilde{s} = 1, 2, \ldots, S.$$

(8C.16)

Note that $(M - y_s)$ is strictly positive since the net premium M in the auction is strictly greater than net customer payouts y_s in state s for $s = 1, 2, \ldots, S$. Based on this fact and rearranging Equation (8C.16) to solve for $\partial p_s / \partial y_{\tilde{s}}$ gives us that

$$\frac{\partial p_s}{\partial y_{\tilde{s}}} = -\frac{p_s}{(M - y_s)} \left(\frac{\partial M}{\partial y_{\tilde{s}}} - I[\tilde{s} = s] \right) \quad s, \tilde{s} = 1, 2, \ldots, S. \quad (8C.17)$$

Now, the self-hedging equation implies that

$$\frac{\theta_s}{M - y_s} = p_s \quad s = 1, 2, \ldots, S.$$

(8C.18)

Multiplying both sides of this equation by p_s / θ_s gives us that

$$\frac{p_s}{M - y_s} = \frac{p_s^2}{\theta_s} \quad s = 1, 2, \ldots, S.$$

(8C.19)

Therefore, substituting for $p_s/(M - y_s)$ from Equation (8C.19) into Equation (8C.17) gives us that

$$\frac{\partial p_s}{\partial y_{\tilde{s}}} = -\frac{p_s^2}{\theta_s} \left(\frac{\partial M}{\partial y_{\tilde{s}}} - I[\tilde{s} = s] \right) \quad s, \tilde{s} = 1, 2, \ldots, S. \quad (8C.20)$$

Now, summing the left-hand side of Equation (8C.20) over s equals 1 to S implies that

$$\sum_{s=1}^{S} \frac{\partial p_s}{\partial y_{\tilde{s}}} = -\sum_{s=1}^{S} \frac{p_s^2}{\theta_s} \left(\frac{\partial M}{\partial y_{\tilde{s}}} - I[\tilde{s} = s] \right) \quad \tilde{s} = 1, 2, \ldots, S$$

$$= -\left(\sum_{s=1}^{S} \frac{p_s^2}{\theta_s} \frac{\partial M}{\partial y_{\tilde{s}}} \right) + \frac{p_{\tilde{s}}^2}{\theta_{\tilde{s}}} \quad \tilde{s} = 1, 2, \ldots, S$$

$$= -\frac{\partial M}{\partial y_{\tilde{s}}} \left(\sum_{s=1}^{S} \frac{p_s^2}{\theta_s} \right) + \frac{p_{\tilde{s}}^2}{\theta_{\tilde{s}}} \quad \tilde{s} = 1, 2, \ldots, S, \quad (8C.21)$$

where the second equality follows from evaluating the indicator function I, and the third equality follows by algebraic manipulation. Equation (8C.11) gives us that

$$0 = -\frac{\partial M}{\partial y_{\tilde{s}}}\left(\sum_{s=1}^{S}\frac{p_s^2}{\theta_s}\right) + \frac{p_{\tilde{s}}^2}{\theta_{\tilde{s}}}. \tag{8C.22}$$

Solving for $\partial M/\partial y_{\tilde{s}}$ implies that

$$\frac{\partial M}{\partial y_{\tilde{s}}} = \frac{\left(p_{\tilde{s}}^2/\theta_{\tilde{s}}\right)}{\sum_{s=1}^{S}p_s^2/\theta_s}. \tag{8C.23}$$

Thus, substituting for $\partial M/\partial y_{\tilde{s}}$ into Equation (8C.20) gives us that

$$\frac{\partial p_s}{\partial y_{\tilde{s}}} = -\frac{p_s^2}{\theta_s}\left(\frac{\partial M}{\partial y_{\tilde{s}}} - I[\tilde{s} = s]\right) \quad s,\tilde{s} = 1,2,\ldots,S$$

$$= -\frac{p_s^2}{\theta_s}\left(\frac{p_{\tilde{s}}^2/\theta_{\tilde{s}}}{\sum_{s=1}^{S}p_s^2/\theta_s} - I[\tilde{s} = s]\right) \quad s,\tilde{s} = 1,2,\ldots,S. \tag{8C.24}$$

Using Equation (8C.24), we can now derive properties 2 and 3.

Property 2: Every diagonal element of $\tilde{\mathbf{D}}$ is greater than zero.

Derivation: To examine the sth diagonal element of $\tilde{\mathbf{D}}$, set $\tilde{s} = s$ and so $I[\tilde{s} = s] = 1$. In this case, Equation (8C.24) simplifies as follows:

$$\frac{\partial p_s}{\partial y_s} = \frac{p_s^2}{\theta_s}\left(1 - \frac{\left(p_s^2/\theta_s\right)}{\sum_{s=1}^{S}p_s^2/\theta_s}\right) \quad s = 1,2,\ldots,S. \tag{8C.25}$$

Since θ_s and p_s are positive for $s = 1,2,\ldots,S$, we note that

$$0 < \frac{p_s^2}{\theta_s} < \sum_{s=1}^{S}\frac{p_s^2}{\theta_s} \quad s = 1,2,\ldots,S. \tag{8C.26}$$

Dividing this equation by $\sum_{s=1}^{S}(p_s^2/\theta_s)$ gives us that

$$0 < \frac{\left(p_s^2/\theta_s\right)}{\sum_{s=1}^{S}p_s^2/\theta_s} < 1 \quad s = 1,2,\ldots,S \tag{8C.27}$$

which implies that

$$0 < \left(1 - \frac{\left(p_s^2/\theta_s\right)}{\sum_{s=1}^{S} p_s^2/\theta_s}\right). \tag{8C.28}$$

Therefore, Equations (8C.25) and (8C.28) imply that

$$\frac{\partial p_s}{\partial y_s} > 0 \quad s = 1, 2, \ldots, S. \tag{8C.29}$$

Hence, each diagonal element of $\tilde{\mathbf{D}}$ is greater than zero and property 2 holds. Property 2 shows that an increase in net customer payouts for a given state increases the price of that state. Thus, property 2 shows that changes in state prices are driven by changes in net customer payouts in those states, reflecting the market-driven nature of the state prices in a parimutuel derivatives auction.

Property 3: Every off-diagonal element of $\tilde{\mathbf{D}}$ is less than zero.

Derivation: Now if $\tilde{s} \neq s$, then $I[\tilde{s} = s] = 0$ and so Equation (8C.24) simplifies as follows:

$$\frac{\partial p_s}{\partial y_{\tilde{s}}} = -\frac{p_s^2 p_{\tilde{s}}^2 / (\theta_s \theta_{\tilde{s}})}{\sum_{s=1}^{S} \frac{p_s^2}{\theta_s}} \quad s, \tilde{s} = 1, 2, \ldots, S, s \neq \tilde{s} \tag{8C.30}$$

Since θ_s and p_s are positive for $s = 1, 2, \ldots, S$, Equation (8C.30) implies that

$$\frac{\partial p_s}{\partial y_{\tilde{s}}} < 0 \quad s, \tilde{s} = 1, 2, \ldots, S, s \neq \tilde{s}. \tag{8C.31}$$

Thus, each off-diagonal element of $\tilde{\mathbf{D}}$ is less than zero and so property 3 holds. Consequently, an increase in net customer payouts for a given state decreases the price of the other states, that is, all prices renormalize so an increase in price for a given state due to increased customer payouts for that state simultaneously depresses all other state prices.

Based on these three properties, we now prove the following theorem.

Theorem 8C.1: $\tilde{\mathbf{D}}$ is symmetric and positive semi-definite.

Proof: Examining Equation (8C.30), we can conclude that

$$\frac{\partial p_s}{\partial y_{\tilde{s}}} = \frac{\partial p_{\tilde{s}}}{\partial y_s} \quad s, \tilde{s} = 1, 2, \ldots, S, s \neq \tilde{s}. \tag{8C.32}$$

Therefore, $\tilde{\mathbf{D}}$ is symmetric. As discussed in Appendix B in Ayazifar (2002), matrices that exhibit properties 1, 2, and 3 are a special class of matrices called "Laplacian."[24] Since $\tilde{\mathbf{D}}$ is Laplacian, Corollary 3.19 of Ayazifar (2002, p. 53) implies that $\tilde{\mathbf{D}}$ is positive semi-definite.[25]

8C.3 Properties of D

Based on the properties of $\tilde{\mathbf{D}}$, we now prove the following theorem for D, the Jacobian of F with respect to the fills.

Theorem 8C.2: D is symmetric and positive semi-definite.

Proof: This proof proceeds from first principles based on the properties of $\tilde{\mathbf{D}}$. To show that D is symmetric, we need to check that $\mathbf{D}^{\mathrm{T}} = \mathbf{D}$. Recall that

$$\mathbf{D} = \tilde{\mathbf{A}}\tilde{\mathbf{D}}\tilde{\mathbf{A}}^{\mathrm{T}}. \tag{8C.33}$$

Therefore,

$$\begin{aligned}
\mathbf{D}^{\mathrm{T}} &= (\tilde{\mathbf{A}}\tilde{\mathbf{D}}\tilde{\mathbf{A}}^{\mathrm{T}})^{\mathrm{T}} \\
&= (\tilde{\mathbf{A}}^{\mathrm{T}})^{\mathrm{T}}\tilde{\mathbf{D}}^{\mathrm{T}}\tilde{\mathbf{A}}^{\mathrm{T}} \\
&= \tilde{\mathbf{A}}\tilde{\mathbf{D}}^{\mathrm{T}}\tilde{\mathbf{A}}^{\mathrm{T}} \\
&= \tilde{\mathbf{A}}\tilde{\mathbf{D}}\tilde{\mathbf{A}}^{\mathrm{T}} \\
&= \mathbf{D}, \tag{8C.34}
\end{aligned}$$

where the second equality follows from the fact that the transpose of a product of matrices is the product of the transpose of each matrix with the order of multiplication reversed, where the third equality follows from the fact that a matrix transposed twice equals the original matrix, where the fourth equality follows from the fact that $\tilde{\mathbf{D}}$ is symmetric, and the fifth equality follows from the formula for D in Equation (8C.33). Thus D is symmetric. To show that D is positive semi-definite, let $\mathbf{z}$ be an arbitrary non-zero column vector with $J + S$ rows and define $\mathbf{q}$ as follows:

$$\mathbf{q} \equiv \tilde{\mathbf{A}}^{\mathrm{T}}\mathbf{z}. \tag{8C.35}$$

Because $\tilde{\mathbf{D}}$ is positive semi-definite, it must be the case that

$$\mathbf{q}^{\mathrm{T}}\tilde{\mathbf{D}}\mathbf{q} \geq 0. \tag{8C.36}$$

Substituting for **q** from Equation (8C.35) yields that

$$(\tilde{\mathbf{A}}^T \mathbf{z})^T \tilde{\mathbf{D}} (\tilde{\mathbf{A}}^T \mathbf{z}) \geq 0 \qquad\qquad (8C.37)$$

which implies that

$$\mathbf{z}^T \tilde{\mathbf{A}} \tilde{\mathbf{D}} \tilde{\mathbf{A}}^T \mathbf{z} \geq 0. \qquad\qquad (8C.38)$$

Therefore, substituting for **D** from Equation (8C.33) into Equation (8C.38) gives us that

$$\mathbf{z}^T \mathbf{D} \mathbf{z} \geq 0. \qquad\qquad (8C.39)$$

Since **z** is arbitrary, Equation (8C.39) implies that **D** is positive semi-definite. This concludes the proof.

CHAPTER 9

Mathematical Properties of Customer Fills in the Parimutuel Equilibrium

For a given set of opening orders and customer orders (the "auction inputs"), the Parimutuel Equilibrium Problem (PEP) has a *unique* set of state prices and derivative strategy prices, as shown in Chapter 8. For a given set of auction inputs, Chapter 8 also shows that there always exists at least one vector of customer fills that satisfy the PEP.[1] There can, in certain cases, be *multiple* vectors of customer fills that satisfy the PEP for a given set of auction inputs. In this chapter, we describe the conditions under which such multiple vectors of customer fills exist.

This chapter proceeds as follows. Section 9.1 motivates the discussion with an auction in which there exist multiple vectors of customer fills. Section 9.2 provides three theorems characterizing the multiple vectors of customer fills. Section 9.3 defines the concept of "competing orders," and Section 9.4 presents two theorems that show that competing orders are required for the existence of multiple vectors of customer fills.[2] Section 9.5 uses linear algebra to present theorems that relate to multiple vectors of customer fills and competing orders.

9.1 EXAMPLE WITH MULTIPLE VECTORS OF CUSTOMER FILLS

We begin in Section 9.1.1 by reviewing the PEP equilibrium conditions. Afterwards, Section 9.1.2 presents an example auction which has multiple vectors of customer fills that satisfy the PEP conditions.

9.1.1 Review of the PEP constraints

Recall from Equation (6.25) that the market exposure per contract for customer order j is defined as

$$
\tilde{\lambda}_j \equiv
\begin{cases}
\pi_j & \text{if customer order } j \text{ is a buy of an option} \\
\pi_j - k_1 & \text{if customer order } j \text{ is a buy of a range forward} \\
\overline{d}_j - \pi_j & \text{if customer order } j \text{ is a sell of an option} \\
k_E - \pi_j & \text{if customer order } j \text{ is a sell of a range forward}
\end{cases}
\quad j = 1, 2, \ldots, J.
$$

$$(9.1)$$

As shown in Equation (6.28), the objective of the PEP is to choose the customer fills that maximize total market exposure $\tilde{M}$, that is,

$$
\max_{x_1, x_2, \ldots, x_J} \tilde{M} = \max_{x_1, x_2, \ldots, x_J} \left(\sum_{s=1}^{S} \theta_s + \sum_{j=1}^{J} x_j \tilde{\lambda}_j \right)
\tag{9.2}
$$

subject to the following four constraints: [3]

$$
\left.
\begin{array}{l}
b_j w_j < b_j \pi_j \Rightarrow x_j = 0 \\
b_j w_j = b_j \pi_j \Rightarrow 0 \leq x_j \leq r_j \\
b_j w_j > b_j \pi_j \Rightarrow x_j = r_j
\end{array}
\right\} \quad j = 1, 2, \ldots, J,
\tag{9.3}
$$

$$
p_s > 0 \quad s = 1, 2, \ldots, S,
\tag{9.4}
$$

$$
\sum_{s=1}^{S} p_s = 1,
\tag{9.5}
$$

$$
\frac{\theta_s}{p_s} + y_s = M \quad s = 1, 2, \ldots, S.
\tag{9.6}
$$

Equation (9.3) represents the "limit-order" conditions. Equations (9.4) and (9.5) are "no-arbitrage" conditions that restrict the state prices to be positive and to sum to one. Equation (9.6) contains the "self-hedging" conditions, which ensure that in every state the net payouts equal the net premium collected.

9.1.2 A new auction example

The Consumer Price Index (CPI) example discussed in Chapters 5, 6, and 7 had a unique vector of customer fills. In other words, for the submitted

Table 9.1 The customer orders and replication weights for the parimutuel derivatives auction on CPI

Customer order j	Derivative strategy	Strike(s)	Side b_j	Requested number of contracts r_j	Limit price w_j	$d_j(u_1)$ or $a_{j,1}$	$d_j(u_2)$ or $a_{j,2}$	$d_j(u_3)$ or $a_{j,3}$	$d_j(u_4)$ or $a_{j,4}$
1	Digital call	0.3	1	100,000	0.41	0	0	1	1
2	Digital put	0.2	1	125,000	0.20	1	0	0	0
3	Digital range	0.2 and 0.3	1	125,000	0.40	0	1	0	0
4	Digital put	0.3	1	125,000	0.60	1	1	0	0

opening orders and customer orders, there exists only one vector of customer fills that satisfy the PEP conditions.[4] Thus, this example cannot be used for illustrating when there are multiple vectors of customer fills. Consequently, to illustrate the case of multiple customer fills, we now introduce a related example. As before, let the underlying be the monthly percentage change in US CPI, let the tick size be $\rho = 0.1$, and let the auction strikes be 0.2, 0.3, and 0.4. Customers submit $J = 4$ orders, all of which are buy orders for digital options. Table 9.1 displays information on these customer orders, including these orders' replication weights. These four customer orders are identical to the four customer orders in the example in Section 8.1.4, except that the orders here are limit orders, not market orders.

Based on the auction strikes of 0.2, 0.3, and 0.4 and the tick size of 0.1, Equation (5.18) implies that there are $S = 4$ state claims. We display information on the state claims and opening orders for this auction in the first five columns of Table 9.2.[5] Based on these opening orders and the customer orders, we can solve for the state prices using the algorithm described in Chapter 7. These state prices are unique (as proven in Chapter 8), and they are displayed in column six of Table 9.2. We can check that the state prices are positive and sum to one, satisfying the PEP no-arbitrage restrictions from Equations (9.4) and (9.5).

The first four columns of Table 9.3 display requested information from the four customer orders in the auction. The fifth column of Table 9.3 shows the equilibrium prices of the requested options. We calculate the option prices based on (1) the replication weights from the last four columns of Table 9.1; (2) the state prices from column six of Table 9.2; and (3) the following equation:

$$\pi_j = \sum_{s=1}^{4} a_{j,s} p_s \quad j = 1, 2, 3, 4. \tag{9.7}$$

Table 9.2 Information on the state claims and the opening orders for the parimutuel derivatives auction on CPI

State claim s	State	Strategy for state claim	Strike(s)	Opening-order premium θ_s in \$	State price p_s
1	$U < 0.2$	Digital put	0.2	100	0.2000
2	$U = 0.2$	Digital range	0.2 and 0.3	200	0.4000
3	$U = 0.3$	Digital range	0.3 and 0.4	200	0.2667
4	$U \geq 0.4$	Digital call	0.4	100	0.1333

Table 9.3 Information on the customer orders for the parimutuel derivatives auction on CPI

Customer order j	Derivative strategy	Strike(s)	Side b_j	Derivative strategy price π_j	First set of fills $x_{1,j}$	Second set of fills $x_{2,j}$	Third set of fills $x_{3,j}$
1	Digital call	0.3	1	0.40	100,000	100,000	100,000
2	Digital put	0.2	1	0.20	0	100,250	50,125
3	Digital range	0.2 and 0.3	1	0.40	0	100,250	50,125
4	Digital put	0.3	1	0.60	100,250	0	50,125

As we know from Chapter 8, the state prices and the prices of the options are unique. For this particular example, there are multiple vectors of customer fills possible, and columns six, seven, and eight of Table 9.3 show three such vectors of customer fills.[6] For notation, let x_1, x_2, and x_3 denote those three vectors of customer fills. Let $x_{n,j}$ denote the value of the nth vector in the jth row (for the jth customer order) for $n = 1, 2, 3$ and $j = 1, 2, 3, 4$.

To confirm that each of these vectors of customer fills satisfy the PEP conditions, we need to check that each of these vectors meet the PEP limit-order conditions, the PEP self-hedging conditions, and maximize market exposure subject to the PEP restrictions.

The PEP limit-order conditions: The first customer order is better than the market, and it is fully filled in all three vectors ($x_{1,1} = x_{2,1} = x_{3,1} = r_1 = 100,000$). The second, third, and fourth customer orders are all at the market, and their fills are all greater than or equal to zero and less

Table 9.4 State-payout information for the parimutuel derivatives auction on CPI

State claim s	Payout to the sth opening order if sth state claim expires in-the-money θ_s/p_s in $	Formula for $y_{n,s}$ based on Equation (9.8)	Net customer payouts if sth state claim expires in-the-money $y_{n,s}$ in $	Total payouts if the sth state claim expires in-the-money θ_s/p_s $+y_{n,s}$ in $
1	500	$x_{n,2} + x_{n,4}$	100,250	100,750
2	500	$x_{n,3} + x_{n,4}$	100,250	100,750
3	750	$x_{n,1}$	100,000	100,750
4	750	$x_{n,1}$	100,000	100,750

than or equal to their requested amounts. Thus, these three vectors of customer fills satisfy the limit-order logic of Equation (9.3).

The PEP self-hedging conditions: We now check that the net payouts equal the net premium regardless of the value of CPI (Equation (9.6)).

Net payouts: The second column of Table 9.4 shows the payouts for the opening orders based on the state prices and the opening-order allocations. Let $y_{n,s}$ denote the net customer payout in the sth state based on the nth vector of customers fills. Then, the formula for the net customer payouts is

$$y_{n,s} = \sum_{j=1}^{4} a_{j,s} b_j x_{n,j} \quad n = 1, 2, 3 \text{ and } s = 1, 2, 3, 4. \tag{9.8}$$

Using Equation (9.8) and the replication weights from the last four columns of Table 9.1, we derive the formulas for the net customer payouts, which are displayed in column three of Table 9.4. Using these formulas and the customer fills from Table 9.3, it is straightforward to check that the net customer payouts are equal for all three vectors of customer fills.[7] The fourth column of Table 9.4 shows these net customer payouts. Column five of Table 9.4 shows the payouts if each state occurs, which is simply the sum of the second column and the fourth column. Note that the net payouts equal $100,750 for all four states.

Net premium collected: All four customer orders are buys of options. The premium paid for an option is the option's fill multiplied by the option's price. Columns two, three, and four of Table 9.5 display the

Table 9.5 Customer premium amounts for the parimutuel derivatives auction on CPI

Customer order j	Premium for first vector of fills $x_{1,j}\lambda_j$ in $	Premium for second vector of fills $x_{2,j}\lambda_j$ in $	Premium for third vector of fills $x_{3,j}\lambda_j$ in $
1	40,000	40,000	40,000
2	0	20,050	10,025
3	0	40,100	20,050
4	60,150	0	30,075
Total	100,150	100,150	100,150

premiums paid for each of the three vectors of customer fills. The final row of each column displays the total premium paid by the customers for each vector. Note that the total premium paid is $100,150 for all three vectors of customer fills. Since the opening orders total $600 in premium, the total auction premium equals $100,750.

Since the net payouts in every state equal $100,750, and the net premium collected equals $100,750, the self-hedging conditions hold.

Maximizing market exposure: Since all customer orders are buys of options, the premium paid for each option is equal to the order's market exposure. Thus, the market exposure in the auction is equal to the total premium in the auction, which is $100,750. It can be shown that this amount is the maximum amount of market exposure for this auction.

Since these PEP conditions are met, these three vectors of customer fills are all solutions to the PEP.

This example leads us to observe the following:

1. The customer orders with different fills in the three equilibria are the second, third, and fourth customer orders, which are all at the market. In contrast, the customer order that has the same fill in all three equilibria, the first customer order, is not at the market.

2. None of the three equilibria have fills that are all greater than or equal to the fills from either of the other two equilibria. Instead, there is a tradeoff between the fills across the three equilibria.

3. The three vectors of customer fills are related in that the average of an order's fill in the first and second equilibria equals the order's fill in the third equilibria.

Section 9.2 presents theorems that show that these three results hold more generally.[8]

9.2 THEOREMS RELATED TO MULTIPLE VECTORS OF CUSTOMER FILLS

The previous section showed (by way of an example) that there can be multiple vectors of customer fills for a given set of auction inputs. We now present three related theorems.

Recall from Chapter 8 that for a particular set of auction inputs, the derivative strategy prices are unique. So, even if there exist multiple vectors of customer fills for a given set of auction inputs, the limit-order logic of Equation (9.3) implies that

1. A customer order that is worse than the market in one vector of customer fills is worse than the market in every vector of customer fills. Therefore, this customer order's fill equals zero in every vector of customer fills.

2. A customer order that is at the market in one vector of customer fills is at the market in every vector of customer fills.

3. A customer order that is better than the market in one vector of customer fills is better than the market in every vector of customer fills. Therefore, this customer order's fill equals its requested amount in every vector of customer fills.

Because of these results, the following theorem holds.

Theorem 9.1: If there exist multiple vectors of customer fills for a given set of auction inputs, then these fills only differ for customer orders that are at the market.[9]

Thus, if there exist multiple vectors of customer fills, fills can only differ for customer orders that are at the market. For all vectors of customer fills, customer orders that are better than the market are fully filled, and customer orders that are worse than the market receive no fill. For example, note that the first customer order has a limit price of $w_1 = 0.41$ (column six of Table 9.1) and a market price of $\pi_1 = 0.40$ (column five of Table 9.3). Theorem 9.1 implies that the first customer order is fully filled for every vector of customer fills. This is the case with the three vectors of customer fills in columns six, seven, and eight of Table 9.3. We can check that customer orders two, three, and four are at the market, and so the fact that they have different fills in the three vectors is consistent with this theorem.

Theorem 9.2: For a given set of auction inputs, let x_1 and x_2 be two distinct J by 1 column vector of customer fills. There exists a customer order whose fill in the first vector is greater than its fill in the second vector. Similarly, there exists a customer order whose fill in the second vector is greater than its fill in the first vector.

This theorem implies that there is a *tradeoff* between vectors of fills of customer orders in the PEP. At least one fill for a particular customer order in the first vector will be above the fill for that customer order in the second vector, and visa versa. For illustration, note that for the first vector of fills listed in Table 9.3, the fourth customer order receives a fill of 100,250 contracts ($x_{1,4} = 100, 250$), while in the second vector of fills, the fourth customer order receives no fill ($x_{2,4} = 0$). Consequently, the fill for the fourth customer order is greater in the first vector than in the second vector ($x_{1,4} > x_{2,4}$). Next, note that for the first vector of customer fills, the second customer order receives no fill ($x_{1,2} = 0$), while for the second vector, the second customer order receive fills of 100,250 contracts ($x_{2,2} = 100, 250$). Therefore, the second customer order has a fill in the second vector that is greater than its fill in the first vector ($x_{2,2} > x_{1,2}$). Thus, these two vectors of customer fills illustrate the tradeoff between different customer fills when there are multiple vectors of customer fills.

This theorem implies that, for a particular set of auction inputs, there cannot exist two vectors, where the jth element in the first vector is greater than or equal to the jth element in the second vector for every j from 1 to J. Why is this never the case? Recall from Equation (9.2) that the PEP maximizes market exposure. Consequently, any two equilibrium vectors of customer fills (for a given set of auction inputs) have the same market exposure. For example, all three vectors of customer fills in the example from Section 9.1.2 lead to market exposure (which includes the contribution of the opening orders) of $100,750 (see Table 9.4). Recall that market exposure is a linear and increasing function of each customer fill by Equation (9.2). Thus, two distinct vectors of customer fills with the same market exposure must each have a customer order with one fill higher (or lower) than the other.

Theorem 9.3: Let x_1 and x_2 be unique vectors of customer fills for a particular PEP. Define x_3 as

$$x_3 = \alpha x_1 + (1 - \alpha)x_2, \tag{9.9}$$

where α is such that $0 < \alpha < 1$. Then, x_3 is a vector of customer fills that satisfy the PEP conditions.

This theorem implies that for a particular set of auction inputs, a "convex" combination of any two vectors of customer fills equals a third vector of customer fills. Since α can equal any value between zero and one, this theorem further implies that if there are two vectors of customer fills for a given set of auction inputs, then there are an infinite number of vectors of customer fills.

To illustrate this theorem, let x_1 and x_2 denote the column vectors with four rows of customer fills from columns six and seven of Table 9.3, respectively. Therefore,

$$x_1 = \begin{bmatrix} 100,000 \\ 0 \\ 0 \\ 100,250 \end{bmatrix} \tag{9.10}$$

and

$$x_2 = \begin{bmatrix} 100,000 \\ 100,250 \\ 100,250 \\ 0 \end{bmatrix}. \tag{9.11}$$

Now, set α equal to 0.5. Using Equation (9.9), we determine that

$$x_3 = \alpha x_1 + (1 - \alpha) x_2$$

$$= (0.5) \times \begin{bmatrix} 100,000 \\ 0 \\ 0 \\ 100,250 \end{bmatrix} + (0.5) \times \begin{bmatrix} 100,000 \\ 100,250 \\ 100,250 \\ 0 \end{bmatrix}$$

$$= \begin{bmatrix} 100,000 \\ 50,125 \\ 50,125 \\ 50,125 \end{bmatrix}. \tag{9.12}$$

Theorem 9.3 implies that these fills satisfy the PEP conditions. These customer fills, which are an average of the first and second vectors of customer fills, are displayed in the final column of Table 9.3.[10] Similarly, Theorem 9.3 implies that *any* weighted average of the first and second vectors of customer fills also satisfies the PEP conditions.

9.3   COMPETING ORDERS

To better understand when there are multiple vectors of customer fills for a particular set of auction inputs, we now define what it means for a set of customer orders to compete for available liquidity. As a simple example, customers who are bidding (or offering) on the same derivative are often described as competing with each other for available liquidity (see, e.g., Harris (2003, p. 226)). Our mathematical definition of competing orders includes this situation as a special case. However, orders on one derivative can impact the liquidity in other derivatives in a parimutuel derivatives auction. For instance, in the example of Section 9.1.2, we observed a tradeoff between the fills for the second, third, and fourth customer orders, all of which requested different derivatives. Because of this, we extend the concept of competing orders to include more general cases. Section 9.4 will relate competing orders to theorems regarding multiple vectors of customer fills. Competing orders will have certain similarities to complementary orders, which were introduced in Section 7.3.

We now construct a portfolio (of competing orders) based on the J customer orders in an auction. Assume that $\mathbf{C}$ is a non-empty subset of $\{1, 2, \ldots, J\}$. We use $\mathbf{C}$ to represent a subset of the J customer orders. To illustrate this and related concepts in this section, we will rely upon the auction example from Section 9.1.2, where there were $J = 4$ customer orders. In this case, let $\mathbf{C} = \{2, 3, 4\}$, so $\mathbf{C}$ is comprised of the second, third, and fourth customer orders.

Based on a set of constants $c_1, c_2, \ldots, c_J$, we construct the portfolio as follows for $j = 1, 2, \ldots, J$:

1. The portfolio is long c_j contracts of the derivative requested in the jth customer order if $b_j c_j > 0$;

2. The portfolio has no contracts of the derivative requested in the jth customer order if $b_j c_j = 0$; and

3. The portfolio is short c_j contracts of the derivative requested in the jth customer order if $b_j c_j < 0$.

Table 9.6 shows the portfolio composition based on the sign of c_j and whether the jth customer order is a buy or a sell.

For a set of customer orders $\mathbf{C}$ to be competing orders, they have to satisfy three properties. The first property is that $c_1, c_2, \ldots, c_J$ satisfy the following based on $\mathbf{C}$:

$$\begin{cases} c_j \neq 0 & \text{if } j \in \mathbf{C} \\ c_j = 0 & \text{if } j \notin \mathbf{C} \end{cases} \quad j = 1, 2, \ldots, J. \tag{9.13}$$

Table 9.6 Portfolio composition based on different values of c_j and b_j

Cases	$b_j = 1$	$b_j = -1$
$c_j > 0$	Long c_j contracts of the derivative strategy requested in customer order j	Short c_j contracts of the derivative strategy requested in customer order j
$c_j < 0$	Short c_j contracts of the derivative strategy requested in customer order j	Long c_j contracts of the derivative strategy requested in customer order j

Consequently, c_j is non-zero if and only if $j \in \mathbf{C}$.[11] Returning to our example with $\mathbf{C} = \{2, 3, 4\}$, set $c_1 = 0, c_2 = c_3 = 1$, and $c_4 = -1$. We can check easily that c_1, c_2, c_3, and c_4 satisfy Equation (9.13).

The following equation represents the second property for competing orders:

$$\sum_{j=1}^{J} c_j \tilde{\lambda}_j = 0. \tag{9.14}$$

This condition is that a weighted sum of the market exposures $\tilde{\lambda}_1, \tilde{\lambda}_2, \ldots, \tilde{\lambda}_J$, where the weights are $c_1, c_2, \ldots, c_J$, equals zero. For intuition regarding Equation (9.14), consider the case where the customer orders in $\mathbf{C}$ are all buys of options. In this case, $\tilde{\lambda}_j$ equals π_j for $j \in \mathbf{C}$, and Equation (9.14) becomes

$$\sum_{j=1}^{J} c_j \pi_j = 0. \tag{9.15}$$

Thus, when the customer orders in $\mathbf{C}$ are buys of options, the portfolio of $c_1, c_2, \ldots, c_J$ contracts costs zero premium up front.

To illustrate Equation (9.14), let us return to the auction example from Section 9.1.2. The second customer order is for a digital put struck at 0.2, the third customer order is for a digital range with strikes of 0.2 and 0.3, and the fourth customer order is for a digital put struck at 0.3. Examine the replication weights in Table 9.1, and note that

$$a_{2,s} + a_{3,s} - a_{4,s} = 0 \quad s = 1, 2, 3, 4. \tag{9.16}$$

Multiplying both sides of this equation by p_s gives that

$$a_{2,s}p_s + a_{3,s}p_s - a_{4,s}p_s = 0 \quad s = 1, 2, 3, 4. \tag{9.17}$$

Summing Equation (9.17) from s equals 1 to 4 gives that

$$\sum_{s=1}^{4} a_{2,s}p_s + \sum_{s=1}^{4} a_{3,s}p_s - \sum_{s=1}^{4} a_{4,s}p_s = 0. \tag{9.18}$$

Since these customer orders are for options, Equations (9.7) and (9.18) imply that

$$\pi_2 + \pi_3 - \pi_4 = 0. \tag{9.19}$$

Since these three orders are buys of options, the definition of market exposure from Equation (9.1) implies that

$$\tilde{\lambda}_2 + \tilde{\lambda}_3 - \tilde{\lambda}_4 = 0. \tag{9.20}$$

As before, let $\mathbf{C} = \{2, 3, 4\}, c_1 = 0, c_2 = c_3 = 1$, and $c_4 = -1$. Then,

$$\sum_{j=1}^{4} c_j \tilde{\lambda}_j = 0 \tag{9.21}$$

and so Equation (9.14) holds for this portfolio. Consequently, a portfolio that is long one contract of the digital put struck at 0.2, long one contract of the digital range with strikes of 0.2 and 0.3, and short one contract of a digital put struck at 0.3 costs zero premium up front. Thus, Equations (9.14) and (9.15) hold for these portfolio weights.

As discussed previously in Chapter 6, $\tilde{\lambda}_j$ is positive for every customer order j, and so Equation (9.14) implies that

$$\min[c_1, c_2, \ldots, c_J] < 0, \tag{9.22}$$
$$\max[c_1, c_2, \ldots, c_J] > 0. \tag{9.23}$$

Consequently, at least one of $c_1, c_2, \ldots, c_J$ must be positive and at least one of $c_1, c_2, \ldots, c_J$ must be negative. As we see in a moment, the signs of the contract amounts have a useful interpretation.

The third property for competing orders is that

$$\sum_{j=1}^{J} a_{j,s}b_jc_j = \kappa \quad s = 1, 2, \ldots, S \tag{9.24}$$

for a constant κ. If this equation holds, then a portfolio with contract amounts $c_1, c_2, \ldots, c_J$ has the same payout in every state, and thus this portfolio is risk-free.[12] To check that this equation holds for our canonical example, note that Equation (9.16) implies that

$$a_{2,s}b_2 + a_{3,s}b_3 - a_{4,s}b_4 = 0 \quad s = 1, 2, 3, 4. \tag{9.25}$$

Further, we can check that

$$\sum_{j=1}^{4} a_{j,s}b_jc_j = 0 \quad s = 1, 2, 3, 4. \tag{9.26}$$

Consequently, the portfolio that is long one contract of the digital put struck at 0.2 (the option requested in the second customer order), long one contract of the digital range with strikes of 0.2 and 0.3 (the option requested in the third customer order), and short one contract of the digital put struck at 0.3 (the option requested in the fourth customer order) pays out \$0 in all four states. Therefore, Equation (9.24) holds with $\kappa = 0$.

We say that the customer orders in $\mathbf{C}$ form a set of competing orders if there exist $c_1, c_2, \ldots, c_J$ that satisfy Equations (9.13), (9.14), and (9.24).[13] Table 9.7 shows these the three conditions. Note that competing orders depend on the side of the order and the derivative strategy, but not on the requested amount and the limit price. As we show below, competing orders are vying for access to the same liquidity in a parimutuel derivatives auction. The signs of $c_1, c_2, \ldots, c_J$ are important, and we say that the customer orders that have positive contract amounts "compete directly" against the customer orders that have negative contract amounts.

Table 9.7 The definition of competing orders

In a parimutuel derivatives auction with J customer orders,
a subset of those customer orders $\mathbf{C}$ are competing orders if there
exist $c_1, c_2, \ldots, c_J$ that satisfy all of the following three properties:

Property 1	$\begin{cases} c_j \neq 0 & \text{if } j \in \mathbf{C} \\ c_j = 0 & \text{if } j \notin \mathbf{C} \end{cases} \quad j = 1, 2, \ldots, J$
Property 2	$\sum_{j=1}^{J} c_j \tilde{\lambda}_j = 0$
Property 3	$\sum_{j=1}^{J} a_{j,s}b_jc_j = \kappa \quad s = 1, 2, \ldots, S \quad \text{for a}$ constant κ

To better understand competing orders, we now consider two examples. Recall our example from Section 9.1.2 with $\mathbf{C} = \{2, 3, 4\}$, $c_1 = 0$, $c_2 = c_3 = 1$, and $c_4 = -1$. We checked above that Equations (9.13), (9.14), and (9.24) hold with $\kappa = 0$. Therefore, the second, third, and fourth customer orders are competing orders. Thus, we can create a portfolio based on these three customer orders that costs zero premium up front, and pays out zero in every state (and so is a risk-free portfolio). Since c_2 and c_3 are positive, and c_4 is negative, we say that the second and third customer orders compete directly against the fourth customer order for liquidity. This can be seen explicitly in columns six and seven of Table 9.3, where there is a tradeoff between filling the second and third customer orders, and filling the fourth customer order.

As another example, assume that the first customer order and the second customer order request the same derivative and with the same side. Let $\mathbf{C} = \{1, 2\}$. Let $c_1 = 1$, $c_2 = -1$, and let $c_3 = c_4 = \cdots = c_J = 0$. It is not hard to check that $c_1, c_2, \ldots, c_J$ satisfy Equation (9.13). Since these two customer orders are for the same derivative,

$$\tilde{\lambda}_1 = \tilde{\lambda}_2. \tag{9.27}$$

Therefore, we can check immediately that Equation (9.14) holds. These first two orders are for the same derivative, and so

$$a_{1,s} = a_{2,s} \quad s = 1, 2, \ldots, S \tag{9.28}$$

and since these two orders have the same side

$$b_1 - b_2 = 0 \tag{9.29}$$

which implies that

$$a_{1,s}b_1 - a_{2,s}b_2 = 0 \quad s = 1, 2, \ldots, S \tag{9.30}$$

which further implies that

$$\sum_{j=1}^{J} a_{j,s}b_jc_j = 0 \quad s = 1, 2, \ldots, S. \tag{9.31}$$

Therefore, $c_1, c_2, \ldots, c_J$ satisfy Equation (9.24) with $\kappa = 0$. Since $c_1, c_2, \ldots, c_J$ satisfy Equations (9.13), (9.14), and (9.24), we conclude that the first and second customer orders form a set of competing orders. Further, the first customer order competes directly against the second customer order (since c_1 and c_2 have opposite signs). This analysis shows that orders for the same derivative with the same direction compete directly against each other. Thus, our definition of competing orders handles this special case in a nature way.[14]

It is worth briefly comparing competing orders to complementary orders, a related concept that was introduced in Section 7.3. All complementary orders have non-negative contract amounts, and such orders do in fact complement each other in the sense that their presence can lead to increased volume in the auction (through the linear program). In contrast, competing orders have both positive and negative contract amounts, and as we see in a moment, their existence can lead to multiple vectors of customer fills. Within a set of competing orders, there is a tradeoff between filling customer orders with positive contract amounts and filling customer orders with negative contract amounts. The next section shows that the existence of competing orders is a necessary condition for the existence of multiple vectors of customer fills, because in certain cases, competing orders allow us to increase fills on customer orders in C who have positive (resp., negative) contract amounts and decrease fills on customer orders in C with negative (resp., positive) contract amounts, while still satisfying the PEP equilibrium conditions.

9.4 COMPETING ORDERS AND ADDITIONAL THEOREMS

We now present two theorems that relate multiple vectors of customer fills to competing orders.

Theorem 9.4: If there are multiple vectors of customer fills for a particular set of auction inputs, then there exist a set of customer orders C that satisfy all four of the following conditions:

Condition 1: The customer orders in C are competing orders;

Condition 2: All customer orders in C are at the market;

Condition 3: For any vector of customer fills, at least one of the customer orders that is an element of C is not fully filled;

Condition 4: For any vector of customer fills, at least one of the customer orders that is an element of C has a positive fill.

The first condition is that there are competing customer orders in the auction. Competing orders are a *necessary* condition for multiple vectors of customer fills, because only when competing orders exist, can we increase fills on one set of orders and correspondingly decrease fills on another set of orders, while still satisfying the PEP conditions. The second condition is that the competing customer orders are all at the market. Note that the fill for a customer order that is at the market can vary between zero and its requested amount, and this creates slack to adjust customer fills in equilibrium. In contrast, the fill for a customer order that is better or worse than the market is pinned to a specific value (the order's requested amount or zero, respectively). The third condition, that there exists at least one customer order that is not fully filled, means that there must be "excess demand" for at least one of the derivatives requested for there to be multiple vectors of customer fills.[15] The fourth condition implies that there must exist supply for at least one of the derivatives requested. Without this supply, all competing orders have zero fill, and there is no available liquidity to move between orders.

In any particular auction, there may be multiple sets of competing orders. Theorem 9.4 does not mean that multiple vectors of customer fills imply that *all* sets of competing orders satisfy conditions two, three, and four. This theorem is a narrower result – it states that multiple vectors of customer fills imply that *at least one* set of competing orders satisfy conditions two, three, and four.

We now illustrate Theorem 9.4 using the auction example of Section 9.1.2. In particular, we verify that the four conditions hold for this auction for $\mathbf{C} = \{2, 3, 4\}$. Since we showed that the second, third, and fourth customer orders are competing in Section 9.3, condition 1 is met. Comparing the limit prices in column six of Table 9.1 with the market prices in column five of Table 9.3, we can confirm that the second, third, and fourth customer orders are at the market. Thus, condition 2 is also met for these orders.[16] In all three equilibria listed in Table 9.3, customer orders two, three, and four are less than fully filled so there exists excess demand, and condition 3 is met. Finally, for all three of these vectors of customer fills at least one of the three competing orders has some fill and so condition 4 (the existence of supply) is also satisfied. Consequently, conditions 1 through 4 are satisfied for this example. Therefore, Theorem 9.4 confirms that there exist multiple vectors of customer fills for this particular set of auction inputs.

If there are no competing orders in an auction, then Theorem 9.4 implies that there is exactly one vector of customer fills that satisfies the PEP conditions. If there are competing orders in the auction, then there may be a single vector of customer fills if some of these competing orders are not at the market (and so condition 2 is not met). If these competing orders are at the market and they are all fully filled (and therefore there is no excess demand, and so condition 3 is not met), then there is a single vector of customer fills. Alternatively, if these competing orders are at the market and have zero fill (and therefore there is no supply for those derivatives, and so condition 4 is not met), then once again there is a single vector of customer fills. Thus, based on Theorem 9.4, we conclude that multiple vectors of customer fills exist only in somewhat restrictive conditions.

To illustrate when the conditions of Theorem 9.4 are *not* met (and so there exists a single vector of customer fills), let us return to the auction example from Chapters 5, 6, and 7. Recall that the fourth customer order is a buy of the vanilla capped call struck at 0.2, and recall that the sixth customer order is a buy of the range forward. By examining the replication weights in Table 7.2, we can check that these two orders are competing orders,[17] and they are the only set of competing orders in the auction. However, the sixth customer order is not at the market, so condition 2 of Theorem 9.4 is not satisfied. Thus, there do not exist multiple vectors of customer fills for this auction. In this case, the customer fills listed in column three of Table 7.5 represent the unique vector of customer fills.

Theorem 9.5: Let x_1 and x_2 be distinct vectors of customer fills for a particular set of auction inputs. Let C denote the set of customer orders whose fills differ in these two equilibria. Then, C are competing orders and the scalars $c_1, c_2, \ldots, c_J$ that satisfy Equations (9.13), (9.14), and (9.24) also satisfy

$$c_j = \beta(x_{2,j} - x_{1,j}) \quad j = 1, 2, \ldots, J \tag{9.32}$$

for a constant β that is non-zero.

Theorem 9.5 states that customer orders whose fills differ between two vectors form a competing set. The differences between the two vectors of customer fills are proportional to the c_j's. Thus, the changes in customer fills are closely related to the c_j's, and positive and negative values of the c_j's denote the orders that are competing directly with one another. For instance, for the auction example from Section 9.1.2, let x_1 and x_2 be as defined in Table 9.3. Here, $C = \{2, 3, 4\}$ are competing orders with $c_1 = 0, c_2 = c_3 = 1$, and $c_4 = -1$. Consequently, we can allocate across competing orders, possibly increasing the fills on the second and third customer orders while decreasing the fill on the fourth customer order, or vice versa. In this case, $\beta = 100, 250$.

9.5   RANK CONDITIONS, COMPETING ORDERS, AND MULTIPLE VECTORS OF CUSTOMER FILLS

This section presents three theorems that relate to competing orders and multiple vectors of customer fills. Using linear algebra, these theorems examine the special cases in which either all competing customer orders are buys of options (Theorem 9.6), or all customer orders are buys of options (Theorems 9.7 and 9.8). These special cases can occur in practice, as many customers in parimutuel derivatives auctions are option buyers.

For a given set of auction inputs, let $\mathbf{A}$ be the J by S matrix of replication weights, where $a_{j,s}$ is the element in the jth row and sth column for $j = 1, 2, \ldots, J$ and $s = 1, 2, \ldots, S$. Therefore,

$$
\mathbf{A} \equiv \begin{bmatrix}
a_{1,1} & a_{1,2} & a_{1,3} & \cdots & a_{1,S} \\
a_{2,1} & a_{2,2} & a_{2,3} & \cdots & a_{2,S} \\
a_{3,1} & a_{3,2} & a_{3,3} & \cdots & a_{3,S} \\
\vdots & \vdots & \vdots & \ddots & \vdots \\
a_{J,1} & a_{J,2} & a_{J,3} & \cdots & a_{J,S}
\end{bmatrix}.
\tag{9.33}
$$

Let $\mathbf{0}$ denote the J by 1 vector containing all zeros. Let $\mathbf{C}$ be a set of competing orders for this set of auction inputs, and let $\mathbf{c}$ be a J by 1 vector whose element in the jth row is c_j for $j = 1, 2, \ldots, J$.

Theorem 9.6: For a given set of auction inputs, if the customer orders in $\mathbf{C}$ are competing orders and they are all buys of options, then there exists a vector $\mathbf{c}$ that satisfies Equations (9.13), (9.14), and (9.24), and

$$
\mathbf{A}^{\mathrm{T}}\mathbf{c} = \mathbf{0},
\tag{9.34}
$$

where "T" denotes the transpose operator.[18]

As described in Strang (1988, Chapter 2), Equation (9.34) is called a "homogenous system." If Equation (9.34) holds, then $\mathbf{A}$ is not of "full rank."[19] This theorem implies that if the customer orders in $\mathbf{C}$ are all buys of options, then $\kappa = 0$ in Equation (9.24).

To illustrate Theorem 9.6, let us return to our auction example from Section 9.1.2. As before, let $\mathbf{C} = \{2, 3, 4\}$, and let

$$
\mathbf{c} = \begin{bmatrix} 0 \\ 1 \\ 1 \\ -1 \end{bmatrix}.
\tag{9.35}
$$

Using the replication weights from Table 9.1, note that

$$
\mathbf{A} = \begin{bmatrix}
0 & 0 & 1 & 1 \\
1 & 0 & 0 & 0 \\
0 & 1 & 0 & 0 \\
1 & 1 & 0 & 0
\end{bmatrix}.
\tag{9.36}
$$

We can check easily that Equation (9.34) holds for these variables (see Equation (9.16)). Further, we note that $\mathbf{A}$ is a four by four matrix that has a rank of three, and so it is not of full rank.

Theorem 9.7: If the customer orders in an auction are all buys of options, and $\mathbf{A}$ is of full rank, then there exists a unique vector of customer fills in the PEP.

Theorem 9.7 relates the rank of $\mathbf{A}$, the matrix of replication weights, to conditions under which there is a unique vector of customer fills. Theorem 9.7 provides a simple sufficient condition, which can confirm that there is a unique vector of customer fills for a particular set of auction inputs. As an example, consider the CPI auction from Section 9.1.2 except that only the first three customer orders are submitted. These three customer orders are all buys of options. In this case,

$$
\mathbf{A} = \begin{bmatrix} 0 & 0 & 1 & 1 \\ 1 & 0 & 0 & 0 \\ 0 & 1 & 0 & 0 \end{bmatrix}. \tag{9.37}
$$

Thus, $\mathbf{A}$ is a three by four matrix that has a rank of three, and so it is of full rank. Consequently, Theorem 9.7 implies that there is a single vector of customer fills that solve the PEP for this set of inputs.

Define $\mathbf{w}$ as the J by 1 vector whose jth element is w_j, the limit price of the jth customer order, for $j = 1, 2, \ldots, J$. Then, Theorems 9.4 and 9.6 can be used to prove the following theorem.

Theorem 9.8: If there exist multiple vectors of customer fills for a set of auction inputs, and if the customer orders are all buys of options, then $\mathbf{A}$, the matrix of replication weights, is not of full rank, and there exists a non-zero vector $\mathbf{c}$ such that $\mathbf{A}^T\mathbf{c} = \mathbf{0}$ and $\mathbf{w}^T\mathbf{c} = 0$. If $\mathbf{C}$ is comprised of the row numbers of $\mathbf{c}$ that are non-zero, then $\mathbf{C}$ is a set of competing orders.[20]

The auction example of Section 9.1.2 has multiple vectors of customer fills. We have already checked that for this example that (1) $\mathbf{A}$ is not of full rank (see Equation (9.36)); and that (2) $\mathbf{A}^T\mathbf{c} = \mathbf{0}$ for $\mathbf{c}$ defined in Equation (9.35). Now, note that

$$
\mathbf{w}^T\mathbf{c} = \begin{bmatrix} 0.41 & 0.2 & 0.4 & 0.6 \end{bmatrix} \begin{bmatrix} 0 \\ 1 \\ 1 \\ -1 \end{bmatrix}
$$

$$
= 0 \tag{9.38}
$$

as predicted by Theorem 9.8. This implies immediately that $\mathbf{C} = \{2, 3, 4\}$ is a set of competing orders for this auction.

APPENDIX 9A: PROOFS OF THE THEOREMS

The main text of this chapter presented Theorems 9.1 through 9.8. Theorems 9.1 and 9.2 were derived in the text. We now prove Theorems 9.3 through 9.8.

9A.1   Proof of Theorem 9.3

To prove that $\mathbf{x_3}$ as defined in Equation (9.9) represents a vector of customer fills for the PEP, we need to check that $\mathbf{x_3}$ has the following properties:

Property 1: $\mathbf{x_3}$ satisfies the PEP limit-order restrictions;

Property 2: $\mathbf{x_3}$ and the variables based on $\mathbf{x_3}$ satisfy the PEP self-hedging conditions;

Property 3: The market exposure associated with the customer fills $\mathbf{x_3}$ is the largest possible market exposure for vectors of fills that satisfy the PEP conditions.

We now check these three properties.

Derivation of Property 1: Note that if customer order j is worse than the market for the first vector of customer fills, then it is also worse than the market for the second vector of customer fills since the side b_j, the limit price w_j, and the derivative strategy price π_j are the same regardless of the customer fills. Therefore, in both vectors, the fill for customer order j equals zero, that is,

$$b_j w_j < b_j \pi_j \implies x_{1,j} = x_{2,j} = 0. \tag{9A.1}$$

Equation (9.9) implies that

$$x_{3,j} = \alpha x_{1,j} + (1 - \alpha) x_{2,j}. \tag{9A.2}$$

Equations (9A.1) and (9A.2) together imply that

$$b_j w_j < b_j \pi_j \implies x_{3,j} = 0. \tag{9A.3}$$

Thus, if customer order j is worse than the market, then it also has zero fill for this third vector of customer fills. Similar reasoning implies that if the jth customer order is better than the market for the first and second vectors of customer fills, then it is fully filled for this third vector of customer fills. If the jth customer order is at the market, then

$$b_j w_j = b_j \pi_j \;\Rightarrow\; 0 \le x_{1,j} \le r_j \quad \text{and} \quad 0 \le x_{2,j} \le r_j. \tag{9A.4}$$

Since $0 < \alpha < 1$, Equation (9A.4) implies that

$$0 \le \alpha x_{1,j} + (1 - \alpha)x_{2,j} \le r_j. \tag{9A.5}$$

Therefore,

$$b_j w_j = b_j \pi_j \;\Rightarrow\; 0 \le x_{3,j} \le r_j. \tag{9A.6}$$

Consequently, we conclude that the limit-order logic holds for the vector of customer fills $\mathbf{x_3}$.

To show that properties 2 and 3 hold, we first prove the following lemma.

Lemma: Let f be a linear function such that $f \colon \mathbb{R}^J \to \mathbb{R}^1$. If

$$\mathbf{x_3} \equiv \alpha \mathbf{x_1} + (1 - \alpha)\mathbf{x_2}, \tag{9A.7}$$

then,

$$f(\mathbf{x_3}) = \alpha f(\mathbf{x_1}) + (1 - \alpha)f(\mathbf{x_2}). \tag{9A.8}$$

Proof of Lemma: Let $\mathbf{x}$ be a J by 1 column vector. Since f is linear, it can be written as

$$f(\mathbf{x}) = a + \mathbf{b}^\mathsf{T}\mathbf{x}, \tag{9A.9}$$

where a is a scalar and $\mathbf{b}$ is a J by 1 vector. Therefore,

$$\begin{aligned}
\alpha f(\mathbf{x_1}) + (1 - \alpha)f(\mathbf{x_2}) &= \alpha(a + \mathbf{b}^\mathsf{T}\mathbf{x_1}) + (1 - \alpha)(a + \mathbf{b}^\mathsf{T}\mathbf{x_2}) \\
&= a(\alpha + (1 - \alpha)) + \mathbf{b}^\mathsf{T}(\alpha \mathbf{x_1} + (1 - \alpha)\mathbf{x_2}) \\
&= a + \mathbf{b}^\mathsf{T}\mathbf{x_3} \\
&= f(\mathbf{x_3}), \tag{9A.10}
\end{aligned}$$

where the first equality follows by Equation (9A.9), where the second equality follows by algebraic manipulation, where the third equality follows by the definition of $\mathbf{x_3}$ in Equation (9A.7), and where the fourth equality follows from Equation (9A.9). Thus, the lemma holds.

Derivation of Property 2: Next, we check that $\mathbf{x_3}$ and the variables based on $\mathbf{x_3}$ satisfy the self-hedging conditions. Let $\mathbf{x}$ denote a J by 1 vector of customer fills that satisfies the PEP conditions for a particular set of auction inputs. Define the function f_s as follows:

$$f_s(\mathbf{x}) = \frac{\theta_s}{p_s} + y_s(\mathbf{x}) - M(\mathbf{x}) \quad s = 1, 2, \ldots, S. \tag{9A.11}$$

We write y_s and M as functions of the argument $\mathbf{x}$ to denote their dependence on the vectors of customer fills explicitly. In this case, state prices are the same across all such vectors $\mathbf{x}$ (see Chapter 8 for the uniqueness of state prices in this scenario), and so we do not represent the state prices as functions of the argument $\mathbf{x}$.[21] Note that the formula for net customer payouts (see, for example, Equation (9.8)) implies that net customer payouts are linear functions of the customer fills, and so y_s is a linear function of $\mathbf{x}$. Similarly, Equation (7.20) implies that net premium M is also a linear function of the customer fills, so M is also a linear function of $\mathbf{x}$. Therefore, f_s is a linear function of $\mathbf{x}$, and so the lemma above implies that

$$f_s(\mathbf{x_3}) = \alpha f_s(\mathbf{x_1}) + (1 - \alpha)f_s(\mathbf{x_2}) \quad s = 1, 2, \ldots, S$$

$$= \alpha \left(\frac{\theta_s}{p_s} + y_s(\mathbf{x_1}) - M(\mathbf{x_1}) \right)$$

$$+ (1 - \alpha) \left(\frac{\theta_s}{p_s} + y_s(\mathbf{x_2}) - M(\mathbf{x_2}) \right)$$

$$s = 1, 2, \ldots, S. \tag{9A.12}$$

Since $\mathbf{x_1}$ and $\mathbf{x_2}$ are customer fills, we know that the self-hedging conditions hold for $\mathbf{x_1}$ and $\mathbf{x_2}$. Therefore,

$$\frac{\theta_s}{p_s} + y_s(\mathbf{x_1}) - M(\mathbf{x_1}) = 0 \quad s = 1, 2, \ldots, S \tag{9A.13}$$

and

$$\frac{\theta_s}{p_s} + y_s(\mathbf{x_2}) - M(\mathbf{x_2}) = 0 \quad s = 1, 2, \ldots, S. \tag{9A.14}$$

Consequently, substituting Equations (9A.13) and (9A.14) into Equation (9A.12) implies that

$$f_s(\mathbf{x_3}) = 0 \quad s = 1, 2, \ldots, S \tag{9A.15}$$

which shows that

$$\frac{\theta_s}{p_s} + y_s(\mathbf{x_3}) = M(\mathbf{x_3}) \quad s = 1, 2, \ldots, S \tag{9A.16}$$

by Equation (9A.11). Consequently, we conclude that the self-hedging conditions hold for this third vector of customer fills $\mathbf{x_3}$.

Derivation of Property 3: Let $\widetilde{M}(\mathbf{x_1})$ and $\widetilde{M}(\mathbf{x_2})$ denote the market exposure for the first and second vectors of customer fills, respectively. We write these variables as functions with the arguments $\mathbf{x_1}$ and $\mathbf{x_2}$ to denote their dependence on the customer fills explicitly. Since the state prices are known, we can easily confirm that market exposure is a linear function of the customer fills by examining Equation (9.2). Therefore, the lemma above and Equation (9.10) imply that

$$\widetilde{M}(\mathbf{x_3}) = \alpha\widetilde{M}(\mathbf{x_1}) + (1 - \alpha)\widetilde{M}(\mathbf{x_2}). \tag{9A.17}$$

Now, note that the PEP maximizes market exposure, so the market exposure for the first and second vectors of customer fills must be the same, that is,

$$\widetilde{M}(\mathbf{x_1}) = \widetilde{M}(\mathbf{x_2}). \tag{9A.18}$$

Equations (9A.17) and (9A.18) together imply that

$$\widetilde{M}(\mathbf{x_1}) = \widetilde{M}(\mathbf{x_2}) = \widetilde{M}(\mathbf{x_3}). \tag{9A.19}$$

Thus, the market exposure for the third vector of customer fills equals the market exposure for the first and second vectors of customer fills. Since the first and second customer fills maximize market exposure for the auction inputs, Equation (9A.19) confirms that the third vector of customer fills also maximizes market exposure for the same auction inputs.

Since $\mathbf{x_3}$ satisfies these three properties, we conclude that $\mathbf{x_3}$ is a vector of customer fills that satisfy the PEP conditions. This concludes the proof of Theorem 9.3.

9A.2 Proof of Theorem 9.4

From the multiple vectors of customer fills, consider two vectors $\mathbf{x_1}$ and $\mathbf{x_2}$, where $\mathbf{x_1} \neq \mathbf{x_2}$. Define $\mathbf{C}$ as the set of customer orders whose fills differ in these two equilibria. We now check that $\mathbf{C}$ satisfies conditions 1, 2, 3, and 4 of this theorem.

Condition 1: To confirm that the customer orders $\mathbf{C}$ are competing orders, let the variables $c_1, c_2, \ldots, c_J$ be defined as follows:

$$c_j = x_{2,j} - x_{1,j} \quad j = 1, 2, \ldots, J. \tag{9A.20}$$

We now check that Equations (9.13), (9.14), and (9.24) hold.

Equation (9.13): Based on Equation (9A.20), if c_j is non-zero, then c_j is an element of $\mathbf{C}$. Similarly, if c_j equals zero, then c_j is not an element of $\mathbf{C}$. Consequently, Equation (9.13) is satisfied.

Equation (9.14): The market exposure for the first vector of customer fills $\mathbf{x_1}$ is

$$\widetilde{M}(\mathbf{x_1}) = \sum_{s=1}^{S} \theta_s + \sum_{j=1}^{J} x_{1,j} \tilde{\lambda}_j \tag{9A.21}$$

Similarly, we can write for the second vector of customer fills $\mathbf{x_2}$ that

$$\widetilde{M}(\mathbf{x_2}) = \sum_{s=1}^{S} \theta_s + \sum_{j=1}^{J} x_{2,j} \tilde{\lambda}_j \tag{9A.22}$$

Subtracting Equation (9A.21) from Equation (9A.22) gives us that

$$\widetilde{M}(\mathbf{x_2}) - \widetilde{M}(\mathbf{x_1}) = \sum_{j=1}^{J} x_{2,j} \tilde{\lambda}_j - \sum_{j=1}^{J} x_{1,j} \tilde{\lambda}_j$$

$$= \sum_{j=1}^{J} (x_{2,j} - x_{1,j}) \tilde{\lambda}_j$$

$$= \sum_{j=1}^{J} c_j \tilde{\lambda}_j, \tag{9A.23}$$

where the third equality follows from the definition of c_j in Equation (9A.20). Since the market exposures $\widetilde{M}(\mathbf{x_1})$ and $\widetilde{M}(\mathbf{x_2})$ are equal, we conclude that

$$\sum_{j=1}^{J} c_j \tilde{\lambda}_j = 0 \tag{9A.24}$$

and so Equation (9.14) holds.

Equation (9.24): Note that both $\mathbf{x_1}$ and $\mathbf{x_2}$ are PEP customer fills for the auction inputs, and so the variables based on them satisfy the PEP self-hedging conditions. Following the notation used in the proof of Theorem 9.3, we can write that

$$\frac{\theta_s}{p_s} + y_s(\mathbf{x_1}) = M(\mathbf{x_1}) \quad s = 1, 2, \ldots, S \tag{9A.25}$$

and

$$\frac{\theta_s}{p_s} + y_s(\mathbf{x_2}) = M(\mathbf{x_2}) \quad s = 1, 2, \ldots, S. \tag{9A.26}$$

Subtracting Equation (9A.25) from Equation (9A.26) gives

$$y_s(\mathbf{x_2}) - y_s(\mathbf{x_1}) = M(\mathbf{x_2}) - M(\mathbf{x_1}) \quad s = 1, 2, \ldots, S. \tag{9A.27}$$

Now, the formula for y_s (see Equation (9.8)) implies that

$$y_s(\mathbf{x_2}) - y_s(\mathbf{x_1}) = \sum_{j=1}^{J} a_{j,s} b_j x_{2,j} - \sum_{j=1}^{J} a_{j,s} b_j x_{1,j} \quad s = 1, 2, \ldots, S$$

$$= \sum_{j=1}^{J} a_{j,s} b_j (x_{2,j} - x_{1,j}) \quad s = 1, 2, \ldots, S$$

$$= \sum_{j=1}^{J} a_{j,s} b_j c_j \quad s = 1, 2, \ldots, S, \tag{9A.28}$$

where the second equality follows from algebraic manipulation, and the third equality follows by the definition of c_j in Equation (9A.20). Therefore,

$$y_s(\mathbf{x_2}) - y_s(\mathbf{x_1}) = \sum_{j=1}^{J} a_{j,s} b_j c_j \quad s = 1, 2, \ldots, S. \tag{9A.29}$$

Equations (9A.27) and (9A.29) together imply that

$$\sum_{j=1}^{J} a_{j,s} b_j c_j = M(\mathbf{x_2}) - M(\mathbf{x_1}) \quad s = 1, 2, \ldots, S. \tag{9A.30}$$

Therefore, Equation (9.24) holds with $\kappa = M(\mathbf{x_2}) - M(\mathbf{x_1})$.

Since $c_1, c_2, \ldots, c_J$ satisfy Equations (9.13), (9.14), and (9.24), the orders in $\mathbf{C}$ are competing orders. This concludes the proof of condition 1.

Condition 2: The customer orders in $\mathbf{C}$ have different fills in the two equilibria. Theorem 9.1 implies that customer fills can only be different for orders that are at the market, so every customer order in $\mathbf{C}$ is at the market.

Condition 3: As discussed above in proof of condition 1, there exists (by Theorem 9.2) a j such that $x_{1,j} < x_{2,j}$. The PEP limit-order logic implies that every customer order's fill is less than or equal to the order's request amount, so $x_{2,j} \leq r_j$. This implies that $x_{1,j} < r_j$, and so at least one of the customer orders in the first vector is less than fully filled. Similarly, there exists a j such that $x_{2,j} < x_{1,j}$. Since $x_{1,j} \leq r_j$, this implies that $x_{2,j} < r_j$, and so at least one of the customer orders in the second vector is less than fully filled. Thus, condition 3 holds.

Condition 4: We can derive condition 4 following the approach we used to derive condition 3. Theorem 9.2 implies that there exists a j such that $x_{2,j} < x_{1,j}$. The PEP limit-order logic implies that every customer order's fill is non-negative so $0 \leq x_{2,j}$. Therefore, $0 < x_{1,j}$, which implies that at least one of the customer orders in the first vector has a positive fill. Further, there exists a j such that $x_{1,j} < x_{2,j}$. Since $0 \leq x_{1,j}$, this implies that $0 < x_{2,j}$. Consequently, at least one of the customer orders in the second vector has a positive fill. Consequently, condition 4 holds.

Since all four conditions hold, Theorem 9.4 has been verified.

9A.3   Proof of Theorem 9.5

Based on the statement of this theorem, let $\mathbf{C}$ denote the set of customer orders that have different fills in the two equilibria. Further, define

$$c_j = x_{2,j} - x_{1,j} \quad j = 1, 2, \ldots, J. \tag{9A.31}$$

Following the proof of condition 1 of Theorem 9.4 from above, it is straightforward to check that $c_1, c_2, \ldots, c_J$ satisfy Equations (9.13), (9.14), and (9.24), and so $\mathbf{C}$ represents a set of competing orders. Setting β equal to 1 implies that Equation (9.32) holds as well. Thus, Theorem 9.5 is proven.

9A.4   Proof of Theorem 9.6

If $\mathbf{C}$ is a set of competing orders, and all customer orders in $\mathbf{C}$ are buys of options, then $b_j = 1$ for $j \in \mathbf{C}$. Therefore, Equation (9.24) simplifies as follows:

$$\sum_{j=1}^{J} a_{j,s} c_j = \kappa \quad s = 1, 2, \ldots, S. \tag{9A.32}$$

Using the fact that the customer orders in $\mathbf{C}$ are at the market, the analysis in Appendix 7C (see in particular Equation (7C.7)) can be used to show that Equation (9A.32) implies that [22]

$$\kappa = \sum_{j=1}^{J} c_j \pi_j. \tag{9A.33}$$

Since the customer orders in $\mathbf{C}$ are buys of options, we have that

$$\pi_j = \tilde{\lambda}_j \quad \forall j \in \mathbf{C}. \tag{9A.34}$$

Therefore,

$$\kappa = \sum_{j=1}^{J} c_j \tilde{\lambda}_j. \tag{9A.35}$$

Since the customer orders in $\mathbf{C}$ are competing orders, Equation (9.14) implies that

$$\sum_{j=1}^{J} c_j \tilde{\lambda}_j = 0. \tag{9A.36}$$

Thus, Equations (9A.35) and (9A.36) imply that κ must equal zero. Therefore, if there exist a set of competing orders $\mathbf{C}$ that are all buys of options, then we can rewrite Equation (9A.32) as

$$\sum_{j=1}^{J} a_{j,s} c_j = 0 \quad s = 1, 2, \ldots, S. \tag{9A.37}$$

We can write this in matrix notation as

$$\mathbf{A}^T \mathbf{c} = \mathbf{0}. \tag{9A.38}$$

and so Theorem 9.6 holds.

9A.5 Proof of Theorem 9.7

If the customer orders in an auction are all buys of options, and $\mathbf{A}$ is of full rank, then Theorem 9.6 implies that there does not exist a set of competing orders for this set of auction inputs. Thus, Theorem 9.4 implies that there is a unique vector of customer fills, and so Theorem 9.7 holds.[23]

9A.6   Proof of Theorem 9.8

If there exist multiple vectors of customer fills for a given set of auction inputs, and if the customer orders are all buys of options, then Theorem 9.4 implies that there exist competing orders $\mathbf{C}$ in the auction. Theorem 9.6 implies that $\mathbf{A}$ is not of full rank, and so $\mathbf{A}^T\mathbf{c} = \mathbf{0}$. Based on the fact that the customer orders in $\mathbf{C}$ are at the market and that Equation (9.24) holds, the proof of Theorem 7C.1 in Appendix 7C can be used to show that $\mathbf{w}^T\mathbf{c} = 0$. This concludes the proof.

Notes

1 INTRODUCTION TO DERIVATIVES

1. As described in Hull (2006, pp. 35–36), in the case of an exchange-traded derivatives contract with physical delivery, a party with a short position in the derivative delivers the physical underlying to a party designated by the exchange who has a long position in the same derivative. In addition, with certain exchange-traded contracts, the party with the short position may have a choice of what underlying to deliver. For example, a seller of a Chicago Board of Trade (CBOT) US Treasury future can deliver one of a set of delivery-grade bonds. For more details, see the Rules and Regulations on the CBOT website, http://www.cbot.com.

2. Hull (2006, pp. 40–41) provides more details on the institutional differences between futures and forwards. For discrepancies between futures and forward prices, see Hull (2006, pp. 109–110) and see the theoretical discussion in Duffie (1988, pp. 262–263).

3. Another widely traded derivative that pays out linearly in the value of the underlying is a "swap," which is a generalized version of a forward contract. With a forward contract, there is one exchange of cash on a date in the future, while a swap contract has exchanges of cash on multiple dates in the future. See Chapter 7 of Hull (2006) for more details.

4. In addition to European-style exercise, options are often "American-style" exercise. In this case, the option holder can exercise at many different times up to the expiration of the option. For other exotic-option styles, see Chapter 22 of Hull (2006).

5. We avoid using the term "at-the-money" (which means that the value of the underlying is equal to the strike upon expiration) because using this term with digital options can cause confusion. For example, as we see in moment, a digital call pays out if the underlying is equal to the strike upon expiration while a digital put does not pay out if the underlying is equal to the strike upon expiration. See Hull (2006,

p. 188) for alternative definitions of in-the-money, at-the-money, and out-of-the-money.

6. Digital options are also called "binary" options or "all-or-nothing" options.

7. Section 5.1 will discuss these derivatives in more detail.

8. While derivatives-market participants consider digital options to be exotic, academic researchers typically consider digital options to be the fundamental building blocks of finance. See the upcoming discussions in Sections 2.1 and 5.3.

9. For additional details on customers and market makers, see Harris (2003), particularly Sections 3.1 and 19.3.

10. See Chapter 15 of Hull (2006) for further discussion on delta hedging.

11. See Weber (1999) for details on electronic trading of derivatives on an exchange, and see Chapter 6 of Liebenberg (2002) for details on electronic trading of derivatives OTC.

12. See Harris (2003, pp. 90–91) for a brief introduction to call auctions. Garbade and Silber (1979) show that auctions in general can reduce overall transaction costs. Several papers show that call auctions in particular can be useful for aggregating liquidity. See, among many, Economides and Schwartz (1995), Theissen (2000), and Kalay, Wei, and Wohl (2002).

13. Garbade and Ingber (2005) describe the mechanics of the Treasury auctions.

14. Domowitz and Madhavan (2001) discuss of the mechanics of the opening of NYSE equity markets.

15. See Hull (2006, pp. 36–37) for a brief discussion of these and other order types. For further details, see Chapter 4 of Harris (2003).

16. See Chapter 18 of Bernstein (1996) for an overview of early derivatives trading.

17. See Barbour (1963, pp. 74–84), and De La Vega (1996) for details on trading in Amsterdam during the 1600s.

18. See Paul (1985, pp. 277–278).

19. See Gates (1973) for a history of early options trading in the US, and see Lurie (1979) for a history of the early years of the CBOT.

20. For more details, see Silber (1983), Carlton (1984), Van Horne (1985), Miller (1986, 1992), and Merton (1992b).

21. Paul (1985, pp. 276–278) discusses (1) instances of cash settlement outside of the US prior to 1981 and (2) instances of partial cash settlement in the US before 1981.

22. In fact, the BIS reports daily numbers for April 2004. We convert these to annual numbers by assuming 250 trading days in a year. See Bank for International Settlements (2004, p. 14) for more details.

23. See Commodity Futures Trading Commission (2005, pp. 109–137).

24. See Commodity Futures Trading Commission (2005, p. 13).

25. Of particular note are the papers by Silber (1983), Van Horne (1985), Miller (1986), and Merton (1992b). Also, see the books by Allen and Gale (1994) and Shiller (1993, 2003).

26. See Anderson (1984) on the development of the CFTC.

27. See Miller (1986) and Telser (1986) for a discussion of the legal aspects involving the CFTC and cash settlement.

28. Of the top ten contracts listed in Burghardt (2005), the following six are cash-settled: KOSPI 200 options, 3-month Eurodollar futures, 28-day Mexican Peso deposit futures, E-Mini S&P 500 index futures, 3-month Euribor futures, and 3-month Eurodollar options.

29. See Cravath, Swaine, and Moore (2001) and White (2001) for more details on the CFMA.

2   INTRODUCTION TO PARIMUTUEL MATCHING

1. Most financial underlyings are likely to require many more than four states. Parimutuel matching can handle such cases, but we chose a small state-space example here to most simply illustrate the properties of parimutuel matching.

2. State claims are also often called "state-contingent" claims or "Arrow–Debreu" securities.

3. In practice, most parimutuelly traded derivatives expire on the same date as the auction so premium and payouts are often exchanged on the same date, satisfying this assumption. See Sections 3.2 and 3.3 for details.

4. In fact, a customer can approximate selling a state claim as follows. For illustration, consider a customer who wants to sell the first state claim. This customer can submit orders to buy every other state claim. In this case, the customer loses money if the first state occurs and may profit if any of the other states occur, as a seller of the first state claim would. However, this customer pays premium up front (as opposed to receiving premium up front as a seller typically would), and this customer receives different payouts depending on what state occurs (since there is no way to guarantee that the customer receives the same payout for every state purchased, since the state prices are unknown at the time the orders are submitted).

5. In fact, it may be the case that a specific state is sufficiently unlikely that no customer invests premium in that state. However, Equation (2.1) is a convenient assumption that simplifies exposition and avoids any dividing-by-zero issues, which would appear for example in Equation (2.8).

6. Equation (2.4) holds because the premium amounts are non-zero, as specified in Equation (2.1).

7. Chapter 6 will add a third no-arbitrage restriction to handle the pricing of derivatives that pay out in multiple states. See Equation (6.4).

8. Equation (2.8) resembles the result from the classical Arrow-Debreu equilibrium, which shows that the ratio of state prices equals the ratio of marginal utilities in those two states. See Arrow (1964).

9. It is not hard to check that the self-hedging conditions of Equation (2.6) and the relative-demand pricing of Equation (2.8) are mathematically equivalent when state prices are positive and sum to one. Appendix 6D will prove this result.

10. It is worth pointing out that parimutuel matching does not always fill all orders when customers can submit limit orders. See the example in Section 5.2.

11. Although this is somewhat non-standard, in this example we fill customers for a fractional number of contracts to make sure that the self-hedging property of Equation (2.6) is satisfied exactly.

12. Transaction costs may include fees for trading on an exchange, clearing fees, and costs of capital.

13. This example illustrates a very simple no-arbitrage relationship. For a detailed discussion of other no-arbitrage relationships, see Chapter 4 of Cox and Rubinstein (1985).

14. In addition, eliminating arbitrage opportunities helps remove certain pricing anomalies and enforces the "Law of One Price," an important principle of finance as described in LeRoy and Werner (2001) and Lamont and Thaler (2003).

15. In addition to the research described here, parimutuel matching is closely related to the academic field of "combinatorial auctions." Section 3.5 will describe combinatorial auctions and compare them to parimutuel matching.

16. The main difference between parimutuel wagering on horses to win and the framework in Section 2.1 is that the horse racing association typically takes 20 cents of every one dollar bet as a fee, whereas the framework in Section 2.1 assumed that fees equal zero.

17. In parimutuel wagering, arbitrage opportunities are generally not possible within one wagering type.

18. See Edelman and O'Brian (2004) for a discussion of arbitrage between the win pool and other parimutuel pools.

19. For empirical support of the favorite-longshot bias, see, among many, Fabricand (1965), Ali (1977), Snyder (1978), and Asch, Malkiel, and Quandt (1982). To explain the favorite-longshot bias, see the work of Ali (1977), Quandt (1986), Thaler and Ziemba (1988), Golec and Tamarkin (1998), Brown and Lin (2003), and Ottaviani and Sorensen (2003).

20. The strongest evidence that at least some bettors have consistently made money wagering on horse races is with strategies based on computer handicapping systems for Hong Kong races. Benter (1994) and Chapman (1994) describe some of these econometric models for handicapping Hong Kong horse races based on information from past races.

Kaplan (2002) describes Benter's consistent success and the success of others in Hong Kong.

21. In somewhat related work, Chapter 8 will prove that state prices are unique in a more general parimutuel setting (which includes orders for vanilla options and limit orders).

22. Also, Norvig (1967) proves that the Eisenberg and Gale (1959) result holds in a convergence sense, that is, bettors reach the same equilibrium iteratively by being able to respond to changing parimutuel prices by altering their wagers through time.

23. In related work, Levin (1994) provides a comprehensive solution methodology for computing optimal parimutuel wagers under a variety of different assumptions.

24. In addition, Hanson (2003) discusses adapting scoring rules for use as a combinatorial information market mechanism. See Section 3.5.

25. Hanson, Oprea, and Porter (2006) provide additional experimental evidence that it is difficult to distort prices in a related setting.

3   PARIMUTUEL APPLICATIONS

1. See Buck (1977, pp. 3–14) for a history of parimutuel wagering on horse races, and see Epstein (1977, pp. 287–288) for a short history of horse racing. Many lotteries have features in common with parimutuel wagering on horse races and date back to biblical times. See Brenner and Brenner (1990, pp. 1–18) for a detailed history of lotteries. Of further note, insurance or risk-sharing pools have many features in common with parimutuel wagering and existed in ancient Greece. See Bernstein (1996, p. 92).

2. For country by country parimutuel wagering statistics on thoroughbred horse racing, see the International Federation of Horseracing Authorities website: http://www.horseracingintfed.com.

3. Nomoto (2004) reports that Japan wagered 5.7 trillion yen parimutuelly in 2003. Based on an exchange rate of 107 yen per dollar (the exchange rate on 31 December 2003), this converts to 53 billion US dollars.

4. See Freeman, Freeman, and McKinley (1982) for more information on these sports.

5. The International Federation of Horseracing Authorities reports that Hong Kong wagered 65 million Hong Kong dollars parimutuelly in 2003. Based on the exchange rate of 7.8 Hong Kong dollars per 1 US dollar (the exchange rate on 31 December 2003), this converts to 8.3 billion US dollars.

6. For Hong Kong population information, see Chapter 20 of the Hong Kong 2003 Yearbook published on the Hong Kong Special Administrative Region Government website: http://www.info.gov.hk/eindex.htm.

7. Although customers cannot submit limit orders at the racetrack, customers can sometimes cancel wagers after they are made. See Camerer (1998) for further discussion.

8. See the discussion regarding the win, place, and show pools in Section 2.3.3.

9. A financial-method patent is considered to be a type of "business-method" patent. In a recent decision, the USPTO's Board of Patent Appeals overturned a patent examiner's rejection of a business-method patent as "outside the technological arts," finding that there was no basis in law for such a rejection. This reversal is widely viewed as favorable to business-method patents (and by implication for financial-method patents). See Ex Parte Carl A. Lundgren, Appeal No. 2003-2088, heard 20 April 2004. Also, see Falloon (1999), Heaton (2000), and Lerner (2002) for further discussion of the patentability of financial methods.

10. See also Shiller (2003) for some discussion of Longitude.

11. Such short-dated options have very high "gamma" and "theta" exposures. See Hull (2006, Chapter 15) for the definition of these "Greeks."

12. The CME began allowing their customers to trade economic derivatives via their Globex platform in March 2006.

13. For further information, see the newspaper articles by Wessel ("New Futures Could Help Folks Insure Against Economic Risks," *Wall Street Journal*, 5 September 2002), Taylor ("Investors Will Now Find Surprises Less of a Shock," *Financial Times*, 24/25 May 2003), and the editorial by Thind (2002).

14. As discussed by Horrigan (1987), CPI futures were first traded on the Coffee, Sugar, and Cocoa Exchange in the 1980s without generating significant volume.

15. For more details on this contract, see the CME website http://www.cme.com/trading.

16. It is worth noting that Miller (1986) does not discuss the possibility of a *parimutuel* auction for trading futures and options on CPI.

17. In a similar vein to TIPS, several academics and practioneers have proposed trading GDP-indexed bonds. See Shiller (1993, 2003) and Borensztein and Mauro (2004).

18. Wolfers and Zitzewitz (2004) note that such markets are also often called prediction markets, information markets, or event futures.

19. See Wolfers and Zitzewitz (2004) for more details on this episode.

20. Bonds and credit-default swaps have an event-market flavor. For example, a corporate bond makes scheduled payments so long as the company does not default. A catastrophic risk or "CAT" bond makes scheduled payments as long as the underlying event (i.e., the hurricane or earthquake) does not occur.

21. It is worth mentioning two additional call-auction frameworks that were used for trading US equities, although neither is in operation today. Woodward (2001) and Domowitz and Madhavan (2001) describe the Arizona Stock Exchange, which used a standard call auction in

the 1990s. Clemons and Weber (2001) discuss the company Opti-Mark, which employed a sophisticated matching engine with some call-auction features in 1999 and 2000.

22. See Garbade and Ingber (2005) for a description of the mechanics of Treasury auctions.

23. As is frequently noted in this literature, a combinatorial auction is an instance of the well-known "set-packing problem," which itself is of the same class of problem as the "knapsack problem." In the standard version of the knapsack problem, a decision maker can choose from among different types and shapes of objects. Each object type has a size or volume and a value to the decision maker. The goal of the decision maker is to choose a set of objects from among the different types in order to maximize the total value. The decision maker is constrained in that the total volume of objects selected must be below some determined constant or the size of the knapsack.

24. See de Vries and Vohra (2003) for citations on these applications.

25. Recall from endnote 23 that a combinatorial auction is closely related to the knapsack problem. A parimutuel derivatives auction relates to the knapsack problem as follows. We can think of the objects as the derivative strategies, and we can think of their shapes as the payout functions on these orders. The parimutuel knapsack must have a flat edge on top representing the criteria that irrespective of which state occurs, the same level of payout has been provided to the group of auction participants.

26. Sandholm, Suri, Gilpin, and Levine (2001) use the term "combinatorial auction" to strictly mean a multiple-item auction with a single seller where participants bid for bundles of items, while they use the term "combinatorial exchange" to refer to a multiple-item auction with multiple buyers and multiple sellers where participants bid and offer for bundles of items. We use the term "combinatorial auction" more generally to mean any auction where bids and/or offers may be made for bundles of items.

27. As will be shown in Equation (4.4), a parimutuel derivatives auction requires that a customer's fill can equal any value between zero and the customer's requested amount.

28. As discussed by Sandholm, Suri, Gilpin, and Levine (2001), de Vries and Vohra (2003), and Sandholm and Suri (2006), the solution to the standard combinatorial auction problem is "NP-hard," meaning that no "polynomial-time" solution is known to exist and worst-case computation times are high. Although Chapter 2 shows that solving the parimutuel wagering problem is trivial, solving for prices and fills in a parimutuel derivatives auction requires an iterative approach (see Chapter 7). Even in this case, though, computation times for typical auctions are under half a second. Peters, So, and Ye (2006) prove an important and related theoretical result. They show that parimutuel derivatives auctions can be solved in polynomial time.

29.   See http://research.yahoo.com/research/foundations/tech_buzz_game.shtml for more details.

30.   See Chapter 7 for more details.

31.   While advances in computing have helped bring parimutuel matching to the derivatives markets, it is interesting to note that in the past, parimutuel wagering has spurred on innovation in computing. The Julius Totalisator, used for calculating odds on horse races in the early 1900s, was one of the leading computers of its time. See Swade (1987).

32.   Without mentioning parimutuel call auctions specifically, several authors have pointed out the usefulness of *electronic* call auctions. See, for example, Domowitz and Madhavan (2001), the collection of papers in Schwartz (2001), and the collection of papers in Schwartz, Byrne, and Colaninno (2003). Schwartz (2003, p. xvi) argues that "computer technology is essential for unleashing the power of a modern call." Cohen and Schwartz (2001) emphasize that electronic call auctions can be run with low operating costs. Economides and Schwartz (1995) stress the importance of electronic trading for call auctions: "with computerization, participants can see the order flow and interact with the system on a real-time basis, entering their orders while the computer broadcasts the orders and indicated clearing prices."

4   A CASE STUDY USING NONFARM PAYROLLS

1.   Even though NFP is the main variable of interest in the employment report, Fair (2003, p. 311) notes that the unemployment rate and the average-hourly earnings also get some attention.

2.   For more details on how the BLS calculates this statistic, see Chapter 2 of the BLS Handbook of Methods, found on http://www.bls.gov, and see Krueger and Fortson (2003).

3.   Krueger and Fortson (2003, pp. 947–948) show that fixed-income markets respond in a statistically insignificant way to revisions on NFP. Most market participants consider the first released value of NFP to be the "headline" number.

4.   For more recent work in this area, see the papers by Tashjian (1995), Tashjian and Weissman (1995), and Corkish, Holland, and Vila (1997).

5.   See the following six articles in the *Wall Street Journal* in their C Section on 4 June 2004:

   1.   E. S. Browning – "Stocks Fall on Interest-Rate Fears Ahead of Jobs Report;"

   2.   Jesse Eisinger – "A Yawner;"

   3.   Steven C. Johnson, and Tom Barkley – "Dollar Weakens Against Yen, Euro Amid Oil-Price Jitters;"

4.　Michael Mackenzie – "Bond Investors Brace for Jobs Data;"

5.　Karen Talley – "Intel, Agere Fall Amid Broad Selling;" and

6.　Kopin Tan – "Jobs Data, OPEC Prompt Traders to Play Defense."

6.　These forecasts can be accessed on a Bloomberg Terminal™ by typing "ECO" and then hitting the "GO" button.

7.　Note that if indicator 2 holds for an underlying, then it is very likely to be the case that indicator 1 holds as well. In other words, given that the release of an underlying has a large impact on financial markets (indicator 2), then that release is likely to be widely followed and forecasted by financial-market participants (indicator 1).

8.　As discussed by Cornell (1981), Silber (1981), Telser (1981), Van Horne (1985), among many, high *uncertainty* about future values of an underlying leads hedgers to trade derivatives on that underlying.

9.　Academic researchers disagree on whether a close relationship between a new futures contract and existing futures contracts is likely to be associated with the success or failure of the new futures contract. For evidence that a close relationship *decreases* the chance of success, see Duffie and Jackson (1989) and Cuny (1993), who develop theoretical models showing that new futures markets for which there are no close substitutes may have the greatest chance for success. Further, using statistical tests, Black (1986) and Corkish, Holland, and Vila (1997) find empirical evidence that introducing a contract that is highly correlated with other contracts is a negative factor for a contract's success. Our view (which is expressed above) is that the fact that several financial markets have a predictable reaction to NFP *increases* demand for NFP derivatives. Providing evidence consistent with that view, Merton (1992b) postulates that highly correlated contracts may, in certain cases, complement one another as opposed to competing with each other, creating a virtuous circle of liquidity. Further, Tashjian (1995) and Tashjian and Weissman (1995) point out that exchanges often introduce futures contracts with a high correlation to other existing contracts, providing indirect evidence that there must be some advantage to doing so.

10.　Section 4.4.4 discusses the range forward in more detail. In addition, Section 5.1.5 will present the payout on the range forward, and Section 6.2.1 will present the formula for the price of the range forward.

11.　Gürkaynak and Wolfers (2006) show empirically that the forecast from a parimutuel derivatives auction is more accurate than the median from a survey of economists (which is often used to measure the market consensus). More generally, there is a significant body of academic research that shows that forecasts based on real money at stake are more accurate than forecasts based on surveys. See Section 2.3.2 and the box at the end of Section 4.4 for more details.

12.   If the surprise is defined as the difference between NFP and the median forecast of the Bloomberg survey, then the standard deviation of surprises is 101 thousand jobs over the sample period. This value is similar to the standard deviation of surprises based on the auction's range forward price.

13.   In studying other financial markets, Andersen, Bollerslev, Diebold, and Vega (2005) show that NFP has a predictable impact in the five minutes after its release on foreign equity indexes, currency markets, and foreign bond markets.

14.   When the underlying is the traded price of a commodity, similar principles apply. Gray (1978), Jones (1982), Garbade and Silber (1983), and Paul (1985) argue that the underlying used for cash settlement must be a reliable and accurate measure of the commercial value of that commodity. They suggest that the underlying must be immune to manipulation and pricing distortions such as short squeezes. Relatedly, Duffie and Rahi (1995) note that for trading to be successful, there must be confidence that no person trading has material private information on the value of the underlying.

15.   One NFP leak occurred in 1998. As described by Sylvia Nasar ("Agency Tangled in Web by Early Release of Data," New York Times, 6 November 1998, late edition, sec. C), the BLS mistakenly posted the report for October 1998 on its website on Thursday morning 5 November 1998 instead of on Friday morning 6 November 1998.

16.   See, for example, Enders (2004) for a discussion of time-series techniques.

17.   In fact, the standard deviation of surprises is statistically *indistinguishable* from the one-month conditional standard deviation of NFP, as we now show. Define the statistic A as the standard deviation of NFP surprises divided by the one-month conditional standard deviation of NFP.

$$A = \frac{SD[\psi_t]}{SD_{t-1}[u_t]}$$

Consider the null hypothesis H_0 that the population value of A is equal to one, versus the one-sided alternative hypothesis H_1 that the population value of A is less than one. If the random variables in the numerator and the denominator of A are independent and normally distributed, then under the null hypothesis, A^2 is F distributed and the lower A^2 is the greater the evidence against the null hypothesis. In this case, A^2 equals 0.61. Using 34 degrees of freedom for the numerator and the denominator of the F statistic, this value of A^2 equates to a p-value of 8%. Thus, A is statistically indistinguishable from one. See Snedecor and Cochran (1989, pp. 98–99) or another standard statistics text for more details on this type of "equality of variance" test.

18. The BLS publishes the dates and times for the release of economic statistics on their website http://www.bls.gov typically months ahead of each release.

19. In related work, Brenner, Eldor, and Hauser (2001) show that traders are willing to pay a premium for options that are liquid.

20. The diversity of forecasts shows that any measurement of the "market's forecast" for NFP is really an *average* of the forecasts of market participants, as opposed to there being any consensus among market participants on the upcoming value of NFP.

21. Since it represents the monthly *change* in jobs in the nonfarm sector, NFP can be positive or negative. Although the lowest strike in the auctions on August 2005 NFP was 0 jobs, there is nothing that precludes NFP options that have negative strikes. In fact, in several past NFP auctions, customers have traded options with negative strikes.

22. Section 5.1 describes vanilla capped calls, vanilla floored puts, and the range forward in more detail.

23. To keep the notation simple, this section uses the variables $a_s, r, x, w,$ and π without any subscripts to denote a particular customer order. By necessity, however, Chapters 5 and higher use subscripts to indicate that variables are related to specific customer orders. Hence, Chapters 5 and higher use the variables $a_{j,s}, r_j, x_j, w_j,$ and π_j to denote that these variables are related to the jth customer order.

24. Replicating derivatives for these NFP auctions using 377 state claims is computationally very expensive, that is, computing prices and fills takes a long time. Fortunately, derivatives can be replicated using a much smaller set of fundamental building blocks. Longitude's parimutuel matching engine uses such an approach, and that approach is described in Lange, Baron, Walden, and Harte (2003, Chapter 11). This replication approach is related to the "supershare approach," which was introduced by Hakansson (1976, 1978) and discussed in Cox and Rubinstein (1985).

25. To guarantee that each state has a positive price, a small amount of premium is invested in each state at the start of every auction. See the discussion in Section 6.1.

26. Recall the assumptions from Section 2.1 that (1) all auction participants meet their financial obligations, and so there is no credit risk in a parimutuel auction; and (2) there is no discounting required between the date that premium is paid and the date that option payouts are made. These two assumptions are crucial for the second no-arbitrage condition.

27. These three no-arbitrage conditions imply that the prices in a parimutuel derivatives auction satisfy "put-call parity," an important condition in option-pricing theory as described in Hull (2006, pp. 212–215). In this context, put-call parity relates the price of the range forward to the price of vanilla capped calls and vanilla floored puts. See Appendix 6B for further discussion.

28. Section 6.2.4 will discuss this in further detail. In particular, that section will rigorously define auction volume as being equal to a quantity known as the total "market exposure."

29. In fact, Appendix 6D will prove that, under no-arbitrage conditions, the parimutuel principle of self-hedging and relative-demand pricing are equivalent.

30. The fact that prices are available on *all* tradable derivatives is a unique feature of parimutuel derivatives auctions. Section 6.1 will discuss this further.

31. Parimutuel wagering works in a similar fashion to parimutuel derivatives auctions, as bettors can view indicative odds (calculated based on all wagers submitted up to that time) throughout the wagering period.

32. Note that there is no price for the vanilla floored put struck at 0 jobs (the floor) or for the vanilla capped call struck at 375 thousand jobs (the cap). Both of these derivatives pay out zero regardless of the value of the underlying, and consequently, neither derivative is tradable in this auction.

33. The fee for an option is typically 1% of the option's maximum payout. Since a digital option pays out $1 if it expires in-the-money, the fee is $0.01. For example, the price to buy the digital call struck at 275 thousand jobs is 0.111 (0.111=0.101+0.01) and the price to sell the digital call struck at 275 thousand jobs is 0.091 (0.091=0.101−0.01).

34. When the adjacent auction strikes are one NFP outcome or one "tick" apart, the state claims and the digital options in the implied distribution are identical. The strikes in the NFP auctions are 25 ticks apart, and so these derivatives differ.

35. For example, an auction participant might take the view that the implied distribution should be relatively smooth, that is, the price of a digital range should be closely related to the prices of the adjacent digital ranges. Based on this view, an auction participant might buy (resp., sell) a digital range whose price is low (resp., high) relative to the prices of the adjacent digital ranges.

36. Many authors have pointed out the close relationship between the implied probability and the price of a digital option. See, for example, Ingersoll (2000, p. 70) and Hull (2006, p. 535).

37. More generally, each tradable option in a parimutuel derivatives auction can be represented as a portfolio of the state claims.

38. Prices in a parimutuel derivatives auction satisfy the principle of "first degree stochastic dominance," which is described in, for example, Chapter 2 of Huang and Litzenberger (1988). Using first degree stochastic dominance, one can explicitly bound the price of the range forward based on the prices in the implied distribution. Based on this, we can derive that the price of the range forward must lie between 177.5 and 201.1 in the 2 September 2005 auction on August 2005 NFP. Of course, the price of the range forward can be determined *exactly* by using the prices of the state claims. See Equation (6.4).

39. In fact, Gürkaynak and Wolfers (2006) use the "implied market forecast" instead of the range forward price in their analysis. The implied market forecast is based on the range forward price and is an estimate of the price of an *uncapped* forward. The implied market forecast and the price of the range forward are very highly correlated.

40. Fair and Shiller's (1990) methodology relies on a multiple regression that uses both the price of the range forward and the median economist forecast as independent variables. Ironically, most econometricians would refer to this testing methodology as "a horse race" methodology.

41. For related studies based on somewhat smaller data sets, see McCabe (2004) and McKelvey (2004).

5   DERIVATIVE STRATEGIES AND CUSTOMER ORDERS

1. For ease of exposition in Chapters 5 and 6, the no-arbitrage and self-hedging principles, which were the first and second mathematical principles in the wagering framework, are the third and fourth mathematical principles in the derivatives framework.

2. Digital options are also called "binary" options or "all-or-nothing" options.

3. For further details on this material, see Lange and Baron (2002), Baron and Lange (2003), Lange, Baron, Walden, and Harte (2003), and Lange and Economides (2005).

4. Another way to exposit the material in Chapters 5 and 6 would be to present the complete mathematical specification of the PEP before presenting an example with equilibrium values included. Because of the large number of equilibrium equations and variables for this problem, we do not take this approach. Instead, to make the exposition as readable as possible, we present the values of variables in equilibrium before the complete equilibrium specification has been presented.

5. Although this assumption is not required, it is used because it simplifies the replication formulas for vanilla options in Section 5.3.

6. Most financial exchanges list and trade many more than three strikes on a single underlying. Parimutuel derivatives auctions can handle such cases, but we chose a small number of strikes to most simply illustrate the properties of parimutuel derivatives auctions.

7. The variable d typically depends on one or more parameters, such as the option strike. To keep the notation simple, we will suppress that dependence in the notation.

8. As shown in a moment, the function d takes on a finite set of values. Therefore, the minimum and maximum of d are well defined.

9. It is possible to create derivatives with unbounded payouts by including a condition that such derivatives are in zero net supply in a parimutuel derivatives auction.

10. Readers with a derivatives background will recognize that a vanilla capped call struck at k_e is simply a "vanilla call spread" with a lower strike equal to k_e and a higher strike equal to k_E. For a vanilla capped call, k_e must be strictly less than k_E since Equation (5.10) implies that a vanilla capped call struck at k_E pays out zero everywhere.

11. A vanilla floored put struck at k_e is simply a "vanilla put spread" with the higher strike equal to k_e and the lower strike equal to k_1. For a vanilla floored put, k_e must be strictly greater than k_1 since Equation (5.11) implies that a vanilla floored put struck at k_1 pays out zero everywhere.

12. A parimutuel derivatives auction assumes that all derivative payouts are settled based on the value of the underlying at a specific point in time (as opposed to a range of dates). Thus, this chapter studies forwards, instead of futures, because forwards typically have a single date on which the forward contract is settled, whereas futures often have a range of dates for settlement.

13. Of all the derivatives described in this chapter, the forward and the range forward (described in a moment) are the only derivative strategies with negative payouts. This property implies that an owner of a forward or a range forward may have to make a payout upon expiration.

14. Hull (2006, p. 530) defines a range forward somewhat differently.

15. Chapter 6 describes in detail how the price of the range forward is determined.

16. See Hull (2006, pp. 234–237) for the definition of these strategies in unbounded form.

17. Appendix 6A will treat the case where the premium settlement date is on or before the payout settlement date and the discount factor for that time period is greater than zero and less than or equal to one.

18. If $\rho \neq 1$, then it is worth noting that one *point* in-the-money is not the same as one *tick* in-the-money. For example, a vanilla capped call struck at k_e is one point in-the-money if $U = k_e + 1$, whereas a vanilla capped call is one tick in-the-money if $U = k_e + \rho$.

19. Recall from Sections 5.1.4 and 5.1.5 that payouts on vanilla options and the range forward are capped below k_1 and above k_E. See Equations (5.10), (5.11), and (5.13).

20. Section 1.2 introduced market orders and limit orders.

21. Chapters 6 and 7 will describe in more detail how x_j and π_j are determined.

22. Uniform-price auctions are used, for instance, by the US Treasury to auction off new Treasury securities. See, for example, the discussion in Garbade and Ingber (2005).

23. To see why such an order is always fully filled requires material from Chapter 6. Chapter 6 restricts the prices of every state claim to be positive (Equation (6.2)). This implies that the price of an option is strictly greater than the option's minimum payout and strictly less

than the option's maximum payout. Similarly, the price of the range forward is strictly greater than k_1 and strictly less than k_E. Therefore, Equation (5.17) implies that such a market order is fully filled and at a price better than the limit price.

24. The fact that the number of states is finite makes the mathematics in this and in upcoming chapters tractable.

25. Since the strikes are multiples of ρ, Equation (5.18) implies that S, the number of states, is at least one greater than E, the number of option strikes, that is, $S \geq E + 1$.

26. Depending on how far away the strikes are set in an auction, the strikes $k_1 + \rho, k_1 + 2\rho, \ldots, k_E - \rho$ may or may not be tradable by customers. See the discussion in endnote 28.

27. We represent the payout function for the sth state claim with the symbol $\tilde{d}_s$ to evoke that it is similar to the payout function d on a derivative strategy. Thus, the tilde symbol is *not* used to denote that d_s is a random variable, as is sometimes done in the statistics literature.

28. The first state claim is the digital put struck at k_1 and the Sth state claim is the digital call struck at k_E, both of which are tradable by customers in a parimutuel derivatives auction. If adjacent auction strikes are one tick apart, then the 2nd, 3rd, $\ldots, S - 1$st state claims are digital ranges that customers can trade in a parimutuel derivatives auction. However, if all adjacent strikes are more than one tick apart, then customers cannot trade the 2nd, 3rd, $\ldots, S - 1$st state claims in the auction. In fact, when strikes are more than one tick apart, derivatives can be replicated using a much smaller set of fundamental building blocks. Longitude's parimutuel matching engine uses such an approach, and that approach is described in Lange, Baron, Walden, and Harte (2003, Chapter 11). This replication approach is related to the "supershare approach," which was introduced by Hakansson (1976, 1978) and discussed in Cox and Rubinstein (1985).

29. These four state claims were also described in Chapter 2.

30. Each state claim is a digital strategy, so one contract of a state claim pays out one dollar if the state claim expires in-the-money.

31. It is important to note that the replication weights for customer order j neither depend on b_j, the side of the customer order, nor on r_j, the number of contracts requested. Thus, the replication weights are for a unit case of $b_j = +1$ and $r_j = +1$.

32. Section 2.3.2 and 4.3.4 also discussed this property.

6   THE PARIMUTUEL EQUILIBRIUM

1. The principles of no-arbitrage pricing and self-hedging were used in Section 2.1 to develop the parimutuel wagering framework discussed there.

2. For further information on this material, see Lange and Baron (2002), Baron and Lange (2003), Lange, Baron, Walden, and Harte (2003), and Lange and Economides (2005).

3. For the parimutuel derivatives applications described in Section 3.3, Goldman Sachs is the initial-liquidity provider.

4. At the start of the auction (before customers have submitted any orders), the opening orders imply that the initial state prices are

$$p_s = \frac{\theta_s}{\sum_{s=1}^{S} \theta_s} \quad s = 1, 2, \ldots, S$$

Based on these initial state prices, Equation (6.4) can be used to calculate prices on all derivatives in a parimutuel derivatives auction.

5. Endnote 21 provides intuition as to how positive premium amounts for all opening orders guarantee unique prices in a parimutuel derivatives auction. Chapter 8 provides a proof of this result.

6. Equation (6.1) plays a similar role to Equation (2.1) in Chapter 2.

7. Column six of Table 6.2 shows the equilibrium state prices, which will be discussed in more detail in the next section.

8. Chapter 7 will show how the prices and the customer fills are determined in a parimutuel derivatives auction.

9. Appendix 6A will consider the case where the premium settlement date is before the payout settlement date, which implies that the sum of the state prices equals the risk-free discount factor between those two dates.

10. See, for example, Theorem 3.4.1 in LeRoy and Werner (2001, p. 26).

11. See Section 5.3.1 for the definition of $\tilde{d}_s$ and recall that $\tilde{d}_s$ is a function, not a random variable.

12. Note that the left-hand side includes any payments that customers who have sold options must make. These payments are included as negative quantities on the left-hand side.

13. Appendix 8A will show that Equation (6.16) can be represented as an eigensystem.

14. Chapter 9 will discuss this case in detail.

15. See also Tashjian and Weissman (1995), who generalize Duffie and Jackson's (1989) model. For a different approach, see Cuny (1993), who assumes that the exchange maximizes revenue earned from charging its members for seats. See also Duffie and Rahi (1995) and Tashjian (1995) for further discussion on this topic.

16. To derive this result, we can first use Equations (5.6), (5.5), and (5.11) to determine the payout functions on orders A, B, and C, respectively. Next, we can show that: the price of the digital put struck at 0.3 is $p_1 + p_2$ by Equation (6.6); the price of the digital call struck at 0.3 is $p_3 + p_4$ using Equation (6.5), which equals $1 - p_1 - p_2$ by Equation (6.3); and the price of the vanilla floored put is $(p_1 + p_2)/10$ by Equation (6.9).

These results imply that all three orders have P&L profiles as defined in Equation (6.22).

17. The fact that a vanilla order (the buy of ten contracts of the vanilla floored put) has the same P&L profile as the digital orders (the buy of one contract of the digital put and the sell of one contract of the digital call) is somewhat unusual and comes about because the adjacent strikes in this auction are one tick apart.

18. There is no need to take the absolute value of the opening order amounts (since they are positive by Equation (6.1)) or the customer fills (since they are non-negative by Equation (5.17)).

19. The fact that the objective function is a linear function of the customer fills allows us to employ a linear program in part two of our solution algorithm. See Chapter 7 for additional discussion.

20. Other objective functions satisfy our two criteria. For example, the maximum possible gain satisfies both criteria, and the standard deviation of the P&L profile (where the probabilities used in the standard deviation are the state prices) satisfy both criteria.

21. To see how positive premium amounts for all opening orders guarantee unique prices in a parimutuel derivatives auction, let us examine the following simple example. Consider an auction with one strike k_1 and $S = 2$ state claims. Let θ_1 be the premium amount of the opening order for the first state claim, the digital put struck at k_1, and let θ_2 be the premium amount of the opening order for the second state claim, the digital call struck at k_1. Assume there are $J = 2$ customer orders. Let the first customer order be an order to buy 100 contracts of the digital put struck at k_1 with a limit price of 0.6, and let the second customer order be an order to buy 100 contracts of the digital call struck at k_1, also with a limit price of 0.6. Let p_1 denote the price of the digital put struck at k_1, and let p_2 denote the price of the digital call struck at k_1. Note that p_1 and p_2 must sum to one by Equation (6.3). If $\theta_1 = \theta_2 = 0$, then $x_1 = x_2 = 100, y_1 = y_2 = 100, M = 100, 0.4 \leq p_1 \leq 0.6$, and $p_2 = 1 - p_1$ satisfy the parimutuel equilibrium conditions (except for the conditions that θ_1 and θ_2 must be positive). Thus, with opening-order premium amounts equal to zero, the prices p_1 and p_2 are not unique. In contrast, when both opening-order premium amounts are positive, that is, $\theta_1 > 0$ and $\theta_2 > 0$, it is not hard to check in this simple example that there exist unique prices. For example, if $\theta_1 = \theta_2 = 1$, then $x_1 = x_2 = 100, y_1 = y_2 = 100, M = 102$, and $p_1 = p_2 = 0.5$ are the only values that satisfy the parimutuel equilibrium conditions. Chapter 8 provides a rigorous proof that the state prices are unique in the most general case.

22. Chapter 7 will describe how we solve for the unknown variables.

23. Some of this material was first introduced in the parimutuel wagering framework of Chapter 2.

24. Recall that a range forward trade has zero premium exchanged at the time of the trade. Even so, the range forward does contribute to the

individual state premiums, as the range forward has a payout in every state.

25. For this result, see Equation (6D.8) in Appendix 6D.

26. Note that since the p_s's are all positive, Equation (6.32) and $M \neq 0$ implies that $M, m_1, m_2, \ldots, m_S$ are either all positive or all negative. If $M = 0$, then Equation (6.16) implies that $\theta_s + p_s y_s = 0$, and so Equation (6.29) implies that $m_s = 0$ for $s = 1, 2, \ldots, S$. Consequently, in all cases, $M, m_1, m_2, \ldots, m_S$ have the same sign.

27. See Aït-Sahalia and Lo (1998) and the citations therein.

28. See Section 4.4.4 for additional discussion on this topic.

29. As argued in Section 2.2.4, a parimutuel derivatives auction may allow for more active trading of low-delta options since no one party has to be short an option strategy that may result in the seller having to make a large payout.

30. This property will be discussed in more detail in Section 7.3. A portfolio of one contract of each of the derivatives requested in the first three customer orders is risk-free, and so we could also illustrate how parimutuel derivatives auctions aggregate liquidity with these three orders.

31. See also Section 2.3.3 for discussion of the impact of no-arbitrage restrictions on parimutuel prices in the wagering framework.

32. The initial-liquidity provider's worst loss is generally smaller the closer the state prices are to the opening prices. For instance, the initial-liquidity provider's worst loss is zero if the state prices exactly equal the opening prices.

33. See Section 2.3.5, Section 3.2, and Section 4.3.3 for further discussion on this point.

34. To those with a derivatives background, it may not be surprising that prices in a parimutuel derivatives auction satisfy put-call parity, since a parimutuel derivatives auction enforces no-arbitrage restrictions and put-call parity is one such no-arbitrage restriction.

35. Appendix 6A presents put-call parity incorporating a discount factor.

7 THE SOLUTION ALGORITHM FOR THE PARIMUTUEL EQUILIBRIUM PROBLEM

1. For details on such numerical solution techniques in general, see Gill, Murray, and Wright (1981) or Luenberger (2005). The PEP is an example of what is referred to in the academic literature as a "mathematical program with equilibrium constraints." As described in Luo, Pang, and Ralph (1996), such mathematical programs are commonly found in engineering and economics. They are typically two-part or bilevel problems in the sense that there is a variational inequality problem (VIP) nested within an optimization problem. Similarly, part one of our algorithm solves the VIP for the unique set of state and strategy prices,

and then part two of our algorithm maximizes the objective function. See Chapter 8 for further discussion on the relationship between the PEP and a VIP.

2. The no-arbitrage restriction of Equation (6.4) is shown in Equation (7.9).

3. Theorem 8.1 will show that Equation (7.4) can be represented as an eigensystem. Although we do not use this representation in the numerical algorithm presented in this chapter, the eigensystem representation will be used in Chapter 8.

4. Theorem 8.4 will show that these equilibrium state and strategy prices are unique.

5. As shown in the steps below, every unknown variable in the PEP can be determined from the customer fills. Put another way, if the customer fills are known, then all other PEP unknown variables (including prices) can be determined. Thus, constraints (7.1), (7.2), (7.3), and (7.4) can be expressed in terms of the customer fills, though our notation does not represent that explicitly.

6. Although the prices from the final iteration are the equilibrium prices, the customer fills from the final iteration of part one may not maximize the market exposure. As described in Sections 7.2 and 7.3, part two adjusts, if possible, those customer fills to maximize the market exposure.

7. The results from Appendix 7A show that $p_1, p_2, \ldots, p_S$ satisfy constraints (7.2) and (7.3) based on the following. Note that M greater than $\underline{M}$ (see Equation (7A.8)) implies that $M - y_s$ is positive for $s = 1, 2, \ldots, S$. Since θ_s is positive, we conclude by Equation (7.14) that p_s is positive for $s = 1, 2, \ldots, S$. Further, $f(M) = 0$ (see Equation (7A.12)) implies that the sum of the state prices equals one. Consequently, $p_1, p_2, \ldots, p_S$ satisfy constraints (7.2) and (7.3).

8. In practice, we stop stepping either when V equals zero or when V is close to zero, that is, when V is less than one dollar.

9. As a rigorous matter, the results from Appendix 8C (see Theorem 8C.2 in particular) will imply that the Jacobian matrix of changes in derivative strategy prices with respect to changes in customer fills adjusted for the order direction is positive semi-definite.

10. This exercise illustrates the market-driven nature of prices in a parimutuel derivatives auction – the greater the demand for a particular derivative strategy, the greater the price of that strategy.

11. Allowing customer order j to be a sell order and possibly for a vanilla option or range forward does not change the conclusion that modifying x_j based on Equation (7.12) will reduce v_j.

12. Appendix 8C will show analytically that the changes in derivative strategy prices with respect to changes in customer fills are smaller in magnitude when the opening orders are large.

13. Due to space considerations, Table 7.3 does not include the values of the variables between the second iteration and the final iteration.

14. A note on fill precision. Although customers typically receive a whole number of contracts when trading in a parimutuel derivatives auction,

Table 7.3 shows the customer fills $x_1, x_2, \ldots, x_6$ to hundredths of a contract (two decimal places of precision). Doing this gives a reader who is so interested the ability to verify the values of the other variables in Table 7.3, as these variables are computed based on the customer fills before they are rounded to the nearest whole number.

15.   A note on price precision. Exchanges allow customers to trade derivatives that have market prices and limit prices with typically four digits of precision or less. Exchanges restrict price precision for two reasons: first, as the number of decimal places of price precision becomes large, additional price precision becomes more of a nuisance than a help to customers; and second, exchange clearing systems have a fixed number of decimal places that they can handle to process trades. We determine equilibrium prices in the PEP to a large number of decimal places to satisfy constraints more closely (7.1), (7.2), (7.3), and (7.4). To follow standard exchange-traded derivatives conventions, parimutuel derivatives auctions display a pre-determined number of those decimal places of prices to customers. For instance, in this CPI example, we round and display p_1, p_2, p_3, and p_4 and $\pi_1, \pi_2, \ldots, \pi_6$ to four decimal places. In parimutuel derivatives auctions, premium is determined based on the rounded values of $\pi_1, \pi_2, \ldots, \pi_J$.

16.   Table 7.3 contains two rows with dashes, which are used to separate variables with different numbers of decimal places.

17.   For ease of exposition, we use a step size of one in the first and second iteration to keep the numbers simple.

18.   This point was also made in Section 6.3.4.

19.   It is not hard to check that a portfolio containing one contract of the derivative requested in the first customer order (the digital call struck at 0.3), one contract of the derivative requested in the second customer order (the digital put struck at 0.2), and one contract of the derivative requested in the third customer order (the digital range with strikes of 0.2 and 0.3) pays out one dollar in all four states (see the replication weights in Table 7.2). These three orders are complementary orders, as discussed in more detail in Section 7.3.

20.   The algorithm in part one is also an example of an "active set" method, which is a type of primal method. See Luenberger (2005, p. 326) and Gill, Murray, and Wright (1981, p. 168).

21.   The gradient projection method is based on the method of "steepest descent," which is used for unconstrained problems. See the discussion in Chapter 11 of Luenberger (2005).

22.   An algorithm that steps the customer fills *large* distances without sufficient intelligence is not likely to have good convergence properties. For example, if δ_j is too large, then x_j might oscillate between 0 and r_j on successive iterations.

23.   See, for example, Chapter 6 of Luenberger (2005) for a discussion of convex programs. In a convex program, any local minimum is in fact a global minimum.

24. For details on how to solve LPs, see Chapter 5 of Gill, Murray, and Wright (1981) or Part One of Luenberger (2005).

25. The state prices from part one satisfy Equations (7.2) and (7.3), as shown in endnote 7. Since the state prices are the same in part two as in part one, we do not have to re-check that Equations (7.2) and (7.3) are satisfied in part two.

26. Section 6.2.4 argued that the objective function should be an increasing function of the customer fills. Equation (7.22) verifies that this criteria is met here.

27. Section 9.3 will describe "competing orders," which have some similar properties to complementary orders.

28. With some additional notation, we can write Equation (7.26) in matrix form. Let $\tilde{\mathbf{A}}$ denote the J by S matrix whose element in the jth row and sth column is $a_{j,s}b_j$. Let "^{T}" denote the transpose operator. Let $\mathbf{c}$ denote the column vector of length J whose element in the jth row is c_j for $j = 1, 2, \ldots, J$. Let $\mathbf{1}$ denote the S by 1 vector of all 1's. Then,

$$\tilde{\mathbf{A}}^{\mathrm{T}}\mathbf{c} = \kappa\mathbf{1}$$

is the matrix version of Equation (7.26). If $\kappa = 0$, then this equation is called a "homogenous system." See Chapter 2 of Strang (1988) for further discussion.

29. In the special case that all the customer orders in $\mathbf{C}$ are buys of option strategies, then κ is strictly positive.

30. See Pindyck and Rubinfeld (2004) for a discussion of "complementary goods," a somewhat related concept from the field of economics.

31. In addition to these three complementary orders in the CPI auction, one can check that the fourth and fifth customer orders complement one another, and one can check that the fifth and sixth customer orders complement one another.

32. Conditions 1 and 2 imply significant restrictions on the limit prices of complementary orders. See Appendix 7C.

33. Because the customer requested amounts can be different orders of magnitude, one might consider scaling the variables $x_1, x_2, \ldots, x_J$ before calling the LP. See, for example, the scaling discussions in Luenberger (2005).

34. Theorem 8.1 will show that Equation (7A.4) can be represented as an eigensystem. Because of this, a number of results in this appendix can be derived using eigensystem machinery. For example, Equation (7A.8) can be derived using bounds on the "Perron root," as described in Kolotilina (2004, p. 2482). In addition, the uniqueness of M follows from the "Perron Theorem," which will be described in Chapter 8. We avoid introducing that machinery here and instead derive results from first principles.

35. Kolotilina (2004, Equation (1.4), p. 2482) presents a somewhat tighter lower bound in the eigensystem context.

36. See Chapter 4 of Gill, Murray, and Wright (1981) or Chapter 7 of Luenberger (2005) for more details on Newton's method.

37. It is straightforward to check that f has a continuous second derivative over the range $G \in [\underline{M}, \infty)$. Luenberger (2005, p. 202) shows that Newton's method converges at a quadratic rate under this condition provided that the initial value $\underline{M}$ is sufficiently close to M. Regarding the closeness of $\underline{M}$ to M, it is not hard to check that

$$0 < M - \underline{M} < \sum_{s=1}^{S} \theta_s$$

by using the upper bound in Equation (1.3) of Kolotilina (2004, p. 2482).

38. As will be discussed further in Chapter 8, M can be solved for as part of an eigensystem problem. Numerical solution techniques are well known for eigensystems, and Chapter 7 of Strang (1988) provides an overview of some of the standard methods. Newton's method has the advantage that it is computationally inexpensive.

39. To emphasize that these iterations take place inside a particular itera-tion of the part one algorithm, Table 7A.1 shows different iterations in different rows, whereas Table 7.3 shows different iterations in different columns.

40. The variables $p_1, p_2, \ldots, p_S$ do not require superscripts since these variables do not change between part one and part two.

8 MATHEMATICAL PROPERTIES OF PARIMUTUEL EQUILIBRIUM PRICES

1. Eisenberg and Gale (1959), Norvig (1967), and Owen (1997) study the mathematical properties of parimutuel prices in the wager-ing framework described in Chapter 2. See Section 2.3.4 for more details.

2. Section 5.2.2 showed that a market order can also be represented as a limit order with an aggressive enough limit price.

3. See, for example, Chapter 5 of Strang (1988) for more details on eigensystems.

4. We thank Professor Michael Overton of the Courant Institute of New York University for first pointing out that Equation (8.5) might be represented as an eigensystem.

5. The self-hedging restrictions are equivalent to the eigensystem repre-sentation in Equation (8.7) if customers only submit market orders, *or* if customers submit both market orders and limit orders.

6. This eigensystem representation for the PEP was first presented in Lange and Economides (2005, pp. 37–38).

7. We can rearrange the eigensystem of Equation (8.7), as is commonly done, into the following form

$$(\mathbf{H} - M\mathbf{I})\mathbf{p} = \mathbf{0}$$

where **I** is the S by S identity matrix and **0** is the column vector of length S of all zeros. Based on this equation, we say that the vector **p** lies in the "null space" of the matrix $\mathbf{H} - M\mathbf{I}$, and the equilibrium state prices are the prices that drive $\mathbf{H} - M\mathbf{I}$ to zero.

8. Theorem 8.3 can be proven from first principles (and without the eigensystem machinery) based on the approach used in Appendix 7A. Without limit orders, $y_1, y_2, \ldots, y_S$ are known and given by Equation (8.4). Appendix 7A showed that there exists a unique amount of net auction premium M based on a fixed set of net customer payouts $y_1, y_2, \ldots, y_S$. Based on these quantities, Appendix 7A proved that there exists a unique M and a unique set of state prices $p_1, p_2, \ldots, p_S$.

9. As described in Section 5.2.2, one can also think of these four market orders as limit orders with limit prices of one.

10. Note that p_3 and p_4 are close to zero. When customers only submit market orders, it is not unusual for certain state prices to be close to zero.

11. See, for example, Magill and Quinzii (1996) and Starr (1997), who discuss these issues in the context of "incomplete markets" and "general equilibrium theory," respectively.

12. Although the SPEP has an objective function, Section 8.1.3 showed that its objective function is not necessary, since there is only one solution to the problem.

13. Recall that Theorem 8.5 implies Theorem 8.4.

14. The pseudo-orders are not used in the PEP solution algorithm, which was described in Chapter 7.

15. The requested amount for a pseudo-order is arbitrary as long as it is positive.

16. The pseudo-orders resemble the opening orders in that both the pseudo-orders and the opening orders are orders to buy the S state claims. However, the resemblance ends there. The opening orders are always filled, while the pseudo-orders are never filled. Further, the opening orders are submitted in premium terms, while the pseudo-orders request specific numbers of contracts.

17. These four relationships represent step 2 through step 5 of part one of the PEP solution algorithm from Section 7.1.2.

18. See the discussion in Luo, Pang, and Ralph (1996, pp. 54–55) and Iusem (1998).

19. In fact, Theorem 8.2 is often stated in terms of **H** being a non-negative and "irreducible matrix," of which a positive matrix is a special case. See Horn and Johnson (1985, p. 361) for the definition of an irreducible matrix.

20. Recall that the GPEP in Equation (8.14) does not include an objective function, and consequently, it is a more general problem than the PEP. Thus, proving Theorem 8.5 implies that Theorem 8.4 holds.
21. See, among many, Schramm (1996) for definitions of compact and convex.
22. A function G is monotone if and only if $(G(\mathbf{w}) - G(\mathbf{v}))^T(\mathbf{w} - \mathbf{v}) \geq 0 \ \forall \ \mathbf{v,w} \in X$.
23. Equations (8C.4) and (8C.5) do not handle the pricing of the range forward. However, because put–call parity holds in a parimutuel derivatives auction, we can represent a buy (resp., sell) of a range forward with limit price w as a buy (resp., sell) of a vanilla capped call struck at k_1 with a limit price of $w - k_1$. See Appendix 6B for more discussion on put-call parity.
24. Laplacian matrices are used for the study of "networks," and they encode how different "nodes" in a network "communicate." In the parimutuel derivatives auction framework, the nodes are the states, and the matrix of first derivatives tells us that all the states communicate when the price of one state is changed.
25. Note that $\widetilde{\mathbf{D}}$ is also "diagonally dominant," which is defined and discussed in Horn and Johnson (1985, p. 349).

9 MATHEMATICAL PROPERTIES OF CUSTOMER FILLS IN THE PARIMUTUEL EQUILIBRIUM

1. We use the term "vector" in this chapter to describe the J customer fills, as we define below a J by 1 column vector $\mathbf{x}$ with customer fill x_j in the jth row for $j = 1, 2, \ldots, J$.
2. When there are multiple vectors of customer fills that satisfy the PEP for a given set of auction inputs, an objective approach is needed to choose a particular vector of customer fills. As discussed in Harris (2003, pp. 112–120), there are a variety of standard approaches, including "time priority" and "pro-rata allocation." Parimutuel derivatives auctions currently allocate fills using a pro-rata based approach.
3. This representation is the shorthand representation of the PEP. For all the constraints and definitions, see Table 6.7.
4. Section 9.4 will explain why this CPI example has exactly one vector of customer fills.
5. The opening orders for this auction are the same as the opening orders for the auction example from Chapters 5, 6, and 7, and for the auction example in Section 8.1.4.
6. Theorem 9.3 from Section 9.2 will prove that there are not just three, but in fact an infinite number of vectors of customer fills for this example.

7. If an auction has multiple vectors of customer fills and all filled customer orders are orders to buy options, then the net customer payouts are equal across all vectors of customer fills.

8. Theorems 9.1, 9.2, and 9.3 will relate to the first, second, and third observations, respectively.

9. It is worth noting that although the customer orders that are *worse than the market* are the same for every vector of fills, the customer orders that receive *zero fill* can differ for different vectors of customer fills. In Table 9.3, note that: in the first vector, the second and third customer orders receive no fill; in the second vector, the fourth customer order receives no fill; and in the third vector, all customer orders receive some fill. In a similar vein, one can show that although the customer orders that are *better than the market* are the same for every vector of fills, the customer orders that are *fully filled* can differ for different vectors of customer fills.

10. In fact, we verified in Section 9.1.2 that this vector of customer fills satisfies the PEP conditions.

11. Since **C** is non-empty, at least one value of $c_1, c_2, \ldots, c_J$ is strictly non-zero.

12. We can write Equation (9.24) in matrix form. See endnote 28 in Chapter 7, and see Section 9.5.

13. The concept of competing orders is closely related to the concept of "redundant securities." See LeRoy and Werner (2001, pp. 5, 10, 36–37), and see Ingersoll (1987, pp. 49–50) for a discussion of redundant securities. LeRoy and Werner (2001, p. 10) point out that the existence of redundant securities leads to multiple portfolio allocations associated with a "market-clearing consumption allocation." Theorem 9.4 will show a somewhat similar result – that the existence of competing orders is required for there to be multiple equilibrium customer fill vectors.

14. Note that the two examples of competing orders considered here both have $\kappa = 0$ in Equation (9.24). In Section 9.5, Theorem 9.6 shows that κ equals zero if all the customer orders in **C** are buys of options.

15. Domowitz and Madhavan (2001, p. 379) and Harris (2003, p. 134) point out that excess demand can lead to multiple vectors of fills in traditional auctions.

16. See Theorem 9.8 for what these conditions imply about the limit prices of the customer orders in **C**.

17. Here, $\mathbf{C} = \{4, 6\}$, $c_1 = c_2 = c_3 = c_5 = 0$, $c_4 = 1$, $c_6 = -1$, and $\kappa = \pi_6$.

18. Note that **C** is non-empty, which implies that **c** contains at least one non-zero element. Thus, if Equation (9.34) holds, then it holds for a $\mathbf{c} \neq 0$.

19. Based on Equation (9.34), it is easy to see that competing orders are closely related to "redundant securities." See endnote 13.

20. The converse of Theorem 9.8 is worth stating: if all the customer orders in an auction are buy orders, and there does not exist a non-zero

vector $\mathbf{c}$ such that both $\mathbf{A}^T\mathbf{c} = \mathbf{0}$ and $\mathbf{w}^T\mathbf{c} = 0$, then there exists a unique vector of customer fills. Thus, even if $\mathbf{A}$ is not of full rank, there may exist a unique vector of customer fills in the auction, depending on the relationship between the customers' limit prices. This result is (obviously) stronger than Theorem 9.7.

21. The state prices $p_1, p_2, \ldots, p_S$ do not depend on the customer fills over this narrow range of customer fill vectors. However, in the more general case, $p_1, p_2, \ldots, p_S$ do depend on the customer fills.

22. Although the results in Appendix 7C are for complementary orders, those results are based on Equation (7.26), which is identical to Equation (9.24). Thus, those results can be applied here.

23. If the customer orders are all buys of options, and $\mathbf{A}$ has full rank, then we can prove that the PEP has a unique set of prices *and fills* by using the fact that the PEP can be represented as a BVIP (see Chapter 8) which has a positive definite Jacobian (see, e.g., Luo, Pang, and Ralph (1996, pp. 54–55)). Such a proof would parallel the proof of Theorem 8B.2, which relied on a positive semi-definite Jacobian.

References

Abrache, Jawad, Teodor Gabriel Crainic, and Michel Gendreau. "Models for Bundle Trading in Financial Markets." *European Journal of Operational Research* 160, no. 1 (2005): 88–105.

Aït-Sahalia, Yacine, and Andrew W. Lo. "Nonparametric Estimation of State-Price Densities Implicit in Financial Asset Prices." *Journal of Finance* 53, no. 2 (1998): 499–547.

Ali, Mukhtar M. "Probability and Utility Estimates for Racetrack Bettors." *Journal of Political Economy* 85, no. 4 (1977): 803–815.

Allen, Franklin, and Douglas Gale. *Financial Innovation and Risk Sharing.* Cambridge, MA: MIT Press, 1994.

Andersen, Torben G., and Tim Bollerslev. "Deutsche Mark–Dollar Volatility: Intraday Activity Patterns, Macroeconomic Announcements, and Longer-Run Dependencies." *Journal of Finance* 53, no. 1 (1998): 219–265.

Andersen, Torben G., Tim Bollerslev, Francis X. Diebold, and Clara Vega. "Micro Effects of Macro Announcements: Real-Time Price Discovery in Foreign Exchange." *American Economic Review* 93, no. 1 (2003): 38–62.

———. "Real-Time Price Discovery in Stock, Bond and Foreign Exchange Markets." Working Paper, April 2005.

Anderson, Ronald W. "The Regulation of Futures Contract Innovations in the United States." *Journal of Futures Markets* 4, no. 3 (1984): 297–332.

Arrow, Kenneth J. "The Role of Securities in the Optimal Allocation of Risk-Bearing." *Review of Economic Studies* 31, no. 2 (1964): 91–96.

Asch, Peter, Burton G. Malkiel, and Richard E. Quandt. "Racetrack Betting and Informed Behavior." *Journal of Financial Economics* 10, no. 2 (1982): 187–194.

———. "Market Efficiency in Racetrack Betting." *Journal of Business* 57, no. 2 (1984): 165–175.

———. "Market Efficiency in Racetrack Betting: Further Evidence and a Correction." *Journal of Business* 59, no. 1 (1986): 157–160.

Asch, Peter, and Richard E. Quandt. *Racetrack Betting: The Professors' Guide to Strategies*. Dover, MA: Auburn House Publishing, 1986.

Association of Racing Commissioners International. *Pari-Mutuel Racing 2003*. Lexington, KY: Association of Racing Commissioners International, 2005.

Ayazifar, Babak. "Graph Spectra and Modal Dynamics of Oscillatory Networks." PhD Dissertation, Massachusetts Institute of Technology, September 2002.

Balduzzi, Pierluigi, Edwin J. Elton, and T. Clifton Green. "Economic News and Bond Prices: Evidence from the U.S. Treasury Market." *Journal of Financial and Quantitative Analysis* 36, no. 4 (2001): 523–543.

Bank for International Settlements. "Triennial Central Bank Survey of Foreign Exchange and Derivatives Market Activity in April 2004." Research Paper, Monetary and Economic Department, September 2004. http://www.bis.org/publ/rpfx04.pdf

Barbour, Violet. *Capitalism in Amsterdam in the 17thCentury*. Ann Arbor: University of Michigan Press, 1963.

Baron, Ken. "Energy Inventory Options Expand the Risk Management Universe." *NYMEX Energy in the News* 1 (2004): 9–12.

Baron, Ken, and Jeffrey Lange. "From Horses to Hedging." *Risk Magazine* 16, no. 2 (2003): 73–77.

Benter, William. "Computer Based Horse Race Handicapping and Wagering Systems: A Report." In *Efficiency of Racetrack Betting Markets*, edited by Donald B. Hausch, Victor S. Y. Lo, and William T. Ziemba, 183–198. San Diego: Academic Press, 1994.

Berman, Abraham, and Robert J. Plemmons. *Nonnegative Matrices in the Mathematical Sciences*. Philadelphia: SIAM Press, 1994.

Bernstein, Peter L. *Against the Gods: The Remarkable Story of Risk*. New York: John Wiley and Sons, 1996.

Bjorkman, Douglas, and Ed Bukszar. "Efficiency Reigns: Disappearance of the 'Favorite-Longshot Bias' in Pari-Mutuel Racehorse Betting." *Western Decision Sciences Annual Conference Proceedings*. Kauai, Hawaii (2003): 197–201.

Black, Deborah G. "Success and Failure of Futures Contracts: Theory and Empirical Evidence." Monograph 1986-1, Salomon Brothers Center for the Study of Financial Institutions, Graduate School of Business Administration, New York University, 1986.

Black, Fischer, and Myron Scholes. "The Pricing of Options and Corporate Liabilities." *Journal of Political Economy* 81, no. 3 (1973): 637–654.

Bollen, Nicolas P. B., and Robert E. Whaley. "Does Net Buying Pressure Affect the Shape of Implied Volatility Functions?" *Journal of Finance* 59, no. 2 (2004): 711–753.

Borensztein, Eduardo, and Paolo Mauro. "The Case for GDP-Indexed Bonds." *Economic Policy* 19, no. 38 (2004): 165–216.

Bossaerts, Peter, Leslie Fine, and John Ledyard. "Inducing Liquidity in Thin Financial Markets Through Combined-Value Trading Mechanisms." *European Economic Review* 46, no. 9 (2002): 1671–1695.

Boyd, John H., Jian Hu, and Ravi Jagannathan. "The Stock Market's Reaction to Unemployment News: Why Bad News Is Usually Good for Stocks." *Journal of Finance* 60, no. 2 (2005): 649–672.

Brenner, Menachem, Rafi Eldor, and Shmuel Hauser. "The Price of Options Illiquidity." *Journal of Finance* 56, no. 2 (2001): 789–805.

Brenner, Reuven, with Gabrielle A. Brenner. *Gambling and Speculation: A Theory, a History, and a Future of Some Human Decisions*. Cambridge: Cambridge University Press, 1990.

Brockett, Patrick L., Mulong Wang, and Chuanhou Yang. "Weather Derivatives and Weather Risk Management." *Risk Management and Insurance Review* 8, no. 1 (2005): 127–140.

Brown, Lawrence D., and Yi Lin. "Racetrack Betting and Consensus of Subjective Probabilities." *Statistics and Probability Letters* 62, no. 2 (2003): 175–187.

Bruce, Alistair C., and Johnnie E. V. Johnson. "Investigating the Roots of the Favourite-Longshot Bias: An Analysis of Decision Making by Supply- and Demand-Side Agents in Parallel Betting Markets." *Journal of Behavioral Decision Making* 13, no. 4 (2000): 413–430.

Buck, Fred S. *Horse Race Betting: A Comprehensive Account of Pari-Mutuel, Off-Track Betting, and Bookmaking Operations*. 4th edn New York: Arco Publishing, 1977.

Burghardt, Galen. "FIA Annual Volume Survey: The Invigorating Effects of Electronic Trading." *Futures Industry Magazine* 15, no. 2 (2005): 28–42.

Busche, Kelly. "Efficient Market Results in an Asian Setting." In *Efficiency of Racetrack Betting Markets*, edited by Donald B. Hausch, Victor S. Y. Lo, and William T. Ziemba, 615–616. San Diego: Academic Press, 1994.

Busche, Kelly, and Christopher D. Hall. "An Exception to the Risk Preference Anomaly." *Journal of Business* 61, no. 3 (1988): 337–346.

Busche, Kelly, and W. David Walls. "Decision Costs and Betting Market Efficiency." *Rationality and Society* 12, no. 4 (2000): 477–492.

Camerer, Colin F. "Can Asset Markets be Manipulated? A Field Experiment with Racetrack Betting." *Journal of Political Economy* 106, no. 3 (1998): 457–482.

Canina, Linda, and Stephen Figlewski. "The Informational Content of Implied Volatility." *Review of Financial Studies* 6, no. 3 (1993): 659–681.

Carlton, Dennis W. "Futures Markets: Their Purpose, Their History, Their Growth, Their Successes and Failures." *Journal of Futures Markets* 4, no. 3 (1984): 237–271.

Chapman, Randall G. "Still Searching for Positive Returns at the Track: Empirical Results from 2,000 Hong Kong Races." In *Efficiency of Racetrack Betting Markets*, edited by Donald B. Hausch, Victor S. Y. Lo, and William T. Ziemba, 173–181. San Diego: Academic Press, 1994.

Chen, Yiling, Chao-Hsien Chu, Tracy Mullen, and David M. Pennock. "Information Markets vs. Opinion Pools: An Empirical Comparison." Conference Paper, 6th ACM Conference on Electronic Commerce, Vancouver, British Columbia, June 2005.

Cho, Young-Hye, and Robert F. Engle. "Modeling the Impacts of Market Activity on Bid-Ask Spreads in the Option Market." Working Paper 7331, National Bureau of Economic Research, September 1999.

Clemons, Eric K., and Bruce W. Weber. "The OptiMark Experience: What We Learned." In *The Electronic Call Auction: Market Mechanism and Trading*, edited by Robert A. Schwartz, 353–364. Boston: Kluwer Academic Publishers, 2001.

Cohen, Kalman J., and Robert A. Schwartz. "An Electronic Call Market: Its Design and Desirability." In *The Electronic Call Auction: Market Mechanism and Trading*, edited by Robert A. Schwartz, 55–85. Boston: Kluwer Academic Publishers, 2001.

Commodity Futures Trading Commission. *Fiscal Year 2004 Annual Report*. Washington, DC: 2005.

Corkish, Jo, Allison Holland, and Anne Fremault Vila. "The Determinants of Successful Financial Innovation: An Empirical Analysis of Futures Innovation on LIFFE." Working Paper 70, Bank of England, 1997.

Cornell, Bradford. "The Relationship Between Volume and Price Variability in Futures Markets." *Journal of Futures Markets* 1, no. 3 (1981): 303–316.

Cox, John C., and Mark Rubinstein. *Options Markets*. Englewood Cliffs, NJ: Prentice Hall, 1985.

Cravath, Swaine, and Moore. "Commodity Futures Modernization Act of 2000." Memorandum for ISDA Members, New York, 5 January 2001. http://www.isda.org/speeches/pdf/Analysis_of_Commodity-Exchange-Act-Legislation.pdf

Cuny, Charles J. "The Role of Liquidity in Futures Market Innovations." *Review of Financial Studies* 6, no. 1 (1993): 57–78.

De La Vega, Joseph. *Confusión de Confusiones*. In *Extraordinary Popular Delusions and the Madness of Crowds and Confusión de Confusiones*, edited by Martin S. Fridson, 123–214. New York: John Wiley and Sons, 1996.

de Vries, Sven, and Rakesh V. Vohra. "Combinatorial Auctions: A Survey." *INFORMS Journal on Computing* 15, no. 3 (2003): 284–309.

Domowitz, Ian, and Ananth Madhavan. "Open Sesame: Alternative Opening Algorithms in Securities Markets." In *The Electronic Call*

Auction: Market Mechanism and Trading, edited by Robert A. Schwartz, 375–394. Boston: Kluwer Academic Publishers, 2001.

Duffie, Darrell. *Security Markets: Stochastic Models*. San Diego: Academic Press, 1988.

Duffie, Darrell, and Matthew O. Jackson. "Optimal Innovation of Futures Contracts." *Review of Financial Studies* 2, no. 3 (1989): 275–296.

Duffie, Darrell, and Rohit Rahi. "Financial Market Innovation and Security Design: An Introduction." *Journal of Economic Theory* 65, no. 1 (1995): 1–42.

Economides, Nicholas, and Robert A. Schwartz. "Electronic Call Market Trading." *Journal of Portfolio Management* 21, no. 3 (1995): 10–18.

Edelman, David C., and Nigel R. O'Brian. "Tote Arbitrage and Lock Opportunities in Racetrack Betting." *European Journal of Finance* 10, no. 5 (2004): 370–378.

Ederington, Louis H., and Jae Ha Lee. "How Markets Process Information: News Releases and Volatility." *Journal of Finance* 48, no. 4 (1993): 1161–1191.

Eisenberg, Edmund, and David Gale. "Consensus of Subjective Probabilities: The Pari-Mutuel Method." *Annals of Mathematical Statistics* 30, no. 1 (1959): 165–168.

Enders, Walter. *Applied Econometric Time Series*. 2nd edn. Hoboken, NJ: John Wiley and Sons, 2004.

Epstein, Richard A. *The Theory of Gambling and Statistical Logic*. Rev. edn New York: Academic Press, 1977.

Fabricand, Burton P. *Horse Sense: A New and Rigorous Application of Mathematical Methods to Successful Betting at the Track*. New York: David McKay, 1965.

Fair, Ray C. "Shock Effects on Stocks, Bonds, and Exchange Rates." *Journal of International Money and Finance* 22, no. 3 (2003): 307–341.

Fair, Ray C., and Robert J. Shiller. "Comparing Information in Forecasts from Econometric Models." *American Economic Review* 80, no. 3 (1990): 375–389.

Falloon, William. "Patent Power: Who Owns the Ideas that Drive Derivatives?" *Risk Magazine* 12, no. 12 (1999): 22–26.

Fan, Ming, Jan Stallaert, and Andrew B. Whinston. "A Web-Based Financial Trading System." *IEEE Computer* 32, no. 4 (1999): 64–70.

——. "The Internet and the Future of Financial Markets." *Communications of the ACM* 43, no. 11 (2000): 83–88.

Ferris, Michael C., and Jong-Shi Pang. "Engineering and Economic Applications of Complementarity Problems." *SIAM Review* 39, no. 4 (1997): 669–713.

Figlewski, Stephen. "Subjective Information and Market Efficiency in a Betting Market." *Journal of Political Economy* 87, no. 1 (1979): 75–88.

——. "Options Arbitrage in Imperfect Markets." *Journal of Finance* 44, no. 5 (1989a): 1289–1311.

——. "What Does an Option Pricing Model Tell Us About Option Prices?" *Financial Analysts Journal* 45, no. 5 (1989b): 12–15.

Fingleton, John, and Patrick Waldron. "Optimal Determination of Book-makers' Betting Odds: Theory and Tests." *Trinity Economic Paper Series*, Technical Paper No. 96/9, June 2001.

Fleming, Michael J. "The Round-the-Clock Market for U.S. Treasury Securities." *Federal Reserve Bank of New York Economic Policy Review* 3, no. 2 (1997): 9–32.

Fleming, Michael J., and Eli M. Remolona. "What Moves the Bond Market?" *Federal Reserve Bank of New York Economic Policy Review* 3, no. 4 (1997): 31–50.

——. "Price Formation and Liquidity in the U.S. Treasury Market: The Response to Public Information." *Journal of Finance* 54, no. 5 (1999): 1901–1915.

Foroohar, Kambiz. "Online Gambling Raises the Ante." *Bloomberg Markets* 14, no. 10 (2005): 64–72.

Fortnow, Lance, Joe Kilian, David M. Pennock, and Michael P. Wellman. "Betting Boolean-Style: A Framework for Trading in Securities Based on Logical Formulas." *Decision Support Systems* 39, no. 1 (2005): 87–104.

Frame, W. Scott, and Lawrence J. White. "Empirical Studies of Financial Innovation: Lots of Talk, Little Action?" *Journal of Economic Literature* 42, no. 1 (2004): 116–144.

Freeman, Bob, Barbara Freeman, with Jim McKinley. *Wanna Bet? A Study of the Pari-Mutuels System in the United States: How it Works – and the Sports Involved*. N.p.: Freeman Mutuels Management, 1982.

Gabriel, Paul E., and James R. Marsden. "An Examination of Market Efficiency in British Racetrack Betting." *Journal of Political Economy* 98, no. 4 (1990): 874–885.

——. "An Examination of Market Efficiency in British Racetrack Betting: Errata and Corrections." *Journal of Political Economy* 99, no. 3 (1991): 657–659.

Gandar, John M., Richard A. Zuber, and R. Stafford Johnson. "Searching for the Favourite-Longshot Bias Down Under: An Examination of the New Zealand Pari-Mutuel Betting Market." *Applied Economics* 33, no. 13 (2001): 1621–1629.

Garbade, Kenneth D., and Jeffrey F. Ingber. "The Treasury Auction Process: Objectives, Structure, and Recent Adaptations." *Federal Reserve Bank of New York: Current Issues in Economics and Finance* 11, no. 2 (2005).

Garbade, Kenneth D., and William L. Silber. "Structural Organization of Secondary Markets: Clearing Frequency, Dealer Activity and Liquidity Risk." *Journal of Finance* 34, no. 3 (1979): 577–593.

——. "Cash Settlement of Futures Contracts: An Economic Analysis." *Journal of Futures Markets* 3, no. 4 (1983): 451–472.

Gates, Stephen. "The Developing Option Market: Regulatory Issues and New Investor Interest." *University of Florida Law Review* 25, no. 3 (1973): 421–464.

Gill, Philip E., Walter Murray, and Margaret H. Wright. *Practical Optimization.* London: Academic Press, 1981.

Golec, Joseph, and Maurry Tamarkin. "Bettors Love Skewness, Not Risk, at the Horse Track." *Journal of Political Economy* 106, no. 1 (1998): 205–225.

Gorham, Michael. "Event Markets Campaign for Respect." *Futures Industry Magazine* 14, no. 1 (2004): 15–20.

Gray, Roger W. "Why Does Futures Trading Succeed or Fail: An Analysis of Selected Commodities." As reprinted in *Readings in Futures Markets, Vol. 3, Views from the Trade*, edited by Anne E. Peck, 235–248. Chicago: Board of Trade of the City of Chicago, 1978.

Green, T. Clifton. "Economic News and the Impact of Trading on Bond Prices." *Journal of Finance* 59, no. 3 (2004): 1201–1233.

Griffith, Richard M. "Odds Adjustments by American Horse-Race Bettors." *American Journal of Psychology* 62, no. 2 (1949): 290–294.

Gu, Siwei, Andrew B. Whinston, and Jan Stallaert. "Exchange Market Model for Over-the-Counter Equity Derivatives Trading." Working Paper, University of Texas at Austin – Center for Research in Electronic Commerce, October 2001.

Gürkaynak, Refet, and Justin Wolfers. "Macroeconomic Derivatives: An Initial Analysis of Market-Based Macro Forecasts, Uncertainty, and Risk." Working Paper 11929, National Bureau of Economic Research, January 2006.

Hakansson, Nils H. "The Purchasing Power Fund: A New Kind of Financial Intermediary." *Financial Analysts Journal* 32, no. 6 (1976): 49–59.

——. "Welfare Aspects of Options and Supershares." *Journal of Finance* 33, no. 3 (1978): 759–776.

Hanson, Robin. "Combinatorial Information Market Design." *Information Systems Frontiers* 5, no. 1 (2003): 107–119.

Hanson, Robin, Ryan Oprea, and David Porter. "Information Aggregation and Manipulation in an Experimental Market." Forthcoming in *Journal of Economic Behavior and Organization*, 2006.

Harker, Patrick T., and Jong-Shi Pang. "Finite–Dimensional Variational Inequality and Nonlinear Complementarity Problems: A Survey of Theory, Algorithms, and Applications." *Mathematical Programming* 48, no. 2 (1990): 161–220.

Harris, Larry. *Trading and Exchanges: Market Microstructure for Practitioners*. Oxford: Oxford University Press, 2003.

Hausch, Donald B., Victor S. Y. Lo, and William T. Ziemba, eds. *Efficiency of Racetrack Betting Markets*. San Diego: Academic Press, 1994a.

——. "Introduction to the Efficiency of Win Markets and the Favorite-Longshot Bias." In *Efficiency of Racetrack Betting Markets*, edited by Donald B. Hausch, Victor S. Y. Lo, and William T. Ziemba, 251–253. San Diego: Academic Press, 1994b.

Hausch, Donald B., and William T. Ziemba. "Transactions Costs, Extent of Inefficiencies, Entries and Multiple Wagers in a Racetrack Betting Model." *Management Science* 31, no. 4 (1985): 381–394.

Hausch, Donald B., William T. Ziemba, and Mark Rubinstein. "Efficiency of the Market for Racetrack Betting." *Management Science* 27, no. 12 (1981): 1435–1452.

Heaton, J. B. "Patent Law and Financial Engineering." *Derivatives Quarterly* 7, no. 2 (2000): 7–15.

Hodges, Stewart D., Robert G. Tompkins, and William T. Ziemba. "The Favorite-Longshot Bias in S&P 500 and FTSE 100 Index Futures Options: The Return to Bets and the Cost of Insurance." Conference Paper 135, European Finance Association Annual Conference, 2003.

Horn, Roger A., and Charles R. Johnson. *Matrix Analysis*. Cambridge: Cambridge University Press, 1985.

Horrigan, Brian R. "The CPI Futures Market: The Inflation Hedge That Won't Grow." *Federal Reserve Bank of Philadelphia Business Review* 2, no. 3 (1987): 3–14.

Huang, Chi-fu, and Robert H. Litzenberger. *Foundations for Financial Economics*. Englewood Cliffs, NJ: Prentice Hall, 1988.

Hull, John C. *Options, Futures, and Other Derivatives*. 6th edn. Englewood Cliffs, NJ: Prentice Hall, 2006.

Ingersoll, Jonathan E. Jr. *Theory of Financial Decision Making*. Totowa, NJ: Rowman and Littlefield, 1987.

——. "Digital Contracts: Simple Tools for Pricing Complex Derivatives." *Journal of Business* 73, no. 1 (2000): 67–88.

Iusem, Alfredo N. "On Some Properties of Paramonotone Operators." *Journal of Convex Analysis* 5, no. 2 (1998): 269–278.

Jameson, Mel, and William Wilhelm. "Market Making in the Options Markets and the Costs of Discrete Hedge Rebalancing." *Journal of Finance* 47, no. 2 (1992): 765–779.

Jones, Frank J. "The Economics of Futures and Options Contracts Based on Cash Settlement." *Journal of Futures Markets* 2, no. 1 (1982): 63–82.

Kalay, Avner, Li Wei, and Avi Wohl. "Continuous Trading or Call Auctions: Revealed Preferences of Investors at the Tel Aviv Stock Exchange." *Journal of Finance* 57, no. 1 (2002): 523–542.

Kanzow, Christian. "Global Optimization Techniques for Mixed Complementarity Problems." *Journal of Global Optimization* 16, no. 1 (2000): 1–21.

Kaplan, Michael. "The High Tech Trifecta." *Wired* 10, no. 3 (2002): 98–103.

Kolotilina, L. Yu. "Bounds and Inequalities for the Perron Root of a Nonnegative Matrix." *Journal of Mathematical Sciences* 121, no. 4 (2004): 2481–2507.

Krueger, Alan B., and Kenneth N. Fortson. "Do Markets Respond More to More Reliable Labor Market Data? A Test of Market Rationality." *Journal of the European Economic Association* 1, no. 4 (2003): 931–957.

Lamont, Owen A., and Richard H. Thaler. "Anomalies: The Law of One Price in Financial Markets." *Journal of Economic Perspectives* 17, no. 4 (2003): 191–202.

Lange, Jeffrey. "Financial Products Having a Demand-Based, Adjustable Return, and Trading Exchange Therefor." US Patent 6,321,212, filed 21 July 1999, issued 20 November 2001.

Lange, Jeffrey, and Ken Baron. "Derivatives Having Demand-Based, Adjustable Returns, and Trading Exchange Therefor." US Patent Application 20030115128, filed 2 April 2002.

Lange, Jeffrey, Ken Baron, Charles Walden, and Marcus Harte. "Replicated Derivatives Having Demand-Based, Adjustable Returns, and Trading Exchange Therefor." US Patent Application 20030236738, filed 11 February 2003.

Lange, Jeffrey, and Nicholas Economides. "A Parimutuel Market Microstructure for Contingent Claims." *European Financial Management* 11, no. 1 (2005): 25–49.

Lerner, Josh. "Where Does *State Street* Lead? A First Look at Finance Patents, 1971 to 2000." *Journal of Finance* 57, no. 2 (2002): 901–930.

LeRoy, Stephen F., and Jan Werner. *Principles of Financial Economics.* Cambridge: Cambridge University Press, 2001.

Levin, Nissan. "Optimal Bets in Pari-Mutuel Systems." In *Efficiency of Racetrack Betting Markets*, edited by Donald B. Hausch, Victor S. Y. Lo, and William T. Ziemba, 109–125. San Diego: Academic Press, 1994.

Liebenberg, Lauren. *The Electronic Financial Markets of the Future and Survival Strategies of the Broker-Dealers.* London: Palgrave Macmillan, 2002.

Lo, Victor S. Y., John Bacon-Shone, and Kelly Busche. "The Application of Ranking Probability Models to Racetrack Betting." *Management Science* 41, no. 6 (1995): 1048–1059.

Luenberger, David G. *Linear and Nonlinear Programming*. 2nd edn. Reading, MA: Addison-Wesley Publishing Company, 2005.

Luo, Zhi-Quan, Jong-Shi Pang, and Daniel Ralph. *Mathematical Programs with Equilibrium Constraints*. Cambridge: Cambridge University Press, 1996.

Lurie, Jonathan. *The Chicago Board of Trade, 1859–1905: The Dynamics of Self-Regulation*. Urbana: University of Illinois Press, 1979.

Magill, Michael, and Martine Quinzii. *Theory of Incomplete Markets*. Vol. 1. Cambridge, MA: MIT Press, 1996.

McCabe, Jennifer. "An Examination of the Predictive Abilities of Economic Derivative Markets." Student Research Paper, Glucksman Fellowship Program, NYU Stern School of Business, April 2004. http://w4.stern.nyu.edu/glucksman/docs/McCabe%20Paper% 202004.pdf

McCallum, William G., Deborah Hughes-Hallett, Andrew M. Gleason, David Mumford, Brad G. Osgood, Jeff Tecosky-Feldman, Thomas W. Tucker, Douglas Quinney, and Patti Frazer Lock. *Calculus: Multivariable,* 4th edn. New York: John Wiley and Sons, 2004.

McKelvey, Ed. "Payroll Forecasts – How Good Are They?" US Daily Financial Market Comment, Goldman Sachs, 19 August 2004. http://www.gs.com/econderivs/NFPForecastingAnalysis08-19-04.pdf

Merton, Robert C. *Continuous-Time Finance*. Rev. edn. Malden, MA: Blackwell Publishing, 1992a.

——. "Financial Innovation and Economic Performance." *Journal of Applied Corporate Finance* 4, no. 4 (1992b): 12–22.

Miller, Merton H. "Financial Innovation: The Last Twenty Years and the Next." *Journal of Financial and Quantitative Analysis* 21, no. 4 (1986): 459–471.

——. "Financial Innovation: Achievements and Prospects." *Journal of Applied Corporate Finance* 4, no. 4 (1992): 4–11.

Nagurney, Anna. "Variational Inequalities." Lecture Notes, Isenberg School of Management, University of Massachusetts, 2002. http://supernet.som.umass.edu/austria_lectures/fvisli.pdf

Nomoto, Kenichi. "Review of JRA Horseracing in 2003." *Japan Racing Journal* 12, no. 1 (2004). http://www.jair.jrao.ne.jp/journal/v12n1/ main.html

Norvig, Torsten. "Consensus of Subjective Probabilities: A Convergence Theorem." *Annals of Mathematical Statistics* 38, no. 1 (1967): 221–225.

Ottaviani, Marco, and Peter Norman Sorensen. "Late Informed Betting and the Favorite-Longshot Bias." Discussion Paper, University of Copenhagen – Institute of Economics, July 2003.

Owen, Guillermo. "Pari Mutuel as a System of Aggregation of Information." In *Game Theoretical Applications to Economics and Operations Research*, edited by T. Parthasarathy, B. Dutta, J. A. M. Potters, T. E. S. Raghaven, D. Ray, and A. Sen, 183–195. The Netherlands: Kluwer Academic Publishers, 1997.

Paul, Allen B. "The Role of Cash Settlement in Futures Contract Specification." In *Futures Markets: Regulatory Issues*, edited by Anne E. Peck, 271–328. Washington, DC: American Enterprise Institute, 1985.

Pekeč, Aleksandar, and Michael H. Rothkopf. "Combinatorial Auction Design." *Management Science* 49, no. 11 (2003): 1485–1503.

Peltz, Michael. "Hedge Funds Grow Up." *Bloomberg Markets* 14, no. 2 (2005): 30–40.

Pennock, David M. "A Dynamic Pari-Mutuel Market for Hedging, Wagering, and Information Aggregation." *Proceedings of the 5th ACM Conference on Electronic Commerce*, 2004: 170–179.

Peters, Mark, Anthony Man-Cho So, and Yinyu Ye. "A Convex Parimutuel Formulation for Contingent Claim Markets." Working Paper, Stanford University, 2006.

Pindyck, Robert S. and Daniel L. Rubinfeld. *Microeconomics*. 6th edn. Englewood Cliffs, NJ: Prentice Hall, 2004.

Plott, Charles R., Jorgen Wit, and Winston C. Yang. "Parimutuel Betting Markets as Information Aggregation Devices: Experimental Results." *Economic Theory* 22, no. 2 (2003): 311–351.

Polk, Charles W., and Evan Schulman. "Enhancing the Liquidity of Bond Trading." In *The Handbook of Fixed Income Technology: Management Issues for Today and Tomorrow*, edited by Joseph Rosen and Russell D. Glisker, 185–194. New York: The Summit Group Publishing, 2000.

Quandt, Richard. "Betting and Equilibrium." *Quarterly Journal of Economics* 101, no. 1 (1986): 201–207.

Ritter, Jay R. "Racetrack Betting – An Example of a Market with Efficient Arbitrage." In *Efficiency of Racetrack Betting Markets*, edited by Donald B. Hausch, Victor S. Y. Lo, and William T. Ziemba, 431–441. San Diego: Academic Press, 1994.

Sandholm, Tuomas, and Subhash Suri. "Side Constraints and Non-Price Attributes in Markets." Forthcoming in *Games and Economic Behavior*, 2006.

Sandholm, Tuomas, Subhash Suri, Andrew Gilpin, and David Levine. "Winner Determination in Combinatorial Auction Generalizations." Conference Paper, AGENTS 2001 Workshop on Agent-Based Approaches to B2B, Montreal, Canada, 2001.

Sauer, Raymond D. "The Economics of Wagering Markets." *Journal of Economic Literature* 36, no. 4 (1998): 2021–2064.

Schramm, Michael J. *Introduction to Real Analysis.* Englewood Cliffs, NJ: Prentice Hall, 1996.

Schwartz, Robert A. "Introductory Remarks." In *Call Auction Trading: New Answers to Old Questions,* edited by Robert A. Schwartz, John Aidan Byrne, and Antoinette Colaninno, pp. xv–xx. Boston: Kluwer Academic Publishers, 2003.

——, ed. *The Electronic Call Auction: Market Mechanism and Trading.* Boston: Kluwer Academic Publishers, 2001.

Schwartz, Robert A., John Aidan Byrne, and Antoinette Colaninno, eds. *Call Auction Trading: New Answers to Old Questions.* Boston: Kluwer Academic Publishers, 2003.

Shiller, Robert J. *Macro Markets: Creating Institutions for Managing Society's Largest Economic Risks.* Oxford: Oxford University Press, 1993.

——. *The New Financial Order: Risk in the 21st Century.* Princeton: Princeton University Press, 2003.

Shin, Hyun Song. "Measuring the Incidence of Insider Trading in a Market for State-Contingent Claims." *Economic Journal* 103, no. 420 (1993): 1141–1153.

Silber, William L. "Innovation, Competition, and New Contract Design in Futures Markets." *Journal of Futures Markets* 1, no. 2 (1981): 123–155.

——. "The Process of Financial Innovation." *American Economic Review* 73, no. 2 (1983): 89–95.

Snedecor, George W., and William G. Cochran. *Statistical Methods.* 8th edn. Ames, IA: Iowa State University Press, 1989.

Snyder, Wayne W. "Horse Racing: Testing the Efficient Markets Model." *Journal of Finance* 33, no. 4 (1978): 1109–1118.

Sodergreen, John. "Economic Derivatives in the Energy Sector." *Futures Industry Magazine* 15, no. 1 (2005): 41–43.

Srinivasan, Sayee, Jan Stallaert, and Andrew B. Whinston. "Portfolio Trading and Electronic Networks." Working Paper, University of Texas at Austin – Center for Research in Electronic Commerce, February 1998.

Starr, Ross M. *General Equilibrium Theory: An Introduction.* Cambridge: Cambridge University Press, 1997.

Strang, Gilbert. *Linear Algebra and Its Applications.* 3rd edn. Toronto: Thompson Learning, 1988.

Sutphen, Leslie, and Mary Ann Burns. "The E-Trader Factor: Arcades and Prop Shops Grow in Number and Influence." *Futures Industry Magazine* 15, no. 1 (2005): 36–39.

Swade, Doron. "A Sure Bet for Understanding Computers." *New Scientist* 116, no. 1584 (29 October 1987): 49–51.

Tashjian, Elizabeth. "Optimal Futures Contract Design." *Quarterly Review of Economics and Finance* 35, no. 2 (1995): 153–162.

Tashjian, Elizabeth, and Maayana Weissman. "Advantages to Competing with Yourself: Why an Exchange Might Design Futures Contracts with Correlated Payoffs." *Journal of Financial Intermediation* 4, no. 2 (1995): 133–157.

Telser, Lester G. "Why There Are Organized Futures Markets." *Journal of Law and Economics* 24, no. 1 (1981): 1–22.

——. "Futures and Actual Markets: How They Are Related." *Journal of Business* 59, no. 2 pt. 2 (1986): S5–S20.

Thaler, Richard H., and William T. Ziemba. "Anomalies – Parimutuel Betting Markets: Racetracks and Lotteries." *Journal of Economic Perspectives* 2, no. 2 (1988): 161–174.

Theissen, Erik. "Market Structure, Informational Efficiency and Liquidity: An Experimental Comparison of Auction and Dealer Markets." *Journal of Financial Markets* 3, no. 4 (2000): 333–363.

Thind, Sarfraz. "Economic Derivatives Debut." *Risk Magazine* 15, no. 11 (2002): 18.

Tufano, Peter. "Financial Innovation." In *The Handbook of the Economics of Finance, Vol. 1A, Corporate Finance*, edited by George M. Constantinides, Milton Harris, and René M. Stulz, 307–336. Amsterdam: North Holland, 2003.

Van Horne, James C. "Of Financial Innovations and Excesses." *Journal of Finance* 40, no. 3 (1985): 621–631.

Weber, Bruce W. "Next-Generation Trading in Futures Markets: A Comparison of Open Outcry and Order Matching Systems." *Journal of Management Information Systems* 16, no. 2 (1999): 29–45.

White, Frederick L. "The Commodity Futures Modernization Act of 2000: How It Affects Professional and Institutional Users of Derivatives." *Investment Lawyer* 8, no. 3 (2001): 15–21.

Willis, Kenneth E. "Optimum No-Risk Strategy for Win-Place Pari-Mutuel Betting." *Management Science* 10, no. 3 (1964): 574–577.

Wolfers, Justin, and Eric Zitzewitz. "Prediction Markets." *Journal of Economic Perspectives* 18, no. 2 (2004): 107–126.

Woodward, Susan E. "Who Should Trade in a Call Market?" In *The Electronic Call Auction: Market Mechanism and Trading*, edited by Robert A. Schwartz, 155–165. Boston: Kluwer Academic Publishers, 2001.

Working, Holbrook. "Futures Trading and Hedging." *American Economic Review* 43, no. 3 (1953): 314–343.

Ziemba, William T., and Donald B. Hausch. *Dr. Z's Beat the Racetrack*. Rev. edn. New York: William Morrow, 1987.

Author Index

Subject Index